SECRETS *of the*
# TEENAGE
# BRAIN

*To my four adolescents, Jen, Scott, Rachel, and James.*

Sheryl G. Feinstein

Foreword by Eric Jensen

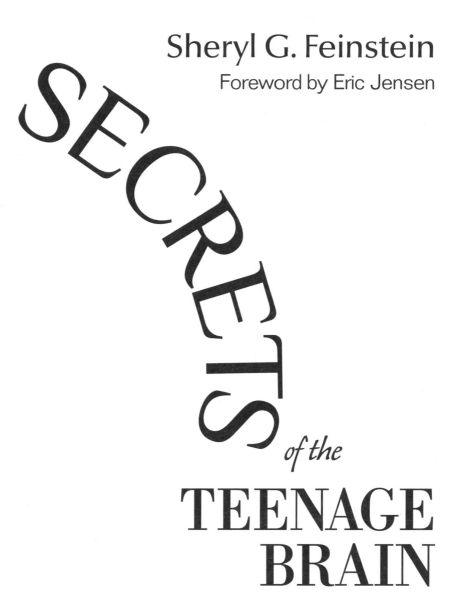

SECRETS

*of the*

# TEENAGE BRAIN

Research-Based Strategies for
Reaching and Teaching Today's Adolescents

Skyhorse Publishing

Skyhorse Publishing books may be purchased in bulk at special discounts for sales promotion, corporate gifts, fund-raising, or educational purposes. Special editions can also be created to specifications. For details, contact the Special Sales Department, Skyhorse Publishing, 307 West 36th Street, 11th Floor, New York, NY 10018 or info@skyhorsepublishing.com.

Skyhorse® and Skyhorse Publishing® are registered trademarks of Skyhorse Publishing, Inc.®, a Delaware corporation.

www.skyhorsepublishing.com

10 9 8 7 6 5 4 3 2 1

Library of Congress Cataloging-in-Publication Data is available on file.

ISBN: 978-1-62087-877-4

Printed in China

# Contents

# Foreword

I am delighted to add my comments to this fabulous resource. Every teacher and parent can relate to the teen years because they've been there. As a teen growing up in the '60s, I was awkward, fearful, excited, risk taking, and cocky but mostly just happy to survive. My grades were all over the place; you would have thought I had multiple personalities attending school under assumed names—it was truly such a crazy time. I was delighted when Dr. Sheryl Feinstein suggested this book and even more so when it became part of my library. I am now pleased to announce that a second edition is being offered, updating everyone on the latest research and strategies for the teenage brain. As a former teenager, you'll relate to so much of this book. If you are the parent of teens, you'll really enjoy it!

When I was a teen, I needed structure but wanted independence. I loved doing risky things even though they rarely paid off. The teachers I had who really cared sure got my attention. For example, my sixth-grade and eighth-grade English teachers were very personable. As a result, I not only worked harder for them, they became role models for me. Years later, I ended up teaching middle school English. There's quite a bit of power in the appropriate role model at the right time in one's life!

What makes adolescents so different from the adults they would become and from the children they used to be? The list of various culprits we've pinpointed is a long one: hormones, rebellious nature, youthful exuberance, and plain old immaturity are among the favorites. No one expected, however, that the teen brain was keeping secrets—and big ones!

Who knew that the teen brain was still growing? Scientists have assumed until just recently that the brain was mostly finished growing in childhood and left it at that. New achievements in brain-imaging technology, especially functional MRIs, finally enabled neuroscientists to look inside the heads of teens and check it out. What they saw took everyone by surprise—the adolescent brain is a hotbed of activity. Even more shocking was the discovery that the brain keeps developing at least into the twenties.

These findings reveal a whole new perspective on the role of secondary education. Teens are neither "big children" practicing to be adults nor are they "adults with a smaller brain"! Rather, they bring different interests and expectations to the classroom. Educators are just starting to view them as a unique group. *Secrets of the Teenage Brain* investigates the neurological and biological changes that teenagers experience. In each chapter are new facts and research findings that topple assumptions we've held about teenagers as well as a comprehensive list of strategies teachers can use with adolescent students.

*Secrets of the Teenage Brain* expands our knowledge on the teenage brain, including cutting-edge research and fresh strategies. Special features include technology and the brain, students with ADHD (attention-deficit/hyperactivity disorder), steroid use, and violence and aggression, giving new perspectives to contemporary issues. I must admit, one of my favorite additions to this book is the book club discussion questions. They are a wonderful way to bring educators together for meaningful dialogue; I can't wait for the conversation to begin.

Hopefully, you'll enjoy learning why teens act like they do; no matter what, you'll definitely see them in a new light when you are done! *Secrets of the Teenage Brain* will reveal the exciting answers to the tantalizing secrets that have eluded educators ever since teenagers have been going to school. As a mother of teens, the author, Dr. Feinstein, also brings quite a bit of firsthand knowledge to these pages. Her experience combined with science should reveal to you, well, the *Secrets of the Teenage Brain!*

—*Eric Jensen*

# Acknowledgments

We gratefully acknowledge  the contributions of the following reviewers:

Barry Corbin
Professor of Education, School of Education
Acadia University
Wolfville, Nova Scotia, Canada

Judy Filkins
Math and Science Curriculum Coordinator
SAU 88 Lebanon School District
Lebanon, New Hampshire

Robert Sylwester
Emeritus Professor of Education
University of Oregon

Brigitte Tennis
Head Mistress and Seventh-Grade Teacher
Stella Schola Middle School
Redmond, Washington

Kathy Tritz-Rhodes
Principal
Marcus-Meriden-Cleghorn Schools
Marcus and Cleghorn, Iowa

# About the Author

 **Sheryl G. Feinstein,** EdD, is an associate professor in the Education Department at Augustana College in Sioux Falls, South Dakota, where she teaches courses in educational psychology and adolescent development. She also serves as an educational consultant for an adolescent correctional facility in Minnesota. She has worked with adolescents as a public school teacher and as a K–12 curriculum coordinator; she has also served as director at an alternative secondary school. She is the author of numerous books, and during the 2007–2008 school year she was a Fulbright Scholar in Tanzania where she continued her research on adolescents. Contact her at sherylfeinstein@yahoo.com

# Introduction

The halls swarm with kids dawdling, talking to friends, obviously in no particular hurry to get to class; a girl slumps in the corner by her locker, priming for a total, tearful meltdown; and two boys circle the lunchroom table, gearing up to lock fists in a knock-down, drag-out brawl. What's going on? What are they thinking? It may seem like a mystery at first, but by taking an extended glimpse at what's happening in the transitioning teenage brain we can better understand, educate, and support this mystifying creature.

Today's educators seek an informed, holistic approach to middle school and high school students. Concepts, such as cost-benefit analysis and calculating the circumference of the circle using pi, are systematically taught while the social and emotional needs of individuality and self-esteem are supported. Teachers strive to ensure that all developmental needs of their students' are valued and tended. At first, their charge of educating youth may seem daunting, but thanks to neuroscience, psychology, and education, the pieces of the puzzle are falling into place.

*Secrets of the Teenage Brain* was written to nourish the inquiring and often overburdened minds of educators. Because the field of neuroscience is continuously and extensively emerging with new research, it was important to supplement this edition with the latest cutting-edge research, fresh instructional strategies, and current insights into trends and topics. Technology and the brain, mirror neurons, and at risk behaviors like cutting, violence, and aggression are just a few of the topics included. Perhaps most exciting is an educator's book club guide that has been added for colleagues wanting to discuss the trials, tribulations, and joys of teaching at the secondary level.

*Secrets of the Teenage Brain* is a hands-on, teacher friendly book. The book is organized around chapters that help educators understand the key issues facing adolescents, including academics, emotional, social, and physical well-being. Each chapter is supported with a with a multitude of instructional strategies that can be modified and adapted to individual content areas. Only the imagination of the teacher is needed to transform each strategy into something that works in their classroom. Special "Secret Revealed" sections go into interesting stories and research that relate to the topic, adding frosting to the cake.

I hope you enjoy the read.

# Teen Brain

*Under Construction*

Neuroscience has recently put forward the startling fact that teen brains resemble blueprints more than they resemble skyscrapers. Secondary educators who once considered a teenage mind an empty house that needed furnishings would do better to understand it as the framing of a house that still needs walls, wiring, and a roof.

**Did you know that . . .**

- The brain, not hormones, is to blame for the inexplicable behavior of teens
- Short-term memory increases by about thirty percent during adolescence
- The activities teens invest their time and energy in influence what activities they'll invest in as adults
- Teens are ruled far more by their emotions than by logic

*A group of middle school boys was sitting around the lunch table telling "Yo' Mama" jokes. Everyone was having fun until one boy went too far; tempers started to flare. A boy at an adjoining table stepped in to avert the fight that threatened to brew. Before anyone knew it, a fight had erupted between two boys who hadn't been telling jokes in the first place! A teacher, Mr. Kenith, broke up the fight and asked them, "Why are you fighting?" Both boys answered, "I don't know." And they really didn't.*

## CATERPILLARS TO BUTTERFLIES

Teenage behavior—nothing is more unpredictable, volatile, or intriguing. Teens want more privacy on the computer and minimize the screen as soon as you enter the room. They cycle earnestly through the roles of vegetarian, stand-up comedian, and swing dancer. They streak around the block in subfreezing weather on New Year's Eve. The sweet boy who blushed and hid his head under a sofa pillow when the Victoria's Secret commercials came on now watches and comments on the models.

Common knowledge used to be that adolescence was a phase all kids went through and that adults should wait it out. Quips like "raging hormones" and "rebel without a clue" attempted to explain the erratic thought patterns and subsequent behavior of adolescents. In their frustration, teachers and parents pondered the question, "Why can't they act like adults?" The real explanation provides a remarkable answer: They can't act like adults because they don't think like adults. Neuroscience confirms what we've always thought—the adolescent brain is still under construction.

The implications of the transitioning state of the adolescent's brain are exciting and unsettling. It's a time of great vulnerability. Teenagers' brains are growing and changing by adding gray matter and pruning old synapses. Choices teens make during adolescence potentially affect their brains for the rest of their lives. For parents and teachers, this discovery can be disconcerting. They had a great deal of power and influence over preschool and elementary school brains. Parents could ensure that young children were not exposed to excessive television, videos, computer games, and other passive activities. Teachers could monitor the books students read in class, assign projects for kids to work on (during academic work and during free time), and design a curriculum that applied to every student. But adult influence is much less effective on adolescents; to a great degree, teenagers are the masters of their own destiny and determine the fate of their brains (Spinks, 2002).

### Secret Revealed

Hormones are off the list of primary suspects! The teenagers-act-crazy-because-of-hormones theory is incomplete. Think of it this way: Adults have hormones in their bodies, too, yet manage to write memos and grade homework even while thinking about a hot date later that evening. Adolescents aren't victims of chemicals coursing through their veins and turning their fancies to thoughts of love or mayhem; if they have trouble sitting still in school and concentrating on their lesson plans, it's because their brains aren't finished yet! MRI scans performed by Dr. Jay Giedd (Giedd, Blumenthal, Jeffries, Rajapakse, et al., 1999) of the National Institute of Mental Health have revealed that rather than leaving childhood with a brain ready to take on the responsibilities of young adulthood, teens have to contend with a brain that is destroying old neural connections and building new ones. Instead of battening down the hatches to wait out some hormonal storm, teens are navigating a cerebral hurricane without a compass. This profound discovery will forever alter how educators and parents interpret the mysterious behaviors of adolescence.

Teenagers also notice the differences between their childhood days and their newfound adolescent interests. One girl said, "I go out more, hang out, talk on the phone." Another said, "I go to the mall, go to parties, dance, listen to music. . . . They're ways to have fun and spend more time with your friends." A middle school boy said simply, "I just chill." These are the same kids who, one year ago, were racing each other to the swings at recess, playing *Candy Land*, and letting Mom pick out their clothes.

## POURING THE FOUNDATION

Understanding the complexity of how the brain grows during adolescence requires knowledge about how the brain is structured. It is composed of two types of cells, neurons and glial cells. Glial cells are the "glue" that binds cells together; they compose ninety percent of the cells in the brain. The other ten percent of brain cells are neurons, cells associated with learning. Neurons hold the secrets of the mind. They are the body's communicators and constantly strike up conversations all over the brain. They coordinate thoughts, ideas, and feelings at breakneck speeds. You can practically hear the neurons roar and rumble in a teenager's head as they fire, ignite, and spring into action!

Neurons are composed of a cell body, dendrites, and one axon. Dendrites, hairlike branches emerging from the plump cell body, receive information from other neurons. Every time an individual has a new experience or gains a bit of information, another connection is made. I once asked a group of middle school and high school students what they had learned in the last month. I was bombarded with responses: I started to drive, I learned how to wait tables, I found out about mono, I learned how to calculate interest, I learned what *jugar* means in Spanish. What a burst of dendrite growth in their minds! Creating dendrites is an exciting proposition to educators; we want our students' brains to teem with them. The more dendrite receptors there are, the better the brain cells' ability to network with one another. And good news—there is plenty of room around the neuron table. Although neurons average about one thousand dendrites, one neuron can have many, many more.

Learning would not occur if neurons were isolated from each other. Each cell's single axon is a long extension from the cell body that sends information to another neuron's dendrite. The space between a dendrite and an axon (where communication between neurons takes place) is called a synapse. Messages sprint from neuron to neuron via the synapses. When the proverbial lightbulb flashes over a student's head in a moment of sudden comprehension, the synapses go wild. Neurons spark and fire across this entire network of cells in the brain. As synapses are strengthened through use, memories are reinforced and the ability to communicate with other neurons increases (Dahl, 2003).

## UPGRADING THE HARD DRIVE

When we think of learning and memory, the cortex is often the first part of the brain to come to mind, but the hippocampus is also involved in learning. This small horseshoe-shaped part of the brain is capable of neurogenesis, the ability to give birth to new neurons. The hippocampus stands in stark contrast to the rest of the brain, which remains infertile. To a large degree, the 100 billion neurons you are born with tend to be your entire slice of the pie. A thought-provoking study of learning done by researchers at the University of Colorado revealed that the cortex finds patterns, integrates information, and attempts to give structure to information (the important stuff); the hippocampus deals with facts and details (rote memory). From this it is inferred that the hippocampus memorizes and the cortex learns (O'Reilly & Rudy, 2000). Like the rest of the brain, the hippocampus creates new dendrites and synapses during adolescence, which increases short-term memory in teenagers. Instead of just five to seven bits of information, teens may now be able to remember seven to nine bits (Woolfolk, 2006). They are better positioned to memorize that wistful sonnet or crucial math theorem.

**Figure 1.1**   Human Brain

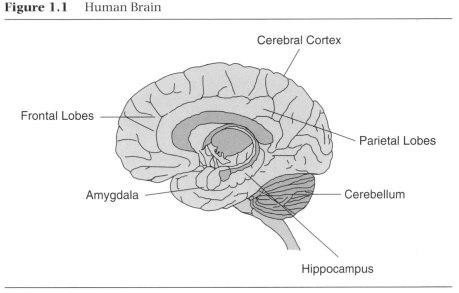

SOURCE: Adapted from Sousa, D. A. (2003), *How the Gifted Brain Learns*, p. 18.

## Secret Revealed

 Remember Piaget's theory of cognition and the information processing model from your Ed Psych classes? They both state that the quality of short-term memory increases when students enter the teenage years, but neither explained why. Dr. Paul Thompson from the UCLA Laboratory of Neuro Imaging put adolescents into an MRI scanner to image their brains and actually witnessed the brains growing in size and power! (Thompson et al., 2000) The formation of new gray and white matter—through dendrites, synapses, and myelination—enables teens to remember more and remember it better. Now, Ed Psych professors can support Piaget's theory and the information processing model with hard data. Finally, teachers in the field and in training have the whole story.

The hippocampus is slow to develop; in fact, there isn't much evidence of activity until about age three. (This probably explains why we have trouble remembering anything in infancy.) The hippocampus is associated with short-term memory—it helps us remember the name and phone number of the person we just met or the location of our favorite pizza place. It acts as a switchboard connecting short- and long-term memory and constantly communicates between the two. This dialogue linking the hippocampus and the cortex helps give meaning to new information (Schacter, 1996).

The cerebral cortex, or neocortex, is the wrinkled outer covering of the brain, the site of higher-level thinking and self-awareness. The most developed part of the human brain, the cerebral cortex allows us to problem solve, think critically, and make decisions. "No, I don't want a beer" or "Sure, I'll have a cigarette" are decisions made in the cortex. Students who say, "Math is my favorite subject," "I like Geography," or "I enjoy my creative writing class" are referring to the content that dwells in the cerebral cortex.

Most mental tasks require communication between both hemispheres of the brain. The corpus callosum acts as a bridge between the two sides, allowing information to cross with ease. Even uncomplicated activities, such as comprehending a joke or singing a song, are not confined to one hemisphere but, rather, require complex connections between both sides of the brain. The more bells and whistles a task has, the more you use the entire brain to complete it (Weissman & Banich, 2000). During adolescence, the corpus callosum increases in size by creating more dendrites and synapses. As the adolescent brain becomes capable of more complex tasks, the corpus callosum becomes larger and thicker, better able to handle the job. Scientists were amazed to discover its long maturation cycle—it continues growing into young adulthood (Keshavan et al., 2002).

A relationship has recently been established between the corpus callosum and self-awareness (the ability to monitor one's own thoughts). New neuroimaging technology has enabled researchers to study the process of self-awareness in the brain. The sense of self seems to be located in the right hemisphere of the brain, and the sense of others in the left (Kircher et al., 2001; Platek, Keenan, Gallup, & Mohammed, 2004). The strengthening corpus callosum enables teens to better understand themselves in relation to others—this budding awareness is part of what turns adolescents into adults.

## USE IT OR LOSE IT

Two processes occur as the human brain develops. The first is an overproduction of dendrites and synapses—gray matter—that results in an overload of dendrites from the cell bodies. Dendrites and synapses are multiplying like crazy in the brain! The second process, the pruning (or elimination) of brain cells, follows this overproduction. Which neurons survive or die is determined by survival of the fittest. The brain selectively strengthens or prunes neurons based on activity. Synapses continually used will flourish; those that are not will wither away. It's "use it or lose it" in action.

This overproduction of neurons, dendrites, and synapses begins at birth and continues until a child is approximately three years old; at this age, the average child has many more synapses than an adult. Obviously, an amazing amount of activity occurs in the brain during this time. From the moment of birth, however, synapses and neurons that are not being used begin to be pruned. This process is very efficient, allowing the brain to invest in strengthening the synapses that the individual finds most necessary and important.

**Figure 1.2**   Significant Brain Changes Occur During Teenage Years

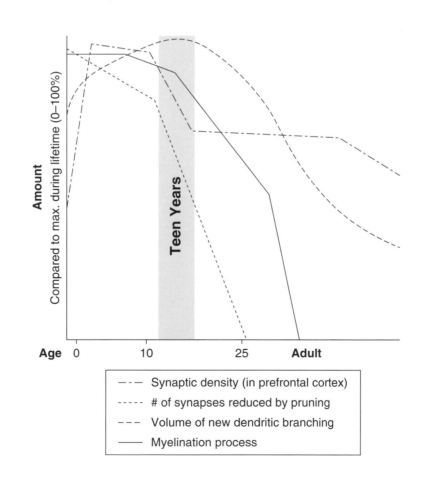

SOURCES: Bourgeois (2001); Huttenlocher and Dabholkar (1997); Sampaio and Truwit (2001).

This period of neural growth has become the focus of popular attention in education, sparking a great deal of excitement from early childhood educators and parents. Research suggests that, as a result of the creation of gray matter, we are biologically primed for learning in the early years. Some individuals have taken this information about the young child to the extreme, claiming that preschoolers who "snooze" will lose the opportunity to grow any more brain cells—ever. This dire prediction places tremendous pressure on preschool children and their parents to fill childhood with as many educational and enrichment activities as possible (Puckett, Marshall, & Davis, 1999).

## Secret Revealed

 Did you go to your high school reunion? Were you surprised that the "Class Clown" was a prosperous salesperson or that "Most Likely to Succeed" did? You shouldn't have been. The girl who spent all those science classes making students laugh when the teacher's back was turned built her brain around the ability to make customers enjoy themselves—and buy products. The boy who spent his time reading, thinking, organizing his notes, and acing projects and exams built into his brain the ability to develop and grow his own business. Any information teens use and learn in school will be hardwired into the brain's structure (good and bad), and anything they ignore will lose its priority. For parents and teachers of preschool children, this concept has been a no-brainer for quite some time. What no one realized until very recently was that teenage brains were still open to this kind of direction and input!

Such emphasis on the preschool brain has overshadowed the opportunities for growth and change in the brain during adolescence. This is known as *plasticity*. Brain plasticity refers to the brain's ability to change as it experiences fresh phenomenon and learns new information. In essence, it means the brain is on a continual course of rewiring in order to make sense of its environment. Amazingly, due to plasticity, changes occur in both the brain's physical structure and in the way it functions throughout our lifespan. This allows the sixty-year-old man to change his golf stroke or the forty-year-old woman to return to school for her master's degree. It also gives special assistance to those with a brain injury, helping them depend more on their remaining brain functions.

Plasticity has promising implications for teachers and students alike. For instance, as a teacher your original course of study may have been social studies, but due to hiring needs you find yourself teaching math. Being pragmatic you hone your math skills, enriching your brain. As a result, there will actually be more gray matter in your brain dealing with math; synapses are being generated. Even if you are not doing a dramatic switch of disciplines, education is an ever-changing field. Fortunately, our minds, and hopefully our spirits, are always up to the challenge. As for students, the same benefits apply; as they learn new information, their brain makes adjustments and grows (Doidges, 2007).

Neuroscience discovered that the brain remains quite malleable in cognitive and emotional development during adolescence and even into adulthood. In the early 1990s, Dr. Jay Giedd of the National Institute of Mental Health began doing MRIs on the brains of 145 healthy children from ages four to twenty-one. The participants selected for the study were scanned every two years to monitor possible anatomical changes occurring with maturation. He noted an undeniable overproduction of gray matter during adolescence (Giedd, Blumenthal, Jeffries, Castellanos, et al., 1999).

This overproduction gives teens the opportunity to excel in all kinds of areas; synapses spawn all over their brains. If teens do a lot of reading, they become better readers; if they are fond of and practice a lot of science, they will probably become scientists; kids who solve problems become great problem solvers. This is a neurological reason to involve adolescents in responsible activities and introduce them to all kinds of new experiences—teens who aren't involved in healthy activities may build their brains around the infamous sex, drugs, and rock 'n' roll! As Dr. Giedd said, "Teens are most likely to experiment with drugs and alcohol. I often show teens my data curve [and say], 'If you do this tonight, you may be affecting your brains not just this weekend but for the next eighty years of your life'" (Vedantam, 2001).

Just as important as the creation of additional gray matter to the adolescent is the process of pruning that follows. The use it or lose it theory pertains to adolescents as well as to ten-year-olds. The neural connections a teenager makes endure a lifetime, and unused connections are lost forever. If they aren't reading, doing science, or solving problems, the synapses for those activities will be pruned. It is hypothesized that pruning at this age permits the adolescent brain to organize its circuitry and refine its thinking processes (Thompson et al., 2000). It is a golden opportunity to build a better brain. It is also a golden opportunity to waste the brain's potential and water it down instead.

The mother of a seventh-grade boy who was getting ready for his first dance said, "His dad and I just could not believe it. He prepped for hours. Lifted weights that afternoon and then went on the treadmill. He took a selection of shirts and jeans into the bathroom—he never does that. He's always particular with his hair, but this time he was overly particular."

A supervisor at a middle school afterschool program said, "There's a group of sixth-grade girls really into boys. Two or three will follow a boy around for a day, take his pencil, that kind of thing. Eighth graders are more subtle. A boy and girl will sit close together, but if you look under the lunch table she'll have her leg over his."

Some scientists even speculate that adolescence is when people learn the mating ritual. Teenagers are very interested in the opposite sex and how to navigate this explosive social field. They commit an extensive amount of time and thought to mastering this particular learning opportunity. As luck would have it, hormones come into play at this very same time, inspiring a mating dance both painful and poetic. The chaos that ensues consumes the minds and lives of teens and everyone else they touch.

With all this restructuring, is it any wonder that the adolescent brain is at times unorganized, spontaneous, and prone to misinterpretations? They have a lot to adjust to. "I can literally stand right in front of my class and say that at 3:00 p.m. we are going to load the bus. The two kids right in front of me will come up one minute later and ask what time the bus will be loaded!" one teacher said. Eighth grader Jamiesha and her mother look at the world from different angles. "Mom tells me I'm supposed to be in at a certain time. I come in late 'cause I decided to go to my friend's house for a little while. She gets all mad. I don't get it." To Jamiesha, being late is no big deal. So what if she changed her plans an hour one way or the other! She came home, didn't she?

## THE INFORMATION SUPER HIGHWAY

After synapses are generated in the brain, myelin—a fatty substance made of glial—is produced to insulate the neurons. Myelin covers the axons of neurons and enables information to travel efficiently. Myelinated tissue is referred to as white matter. The more extensive the myelination of axons, the faster information flows between the cells. At the same time, the ability to use symbolism, metaphors, and analogies increases in older adolescents. They are able to appreciate irony and sarcasm; their sense of humor becomes more sophisticated, and teachers often find themselves the objects of this increased capability (Santrock, 2003). The adolescent is ready to hypothesize, create abstractly, and comprehend complex math theorems. The rampant changes are dynamic and undeniable. The transition from the childhood brain to the adolescent brain is like paving a gravel road with asphalt; teens are on their way to becoming faster, sleeker thinking machines. Their steadfast memory, jaunty step, thinking processes, language skills, and emotions all benefit from this smoother ride.

Construction occurs throughout the teen brain. The parietal lobes (which process and desegregate sensory information like sights, sounds, and smells), temporal lobes (which process language and emotional behavior), occipital lobes (which processes visual information), cerebellum (which processes coordination and thinking skills), and hippocampus (seat of short-term memory) all benefit from the overproduction and pruning of synapses. Researchers at the UCLA Laboratory of Neuro Imaging discovered that the parietal lobes did not complete the creation of gray matter until about the age of twelve—and only then did they start pruning. Temporal lobes limped even further behind—they did not finish growing gray matter or begin the processes of pruning and myelination until the age of sixteen (Giedd, Blumenthal, Jeffries, Castellanos, et al., 1999)! In some areas, pruning and myelination follow even later.

The brain does not release myelin to all neurons at the same time but rather in stages. The timing of the release of myelin appears to be dependent upon the developmental age of the individual, environment, and genetics. One of the last parts of the brain to receive myelin is the frontal cortex, the area responsible for abstract thinking, language, and decision making (Fuster, 2002). As the brain's frontal lobes become myelinated during adolescence, teens develop the ability to hypothesize, look into the future, deduct, analyze, and logically reason.

## Secret Revealed

*There was a time when me and my best friend since first grade got into a fight. She told someone a secret I'd told her. I told her she was a liar; she said I was being paranoid. So I hit her.*

*—Kenisha, eighth grade*

Have you ever felt like hitting your boss because of something he or she said about you? Did you? Why not? No matter how infuriated or exasperated adults become with each other, logic and reason usually prevail. Adults choose their words carefully and try to calmly discuss problems instead of rolling up their shirtsleeves and taking it outside. No matter how

*(Continued)*

(Continued)

good it may feel to indulge in the wild emotions of the moment, adults think through the consequences and make decisions based on what might happen the next day and how their reactions affect things like income, family security, and personal relationships. Teens, however, are famous for not calmly assessing consequences and for making poor, on-the-spot decisions. Teens succumb to the temptation of hitting first and talking later.

In two separate studies, Dr. Deborah Yurgelun-Todd (Yurgelun-Todd, Killgore, & Young, 2002) of McLean Hospital and Dr. Elizabeth Sowell (Sowell, Thompson, Holmes, Jernigan, & Toga, 1999) of the UCLA Laboratory of Neuro Imaging found out why. Until the frontal lobes, the seat of language and reason, are completely formed, teens rely overmuch on their amygdala—the seat of emotion. Not only do the wild emotions get first say about what teens will do next, their ability to negotiate their way out of a tense moment by using carefully chosen, diplomatic language is fledgling at best. Fortunately, the adults and adult brains that are often at the receiving end of adolescent outbursts can understand what is happening and de-escalate confrontations when they do occur.

The frontal lobes are in charge of taming the beast within us, humanizing our nature, and making us be the best we can be. They have an interesting relationship with the amygdala, an organ that controls our often tumultuous array of emotions. Pleasure, anger, and fear all spring from this small but mighty structure located a few inches from the ears in the lower center of the brain. When confronted with information, the adolescent brain reacts quite differently than the adult brain. Adults rely more on the frontal lobes of their brain and less on the amygdala, and therefore respond logically to the input they receive. The adolescent, on the other hand, tends to rely more on the amygdala than the frontal lobes and responds emotionally to stimuli (Baird et al., 1999). This explains the poor decisions they make, like going shopping (instead of doing homework) or having unprotected sex, and their highly emotional responses to ordinary requests, such as remarks like "I hate you!" or "Don't tell me what to do!"

The frontal lobes are also the province of language. Frustrated teens answer frustrated adults with inarticulate expressions like "Whatever" and "I don't know." For years, educational psychologists have documented the vague and mumbled expressions of adolescents (Woolfolk, 2006), but it wasn't until recently that neuroscientists examined the phenomenon. Dr. Elizabeth Sowell examined language production in adolescents and found that there is a shift in function as brains mature (Sowell et al., 1999). Young adolescents have more difficulty generating words and expressing themselves than do older adolescents. By high school, teens start speaking in a more rational and logical manner.

## MIRROR, MIRROR ON THE WALL

One of the most exciting new discoveries in neuroscience is that of mirror neurons. Evidence of mirror neurons was actually discovered in macaque monkeys during the mid-1990s, but not in humans until the early twenty-first century, when neuroimaging technology advanced to the point where studies could be done on humans. The very nature of mirror neurons is found in their name: Neuroscientists discovered that a network of neurons fired when they vicariously experienced something; it was as though another person's action was reflected in a mirror. The same parts of the human brain were activated in the observer as the neurons in the person doing the activity (Iacoboni, 2008; Sylwester, 2007).

Literally speaking, it means we actually experience another person's pain or joy. Early studies are suggesting that mirror neurons may help us understand how empathy, language, self-awareness, intentions, and altruism are developed. Individuals who have a burst of mirror neurons igniting in response to other's facial expressions are able to

empathize with the sadness of failing a test or being rejected by a potential girlfriend and the happiness of scoring an A or getting that first date. These individuals develop a sense of caring, enabling them to share other's emotions and identify other's needs. In contrast, individuals with autism have few mirror neurons igniting in response to others, explaining their lack of social development. It may also add further support to learning through observation and imitation, a theory that Albert Bandura, the psychologist, promoted (see Woolfolk, 2006). There are possibilities for every content area, so stay tuned for exciting discoveries and educational implications in this neuron neighborhood.

## ADOLESCENCE: THE FINAL FRONTIER

Innovations in brain technology have led to discoveries that spark the interest of educators and provide rich possibilities for instruction and assessment. But like the crew of the starship *Enterprise*, teachers and parents must go where no one has gone before—into the uniqueness of the brain that spans the abyss between childhood and adulthood. Teenagers seem irresponsible and unreasonable only when they are compared to people older and younger. But viewed against the backdrop of the profound and rapid neurological and biological changes that are happening in their bodies, their behavior is much more understandable and logical.

Why do adolescents blurt out answers in class? Why do they fall asleep during third period? Why do they fight so bitterly over late homework assignments or missed points on a test? Take comfort in the fact that they do not plot their unruliness; they are just trying to cope in a school run and designed by adults from an adult perspective—adults with brains that are structured and that function in ways vastly different from their own. This book attempts to highlight the primary differences in teen and adult brains and behavior as well as offer suggestions for channeling these differences toward a more productive classroom, academically and emotionally.

# Teen Cognition and Learning

Conventional wisdom about teenagers is wrong. Teenagers are not incoherent, clumsy, sex-crazed, unpredictable, irrational monsters who can't be reasoned with—they are intelligent creatures not yet accustomed to their (unevenly) burgeoning mental strengths and capabilities. Adolescence is a time of startling growth and streamlining in the brain, enabling teens to think abstractly, speak expressively, and move gracefully. Of course, they often use their newfound abilities to talk their way out of homework deadlines or concoct elaborate games to play behind teachers' backs, but it's a good start!

**Did you know that . . .**

- The teen brain is particularly susceptible to novelty
- ADHD is not caused by a bad student, bad parent, or bad teacher; the reason can be found in the brain
- The burst of growth in the frontal lobes means that teens overcomplicate problems, idealize the world, and say one thing while doing another
- The development of the parietal lobes helps teen athletes improve their pace and teen musicians improve their beat
- Physical movement helps the cerebellum develop, thereby helping teens improve their cognitive processing skills
- Feedback improves the brain's efficiency
- Teens crave structure and organization in spite of their attraction to novelty

*The wacky and weird teenagers who filled the hallway of the high school transformed suddenly to zombies as they filed into their English class. With drooping shoulders and shuffling feet, they exchanged resigned looks and rolled their eyes knowingly at one another. They sat in the unbroken silence and waited for their student teacher to enter.*

*She entered the room in the same manner as her students—no welcoming smile, no friendly words. She went to the front of the class with a stiff, swift step and abruptly launched her fifty-minute lecture on punctuation. One boy leaned over to his neighbor and pleaded, "Kill me. Kill me now." The teacher lost everyone's attention by droning on and on about the various uses of the apostrophe. All around the room, students daydreamed and drifted to sleep.*

## ATTENTION-GETTING DEVICES

Our first objective as teachers is to capture students' attention. If we don't gain their attention, the chance that they'll learn anything is remote at best. The process of attention serves two primary purposes, the first of which is survival. The brain kept our ancestors safe by alerting them to possible hazards in their midst like strangers, thunder clouds, or wild animals. Fortunately, it is the rare occasion that survival is at stake in school. Instead, attention serves its second purpose—maintaining pleasurable feelings. The exotic girl with the pierced tongue, a double chocolate ice cream bar, and listening to rock music on the radio are pleasurable diversions for modern teenagers. So are funny stories, terrible tragedies, and the first snowfall.

The brain is bombarded with information from the senses. Everything we see, hear, touch, smell, and taste finds its way to the sensory receptors, from the clothes on your back to the beige walls of the room and the radio playing softly in the background. At the base of the brain is the brain stem, which controls involuntary actions like breathing, blood pressure, and heartbeats. Deep within the brain stem is the reticular formation, a system of neurons that gathers information from all of your senses and controls your awareness levels. Some awareness is at a conscious level (what you see and hear the teacher do and say) and some at an unconscious level (the color of the walls or the socks you are wearing). It would be impossible for the brain to consciously focus on each bit of data it receives. You may be oblivious to the feel of a baseball hat on your head while the cute girl beside you captures your full attention. Considering the immense amount of information the brain is capable of absorbing, from the spinach stuck in your teeth to the lint on your coat, we are fortunate to be able to forget most things. Otherwise, we'd overload.

## Secret Revealed

No matter what you heard in the past, teens can be as interested in photosynthesis as the armpit squelches that come from the back of the classroom! The adolescent brain really does want to learn more about the world we live in and less about the student who enters the classroom to collect the attendance, but it values novelty and unpredictability. Not even a lecture and slide show about alien technology would hold your students' attention for long without these two elements!

Dr. Linda Spear (2000), a behavioral neuroscientist at Binghamton University, studies the teenage propensity for seeking novelty; she finds that the physical changes in the brain during adolescence significantly affect what appeals to teens. Fortunately, novelty and surprise can be planned for any lesson content. Instead of just lecturing about photosynthesis, work with plants and sunlamps. Instead of labeling anatomical charts, dissect a frog. Appeal directly to the teen brain's innate interest in the unexpected and enjoy a more productive classroom.

Ask a group of teenagers what they think about school and you probably won't be surprised by the answers: "Boring." "Stupid." "School sucks." Of course, friends, potential dates, lunchtime, and doodling don't bore them; the adolescent brain is fascinated by (and seeks out) novelty and emotion (Koepp et al., 1998; Spear, 2000). Sitting through classroom instruction that fails to include either is the real test of a teen's attention. Many teaching strategies and testing options have a great deal of difficulty keeping attention and arousing emotion. Worksheets require students to pay attention to something that evolution and instinct quite frankly say is irrelevant to life. Lecture, which can be an efficient way to deliver instruction, is often not emotionally charged. Objective tests, such as those in multiple-choice or true-false formats, rarely generate emotion and are extremely difficult to apply to real-world applications. Yet lecture and worksheets are dismayingly popular means of presenting content. We miss academic opportunities when we overuse strategies that neglect our emotional and cognitive constitution—two powerful memory builders.

Capturing students' attention by engaging them in feel-good experiences is good news for teachers and teens alike; everyone enjoys dwelling on the positive. People who know how to entertain an audience are almost always sure to get their educational messages across. Consider Simon, a spirited ninth grader who definitely captured his classmates' attention when he gave his presentation about a city in America. The students had already heard a dozen speeches about cities from Philadelphia to Portland

and waited politely for another colorless, note-card-heavy tale of yet another metropolis. Nonetheless, Simon strode confidently to the front of the room and began by telling the class to imagine themselves sitting in a lawn chair, gazing at mountains, and sipping a latte. "It was such a beautiful morning. Where could we be? Aspen? Salt Lake City? No, Mianus." In complete earnestness, he continued. "I suppose you're wondering what we can do for fun in Mianus, what people are like in Mianus. That's what I am here to tell you today." Every eye in the room was riveted on Simon, first in disbelief and then in hysterics. Needless to say, Simon had everyone's attention (even if he didn't have all the facts correct).

So did a physics teacher, Mr. Berndt. Mr. Berndt thrilled his students by entering their classroom one day on in-line skates. As if the novelty of skating in class weren't enough, he had brought skates for them to use, too! Soon everyone had taken turns pulling each other around the room to determine force and speed with two different masses. In a biology class, Mr. Gjornes (who is young and in exceptional shape) turned cartwheels to demonstrate the rotation of molecules. These were two classes during which no students daydreamed, no minds drifted, and every brain gave its attention to the teacher and the lesson; not only were the activities fun, they were content meaningful, too.

Attention-getting activities are not required to be amusing or participatory, however. Mr. Hoffman, a high school principal, explained how a guest speaker captivated the entire student body with a story about how his younger brother was killed by a drunk driver and finally revealed himself as the driver. The story had the students so riveted that they carried his message right into their other classes, relating his experiences to their own actions, past and future. The principal even received phone calls from parents explaining how this tale had transformed their teenagers.

## Instructional Strategies

### *May I Have Your Attention Please?*

You can only maintain student attention if you've already captured it. Introducing novelty is one way to do it, so is engaging the physical senses and arousing curiosity. Throw novelty at teens from all sides—vary the pace and tone of your voice, dress in bell-bottoms, circulate around the room, use colored chalk, bring flowers into the room, or add the scent of lemon. Incorporate all the senses in the learning adventure.

Mrs. Reynolds introduced a unit on poetry to her ninth-grade English students by speaking to the class in French. The look of amazement on students' faces made dusting off her high school French book worth the effort. Mr. Amundson strung lights around a bulletin board describing how the legislature passes a bill, literally lighting up the room (to use a sophomoric pun)! But teachers should not always be the performers. Encourage students to act in novel ways themselves. Change their seats or surprise them with a hands-on task. You could even video record them in action and have them analyze what snags their attention.

The flip side of keeping student attention is that they have an easier time watching and listening to you when there are fewer distractions in the room. Not that you should remove a single thing from the walls—but you should be aware of annoying or repetitive mannerisms you may have, such as habitual throat clearing or fidgeting with a necklace. You would hate to discover that a student chose to spend the entire period tallying how many times you tapped your pencil against the desk or said the word *okay*. This is not the attention we're striving for.

### *Things to Try*

- Show a comic strip or a few minutes of a television cartoon to put a smile on their faces.
- Tell a riddle: How many teenagers does it take to screw in a light bulb? (One answer is one to screw in the bulb, one to hold the ladder, and one to order a pizza. You could have students take a minute or two to write their own punch lines, too.)
- Play a song from a popular CD and ask them about why they like it—inquiring about their interests will capture their attention.
- Show a video of a trendy commercial—it's the last thing they'll expect!
- Have every one of your students find a place at the board and start listing all the words that describe what they learned that week.
- Share a story from your own middle school or high school days. Students will connect with you on a personal level, and if told well, the story will draw emotion into the classroom.
- Bring in candy as a writing prompt. You could have students create metaphors for the candy out of class content while they munch and chew.
- Pass around clay, feathers, or pieces of packing foam; hands-on objects arouse curiosity and activate the tactile senses.
- Move the location of your desk periodically. In fact, move everything periodically. Change not just students' seats but also the actual desk arrangement a few times a year.
- Mix it up; occasionally have students stand up to deliver important information or respond to key ideas.
- Read a poem by Shel Silverstein or Emily Dickinson to set a mood and engage emotions.
- Start a service project for immigrant adolescents in your community. The opportunity to contribute directly toward helping a peer is meaningful, specific, and unique. The idea will pique their interest at the very least.
- Surprise them with a celebration for work well done. Make popcorn or roller-skate on the blacktop!

## ATTENTION-DEFICIT/
## HYPERACTIVITY DISORDER (ADHD)

The subject of attention has particular significance for students who have attention-deficit/hyperactivity disorder (ADHD). These students are a challenge to themselves, their parents, and their teachers. Known for being distracted, impulsive, and argumentative, they lack the very cornerstones of what is needed to succeed in the classroom.

Lack of focus is one of the major obstacles students with ADHD face; it negatively impacts every aspect of their lives: academics, friendships, extracurricular, and jobs. Teachers often hear the constant refrain "I don't know" to every question posed. Where is your homework? I don't know. Why are you wandering the room? I don't know. What are you talking to her for? I don't know. This frustrating chant manifests their inability to focus.

Hyperactivity is also associated with ADHD, causing these students and everyone around them grief. Continually wired, teachers often describe the behavior of students with ADHD as "he is literally bouncing off the wall," "he can't sit still, he blurts out answers," and "he doesn't listen, he never pays attention."

Recognizing cause and effect constitutes another challenge for the student with ADHD. While most teenagers are beginning to understand that if they turn their homework in on time they learn more, have better grades, and have less stress in their lives, the teen with ADHD misses the connection.

Hyperfocusing is also a featured attribute of students with ADHD. The activity that triggers hyperfocusing is usually one that requires quick, spontaneous responses. Computer games are the perfect vehicle for this ride. Once something has caught their attention and manages to keep their attention, they are not about to put on the brakes. Interrupting a student with ADHD when they are hyperfocusing is a sure recipe for a meltdown.

Brain differences are abundant between individuals with ADHD and those without. Brain size is about three to four percent smaller in teenagers with ADHD compared to their age-mates. Fortunately, the difference in brain size in no way impacts their intelligence. Other brain differences include the basal ganglia, a part of the brain associated with thinking and emotion, and the frontal lobes, the thoughtful, decision-making center of the brain. Both have reduced activity. This affects their ability to pay attention and control their emotions. Dopamine only adds fuel to the confusion. Dopamine transporters take on too much dopamine before they pass it between brain cells; this

## Instructional Strategies

- Reduce distractions—seat them near the front of the room, clear their desks of objects, and keep their desks away from high traffic areas.
- Give directions one step at a time.
- Allow frequent participation and, if possible, movement.
- Break down objectives and assignments into small segments.
- Use computer-based instruction; it will draw their attention.
- Help their disorganized minds become organized by using planners and directly teaching study skills.
- If they act inappropriately and will not control themselves, remove them from the classroom.
- Reset your expectations: don't be shocked by explosive, unacceptable behavior.
- Stay calm, because they won't. Their lack of self-control means as adults we must have more control.
- Don't engage in an argument when they are out of control.
- Supply accurate information to parents and physicians as to behaviors seen in the classroom. Because of the behavior expectations in school, we are an important part of putting the puzzle together.

misstep further affects attention and impulse control (Bloom, Beal, & Kupfer, 2006).

## THE FOREST OR THE TREES?

The frontal lobes are located in the front of the brain and are the largest part of the cortex. Positioned right behind the forehead, they are responsible for cognitive processing. Speaking, reading, writing, math, and music are all processed in the frontal lobes, along with the ability to analyze, apply, and evaluate. Secondary educators are constantly contemplating how to engage students in higher-order thinking, how to start their cognitive gears turning, and how to activate their frontal lobes. Fully understanding the maturation process during adolescence paves the way for compatible instruction. Neuroscience has allowed us the opportunity to witness the dramatic changes in the frontal lobes between childhood, adolescence, and adulthood.

**Figure 2.1**   Human Brain

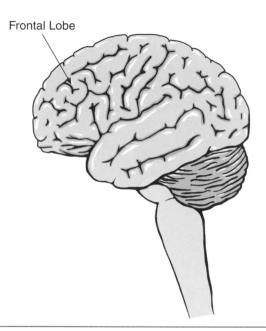

Frontal Lobe

SOURCE: Adapted from Sousa, D. A. (2003), *How the Gifted Brain Learns*, p. 16.

Children look at the world very concretely. When visiting an elementary school, I overheard a group of kindergartners trying to decide who was older between a husband and wife. It was obvious to me at first glance that the husband was older, but the kindergartners gave it an interesting twist. Lety ended the discussion by announcing, in a tone denoting the obviousness of the statement, "She's taller, so she must be the oldest." The children in attendance agreed; Lety's logic apparent to everyone. Later that day, their teacher, Ms. Gibbons, gathered all her students at the front of the room and announced that it was Presidents' Day. "Whose birthdays do we celebrate on Presidents' Day?" she asked. No one responded, so Ms. Gibbons said, "One person is Abraham Lincoln." A hand immediately shot up from the back of the group and Micah hopefully inquired, "Did he bring cupcakes?" Innocent and sweet? Absolutely. But surviving in a concrete world has its limitations. Young children have no sense of the past: Abraham Lincoln is alive, butterflies don't come from caterpillars, and monsters really do live under the bed. Adult brains are necessary to guide and structure the lives of children; they need our fine-tuned frontal lobes to shelter them.

## Secret Revealed

For years, adults have assumed that teenagers are self-absorbed, uncaring, and oblivious to the world around them. Meanwhile, teens have always been certain that they could solve all the world's problems if their stupid parents would only give them a chance. They would never allow the planet to become so polluted; they would never put an extra refrigerator in the garage when so many people are starving! If teens were in charge, all beaches would be clean and there'd be sports drinks for everyone. The world would be a better place.

As the frontal lobes mature, teens are increasingly capable of moral reasoning and idealism. Children's brains may think only in the concrete—Did I get as many cookies as she did?—but adolescence is when the brain's awareness and interest expands. Able to imagine the thoughts of another person and to appreciate the passage of time, teens suddenly become aware that they are not the only people in the world and that actions can have future consequences. They see the world not only as it is but how it could be.

The frontal lobes that distinguish men and women from boys and girls begin to mature during adolescence (Giedd, Blumenthal, Jeffries, Castellanos, et al., 1999). Young teenagers begin to think abstractly and become capable of pondering concepts that have little or no basis in concrete reality. Teens can consider hypothetical questions like "If there are millions of plants found in the rain forests, and if the majority of medicines that are discovered come from plants found in the rain forests, what implications does the deforestation of the rain forests have for our future?" They can embark on discussions ranging from civil rights to the death penalty. Teenagers can analyze, deduce, and make reflective decisions.

Educators know that secondary students need exposure to higher-level thinking skills, but the role of physical development cannot be overstated. It is the combination of biological maturation with thoughtful instructional strategies that creates a better brain. To compare teenagers to computers, we can expose teenagers to all the software we want, but until their "hard drives" are upgraded, it will have minimal impact (Epstein, 2001). "Software" that reinforces the acquisition of abstract thinking skills includes exploring various hypothetical questions, teaching broad concepts, and encouraging scientific reasoning and reflective decision making. Mostly, though, the best way to wait out this period of development is with patience and understanding. The great city of Rome wasn't built in a day, and neither is the teenage brain.

Neuroscientists and educational psychologists concur that not all teenagers develop the capacity for abstract thought at the same time. Concrete learning strategies are still needed at the middle school and high school level (Neimark, 1975). Pierre van Heile, who designed the model of geometric thought, did valuable research in teaching geometry at the high school level (Mason, 1998). He found that many older students still require concrete, hands-on material when initially studying geometry. Teacher expectations were that high school students could handle the complex and often-unfamiliar material without the support of hands-on activities. The result was student frustration and failure in this subject area.

Providing hands-on materials enabled students to quickly transition into abstract thought in geometry. This same premise is true in other areas of the curriculum. Shawna, a vivacious tenth grader, said, "My history teacher just lectures, which is not a good style for me. I daydream in that class. I try not to, but I always do. In biology class, my teacher has us doing things. One week we dissected fetal pigs. It smelled, but it made it easy to understand the parts of the body. I think I finally figured out the different ventricles in the heart." For Jason, a thoughtful boy of seventeen, concrete examples made all the difference in his understanding of upper level math. He commented, "I like my math class. We don't just do worksheets or listen to the teacher talk; we get to actually work with objects. Sometimes I need to see it to understand it."

## BRUSH OFF OLD CLASSROOM FAVORITES

Some of the most traditional lesson elements are well researched and brain friendly. Robert Marzano (Marzano, Pickering, & Pollock, 2001) and his team at MCCREL (Mid-Continent Research for Education and Learning) have led educators to institute ten nonnegotiable strategies in their classrooms. Incorporating some of these following activities will give teens the chance to practice their burgeoning ability to think abstractly while still grounding them firmly in concrete facts and information.

1. *Ask students to write a summary of a lesson.* Despite its reputation, the act of summarizing requires students to delete, substitute, and retain knowledge as they analyze information. Sifting through information during and at the end of a lesson increases their understanding of it—and it doesn't always have to happen in paragraph form. Have students directly connect five concepts that they learned that day in class, write a newspaper headline for what was covered, make a prediction about what they'll learn in the next day's class, or bring technology into the forum; have

them text message a summary. Cell phones aren't a prerequisite (they just add to the ambiance); the text can be written on a sheet of paper.

2. *Identify similarities and differences.* The brain stores by similarity, but retrieves through differences. This is another simple activity that has been shown to increase academic achievement on standardized tests. Higher-order thinking is required to compare and classify information; students must analyze and evaluate information before they can categorize it. Venn diagrams, matrix, and charts add a supportive visual to the process.

**Figure 2.2**   Venn Diagram

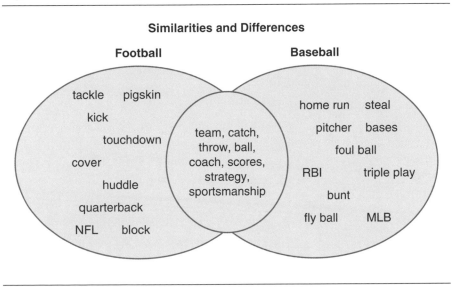

**Similarities and Differences**

3. *Write metaphors and analogies.* Writing metaphors and analogies is an effective way to engage higher-order thinking skills. Imagine how many ways there are to fill in the blanks of the sentence: Adolescents are like _____ because _____. When given this assignment, one veteran teacher wrote, "Adolescents are like TV shows because sometimes you thoroughly enjoy them and other times you wonder who produced them." Students might enjoy filling in the blanks of a sentence like "The Internet is to _____ as the brain is to _____."

4. *Present material nonlinguistically.* Knowledge is stored in two ways, visually and linguistically. Incorporate both for optimal learning. Embracing graphic organizers, body movements, and multiple intelligences will form a firm foundation.

5. *Create and test a hypothesis.* Challenge students to apply their knowledge. Generating a hypothesis, a part of the inquiry process, helps

build a better brain. Examine water quality in school, healthy lifestyles of freshman versus seniors, or ways to make your school more Green. Amazingly, it does not matter if the answer is discovered; the journey is what matters, not the destination.

6. *Reinforce effort and provide recognition for accomplishments.* Make the connection between effort and achievement, show examples of people who overcame the odds, and inspire students to do the same. All the while, praise them for their effort and for taking that risk. Intrinsic, intrinsic, intrinsic—when it comes to recognition, replace the rewards of candy and stickers with feelings of accomplishment, and at the same time build a positive self-concept.

7. *Assign homework and provide practice.* Repeating skills helps them stick in memory. Refiring synapses strengthens the memory and makes it easier to recall; homework provides that memory-producing practice. Homework may take various forms: memorization (ribosomes, cytoplasm, proteins = Robots Can Produce), prep for the next day (read Chapter 2), understanding complex content (compare and contrast energy sources), and increasing speed (flash cards), all valuable avenues for practice. Difficulty in content and time spent on homework should increase with age; remember the fourteen-year-old brain does not have the same capabilities as the seventeen-year-old brain. Interestingly, parental assistance should be kept to a minimum; homework is no time for them to hover.

8. *Facilitate cooperative learning.* In the process, support positive interdependence. Keep the groups small and vary the composition; no one wants to always be in the "average" or the "at-risk" group. Webquests— inquiry-based Internet activities—add novelty to this first-class strategy.

9. *Set objectives and provide feedback.* Teacher objectives help set the direction of learning; when students personalize those objectives, owner-ship occurs. Long-term and short-term objectives, both have a place in the classroom. Feedback resets the direction of learning, immediate and specific is most effective.

10. *Start and reinforce lessons with cues, questions, and advance organizers.* Begin class on the right foot, jog their memory with questions and advance organizers. Focus on what's most important: Don't confuse the issue with trivia; they'll flounder sifting through the muck. While details may be the spice of life (goats in Morocco can climb trees), they shouldn't be the main course. Inspire students to analyze, instead of merely reacting to or describing a situation, by asking questions that force them to view a scenario in a new light. Try "How did you do that?" "What would you do differently next time?" "Why did you make that choice?" "What evidence

substantiates your conclusion?" and "What did you learn that you could apply in another class?" And remember to use wait time, the added return in quality answers is well worth your patience.

# Instructional Strategies

## I Think (and Solve and Inquire), Therefore I Learn

When choosing strategies, it is important to remember three things about the brain: It is capable of multiprocessing, it thrives on challenges, and it makes synapses when actively involved with learning. Instructional strategies that provide complex thinking skills and interaction provide opportunities for the brain to work more efficiently.

Take advantage of the adolescent's new ability to think abstractly by introducing a thinking curriculum into the classroom. Challenge students with assignments that promote higher-level thinking skills, such as problem-based learning, research projects, experimentation, inquiry, authentic data analysis, persuasive writing, presentations, dramas, composing music (even in a nonmusic class), and visual analysis. One day, have the students guess the legal consequences of keeping marijuana in their locker or painting graffiti or gang signs on the bathroom wall; the next day, invite a lawyer or police officer to the class to explain the actual consequences. Create a political comic book, look for a philosophy of life in popular songs, analyze a TV show or discuss hot topics like dating, parents, sex, drinking, drugs, friends, and work.

## Things to Try

- Develop a new strategy for the football team or an election campaign for the candidate running for student counsel. Data mining information from the computer to solve these problems reinforces the positive use of technology.
- Think out loud for your students—verbally go through your thoughts as you decide on a topic for a writing assignment or solve a problem in trigonometry.
- Simulate a crime and investigate it; the continual popularity of this type of TV programming will grab the interest of wannabe detectives.
- Form pairs or small groups and put the students in charge. Let them teach their classmates; reciprocal teaching is one good formula for letting them shine.
- Rewrite a scene from Shakespeare against a modern day setting. Then, identify and explain similarities and differences between the two versions.
- Seek out members of the community: Interview employers about hiring adolescent workers, talk to the elderly for their historical perspective of an important event, or shadow a state legislator or city council member.

*(Continued)*

(Continued)

- Tap into the multiple intelligences of your students: Chart birth rates in the United States or on each continent, listen to and write about bird songs, invent a game, or visit a museum.
- View political debates on television and analyze them; watch fifteen minutes of local news and identify which issues are most likely to affect teenagers; write about contemporary concerns like forest fires, combating terrorism, stem cell research, or the use of steroids by athletes; or search the Internet to identify topics of immediate importance.
- Have students write and distribute a survey to their schoolmates (perhaps about the effect of sports programs on school spirit or academic achievement—something of significance in their lives), and collect and analyze the data.
- Develop a game of chance, like a lottery or raffle, for a charitable cause. Predict earnings and run a simulation of the game.
- Publish a class newspaper from a contemporary (what would biologists want to subscribe to?), historical (during World War I), or fictional perspective (what might Jane Eyre read?). Write engaging headlines and lead stories, draw comic strips, provide entertainment reviews, and include a financial page and advice column.
- Foreign language teachers: Have students study a country and collect information about it for the purpose of writing a tourist guide.
- Middle school teachers: Collaborate on a thematic unit. Host a Renaissance fair, sponsor an archeological dig, or investigate garbage in the community.

## MAKING THE WORLD A BETTER PLACE

Abstract thought is not the only change observable in the adolescent as the frontal lobes bloom. With cognitive maturation emerges idealistic behavior; teenagers are finally able to understand the way the world works as well as envision the possibilities of an ideal place. During this stage, adolescents can become very critical of past generations (in particular, their parents' generation). In middle school, this behavior often manifests only in verbal statements—kids will talk a good game but rarely follow it up with action. For all of Jordan's arguments about the need to recycle and Kajia's concerns about the ways girls are portrayed in the media, fervent words are probably the most they will contribute to the cause. Expect even the most environmentally conscious thirteen-year-old to be assigned school ground cleanup duty for littering at least once!

As they enter high school, teens often turn idealism into activism. Older teenagers may become absorbed in service clubs that meet a variety of real-world needs, such as helping the elderly reset their clocks to daylight savings time, tutoring young children, or participating in a local walk-a-thon. Lars volunteers weekly at the local soup kitchen. He commented, "I feel really good, like I'm making a difference, helping out a lot of less-fortunate people." Mark teaches religious school to second and third graders. "I do it for community service and to help teach youth in my temple about Judaism. I enjoy it because I like working with the kids and I feel good about it because I give them a good role model. Even though they may not appreciate it or show it now, I think they'll remember my positive influence later."

But it is not uncommon for the young adolescent to be somewhat hypocritical in their idealistic behavior. They often have a difficult time practicing what they preach. David Elkind (1978) identified this characteristic as "adolescent hypocrisy" and linked it to intellectual immaturity, as opposed to a character flaw. In the context of brain development, their hypocritical behavior parallels the frontal lobe development and myelin enveloping the frontal lobes as the adolescence matures. The brain is not yet a smooth, paved road—there are still plenty of potholes, dirt paths, and back alleys to even out.

Anita spent hours telling her friends how important honesty was to her and how she would never lie to them. But when her mother asked her with whom she was going to the movies, she conveniently neglected to mention any of the boys' names. Lindsey, Kelsey, and Maggy all joined SALSA (Serve & Learn Student Association), a group committed to service. They talked excitedly about their first project, a highway cleanup south of town, sure that it was a chance to make a real difference in their community. The girls made detailed plans for the day: who would drive them there, what grubby clothes to wear, and what to put in their sack lunches. Yet Maggy's mother—who drove—was perplexed by their behavior. When asked how the day went, she replied, "The girls worked hard and had a lot of fun, but I don't understand teenagers. After picking up trash for two hours in the hot sun, we stopped for a snack; when they were finished eating, the girls left their candy wrappers on the ground! What were they thinking?"

Pseudostupidity is another educational psychology term that describes the transitioning adolescent brain (Elkind, 1978). With the development of the frontal lobes, teens are able to look at a problem from a number of perspectives. No longer is there just one correct answer; instead, they can imagine all kinds of possibilities. It sounds wonderful, but instead of simplifying their lives, it complicates them. Faced with a problem, they will think and think and think, unable to give any answer—not because it is too difficult to solve but because they have made the problem too complex. The answer may be right in front of their noses but they concentrate on every possible solution rather than an obvious one.

Mr. Armstrong, a middle school math teacher, assigned a simple assignment as homework. Students were to use toothpicks to show how one aspect of geometry (exponential growth) worked. All the assignment required was toothpicks, paper, and glue. What could be easier than doubling one toothpick to a group of two, the group of two to a group of four, four to eight, and so on? By doing the assignment, students would learn just how fast exponential growth took place. At 9:30 that evening, Mr. Armstrong received a phone call from a frantic parent whose sixth-grade son, Sam, was in tears. Sam was sure he needed to demonstrate the complexities of the geometric system to the hundredth degree; the family didn't have anywhere near enough toothpicks in the house, and the drugstore was closed. Somehow, in this student's mind, the project had become much more complex than what had been assigned.

Pseudostupidity also appears in social settings. A simple request to hang up a coat in the closet can set the adolescent mind running amuck: "Are they trying to control me? If I refuse am I just doing it because I think they are trying to control me when they aren't? What should I do?" Usually what a teenager does is get mad. An innocent remark becomes fuel for a teenage conflagration—or for a teenage anxiety attack: Amanda, a very likable teenager, was worried about making friends after her family moved to a new school district. One of her teachers reported that she went to extremes to get classmates to like her—brought them treats, agreed with everything they said, just wore herself out to get noticed—when all she really had to do was be herself.

## Instructional Strategies

### Walking the Walk: Countering Teenage Hypocrisy

The best way to counter teenage hypocrisy is to immerse them in the real world and in their community. Exposing adolescents to the way things really work and showing them real-life consequences to their behavior will help make the connection between well-intentioned words and meaningful actions.

- Have students research service agencies and volunteer in the community at soup kitchens or shelters, act as mentors to younger children, or participate in diversity projects.

- Encourage students to offer help on a local political campaign.
- Invite people from the community—an elderly veteran, a local artist, someone who trains Seeing Eye dogs, anyone of interest—to be guest speakers in your class.
- Enact historical or government simulations.
- Compare the experiences of characters on television or in books to the real lives of students.
- Take a trip to a city dump or landfill and talk about recycling and littering on your campus.
- Attend cyberschool—investigate controversial issues on the Internet and discuss how they impact your thinking. Stimulate the conversation further by figuring out solutions. Channel that adolescent energy into positive action.

## Secret Revealed

It may come as some surprise for parents to learn that teenagers aren't claiming the garage for rock band practice just to give them a headache. Research has discovered the real reason behind the sudden enthusiasm for this noisy pastime—the parietal lobes are in full bloom! Suddenly, kids who grumbled about practicing for weekly music lessons can't get enough of playing the guitar or singing into a microphone. Kids who grumbled when Saturday morning cartoons ended now "waste" the day shooting hoops or hitting a tennis ball against the front of the house.

The parietal lobes control our sense of spatial awareness and the fluidity of the body's movements. Teen brains are busy forming new neurons and cleaning up old synaptic connections, fine-tuning adolescents' control over their fingers, arms, and legs. Their interest in all things physical springs from the discovery that, for the first time, they can actually play that tricky chord pattern and predict where that fly ball is going to land. Practice finally is likely to make perfect—the extra effort pays off, and everything is so much more fun.

## BACKSTAGE IN THE THEATER OF THE TEEN MIND

The parietal lobes are located at the top of the brain toward the back of each hemisphere. The front and back areas of the parietal lobes each have separate jobs. The front part receives messages from our senses, like pain, pressure, and temperature. Am I cold? Do I need a jacket? Are these pants too tight? Information from all over the body is sent here and then monitored. Not all areas of the body are represented equally, however; the lips and tongue are particularly sensitive to outside stimulus and have extensive network access to the parietal lobes. The back part of the parietal lobes is responsible for logic and spatial awareness and keeps track of where our fingers, feet, and head are in relation to our surroundings. They keep the rhythms of our motions going and help us avoid that clumsy misstep.

**Figure 2.3**  Human Brain

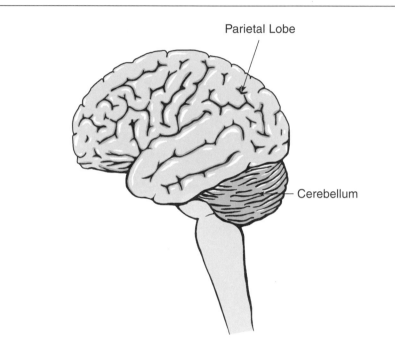

SOURCE: Adapted from Sousa, D. A. (2003), *How the Gifted Brain Learns*, p. 16.

Because early adolescence is when the parietal lobes create gray matter and prune extraneous neurons, it is a critical time for learning. As the parietal lobes mature, the ability to become proficient in sports and musical instruments is particularly enhanced. Caitlin, a track star, exudes enthusiasm as she completes the mile five seconds faster than her personal best. Wyatt practices the piano, playing with an ease and grace that is appreciated by everyone within earshot. Both of these individuals made huge strides in their capabilities during their teenage years.

We see this growth in athletics all the time. The junior varsity basketball team may have a tough time competing against the varsity team today, but the younger athletes keep practicing and learning the plays; next year, they'll be the ones playing varsity. Ninth-grade teachers are probably the most familiar with this transformation—their students go from confused, intimidated, and naïve in September to confident by May. The ninth-grade boy who spent the whole year with all his textbooks in his backpack (because he was too embarrassed to ask for help locating his locker) casually approaches the principal to discuss a class change in tenth grade.

## "EVERY MOVE YOU MAKE, EVERY STEP YOU TAKE . . ."

The cerebellum, located at the back of the brain, looks like a head of cauliflower and has more neurons than any other area of the brain. It is another part of the brain associated with movement. It is particularly linked to balance, posture, and gross motor skills like riding a bike, jogging, or snapping your flip-flops. It does not reach maturation until young adulthood, and its greatest changes happen during adolescence. Although Sting, the lead singer of the band, Police, may not have been referring to the cerebellum with his lyrics, "every move you make, every step you take, I'll be watching you," they certainly apply—the cerebellum guides and modifies our every action! But neuroscience has recently revealed that the cerebellum is also involved in the coordination of cognitive processes. It actually makes thinking tasks easier. Just as it balances and guides our physical movement, it keeps our thought processes moving smoothly. The more complicated a task facing us, the larger the role the cerebellum plays in resolving it (Giedd, Blumenthal, Jeffries, Castellanos, et al., 1999).

---

### Secret Revealed

Maybe we shouldn't have been making jokes about "dumb jocks" for all these years. Have you ever noticed how complicated a football playbook is? Could you memorize all those diagrams and recall them during the stress of competition? New research reveals that physical fitness might be what helps football players keep it in their heads! Dr. Jay Giedd (Giedd, Castellanos, Rajapakse, Vaituzis, & Rapoport, 1997), the neuroscientist from the National Institute of Mental Health (Remember him from Chapter 1?), also discovered that the

*(Continued)*

(Continued)

cerebellum, so long considered the "motor center" of the brain, plays a crucial role in coordinating thought processes and making decisions, too.

Teens need to move! Contradictory though it may seem, cutting PE and intramural sports is not the right way to improve academic programs at schools. A strong cerebellum is essential for efficient problem-solving skills and mental planning. Without regular physical activity, the teen brain gets the signal that the neurons in the cerebellum aren't as important as the neurons in other places (and less important neurons are in danger of being pruned). And without a strong and healthy cerebellum, that multistep math problem and reflective essay are much harder to do.

The cerebellum works in coordination with the motor cortex. When the cortex decides at a conscious level to move, it relays a message to the cerebellum. The cerebellum is connected by neurons to all the muscles in the body; it calculates which muscles are needed to enact the motion, sends them the message to move, and off you go! The cerebellum then continues to monitor and make adjustments to your movements. No wonder some people find it difficult to walk and chew gum at the same time! The combination requires the cerebellum to control two completely different sets of muscle groups.

Just as the abilities to play soccer, dance, or walk to school are guided by the cerebellum, so seem to be the thinking skills involved in planning a party, organizing a research paper, or making a reflective decision (Giedd, Blumenthal, Jeffries, Castellanos, et al., 1999). Your ability to read (although not your ability to comprehend) is stored in the cerebellum, as are song lyrics and lines from favorite movies ("Here's lookin' at you, kid") (Leonard, 1999). Like learning physical skills, the adolescent needs opportunities to practice cognitive processes in order to improve them. Teachers who involve students in thinking skills will help their students' cerebellums refine processing skills. Adolescents involved in bodily kinesthetic movement, whether taking part in a structured physical education class, participating in extracurricular activities, or playing musical instruments, will strengthen the neural connections in their adolescent cerebellum. Use it or lose it applies to the neurons in the cerebellum as much as the neurons in the cortex; they are all strengthened or sacrificed depending on usage.

Sadly, participation in all types of physical activity declines as children advance through school; maintaining moderate activity levels is a greater challenge for the adolescent than the child. As districts face financial challenges, physical education graduation requirements are being reduced throughout the country. For example, districts that once required one credit of physical education for graduation are now considering reducing the requirement to one-half credit. Although most schools still maintain afterschool sports programs and individual students exercise during their (ever-diminishing) free time, the lack of formal physical education classes will ultimately affect student cognition as well as coordination.

It is known that the adolescent who engages in challenging cognitive activities increases and strengthens the neurons involved in coordinating thinking skills (Giedd, Blumenthal, Jeffries, Castellanos, et al., 1999). Actively involving students with brain-compatible learning strategies, such as art or science projects, simulations, and problem-solving activities, will build better cerebellums than will forcing students into the roles of consistently passive recipients of knowledge. Elementary school teachers commonly use body movements to support learning, but secondary teachers aren't always comfortable with such techniques. Even though their students say things like "A math teacher had us move to learn a theorem—it  was helpful," and "In our American Studies class, the teacher had guys act out the characters of different stories. I can still see how they did it!"

Interestingly, the cerebellum is the area of the brain that differs the most between teenage boys and girls. Cerebellums in adolescent boys are about fourteen percent larger than cerebellums in adolescent girls, and the difference remains through adulthood (Raz, Gunning-Dixon, Head, Williamson, & Acker, 2001). It is speculated that the difference between male and female cerebellum size is partially a result of human evolution—males were the ones tracking and hunting while females were the ones keeping the home fires burning. Because the cerebellum controlled the skills the males were using, they developed larger cerebellums. (In general, the size of any brain component is proportionate to the amount of processing it does.) Whether or not this supposition is true, a larger cerebellum may explain why the boys in your class like to be in motion (moving their legs and stretching their arms) and the girls don't mind sitting and listening. Boys and girls both benefit, however, from the cognitive skills that come from physical movement.

# Instructional Strategies

## *Of Sound Mind and Body*

An extensive study of the benefits of active learning was done in elementary and middle schools in Chicago. Classrooms that actively engaged students were compared to classrooms that viewed students as passive receptors, relying on drill and practice to increase learning. The results were impressive. Classrooms that had a great deal of interaction and didactic instruction saw dramatic increases in scores on the Iowa Test of Basic Skills in reading and math over a four-year period (Smith, Lee, & Newmann, 2001).

Active learning doesn't come without challenges: Limited class time, greater prep time, lack of materials, and of course the biggest challenge of all—the possibility that students won't engage, are some of the issues teachers face. Give yourself a break; remember that while creative methods of urging participation are great, simply mixing lecture and discussion creates an actively involved classroom. Whatever method you use to actively engage students, the payback in academic achievement is worth taking the risk.

Teachers come to the same conclusion informally all the time. Mr. Miller, a high school math teacher, was concerned that year after year his students had difficulty understanding the concept of slope. He decided to see if active learning in place of paper and pencil exercises would make a difference. "I had them measuring the slope on the school's handicapped accessible ramps, the football field, and the staircases. I know I had a lot of fun, and I think they did, too. The best news was that their tests showed they had a much better understanding of slope when all was said and done." Active learning works.

So incorporate movement into learning—sit less and move more. Enact simulations, play charades, and do energizers. Choreograph body movements to represent phenomena in nature or the emotions of a character in literature. Allow students to step into the psyche of a new character. Let them act out the experience of being a boring guest speaker, substitute teacher, or the teacher arguing with a student over a grade by stepping into another person's shoes. Compose a song. Create a collage, time capsule, or board game. Conduct a science experiment. Get out the cotton swabs, construction paper, marshmallows, and toothpicks and get busy!

## *Things to Try*

- Have students create time capsules of their lives. "Bury" the collective contributions somewhere on campus (in a safe place) and open them a year or two later. Then, let students take their individual capsules home. The personal connection at both ends of the project will engage all students.
- Simulate a mock Congress. Having representatives from every state will involve every student. Students work individually to gather data but work collectively to present it.
- Make a board game about some lesson in a social studies, English, or math class. Have students exchange games and play them. Small groups of students will form naturally; designing the games is educational, but playing them is fun.

- Design a bumper sticker that reflects political views on an issue—this activity combines creativity with academic research. Have a contest with silly prizes for the best bumper stickers in a variety of categories, such as "Bumper Sticker that Will Fit on the Smallest Car."
- Tour and study historic buildings in your area. Not only will a field trip give students a sense of perspective about their community and times gone by, the novelty of the location will make a better background against which to remember new knowledge. The effort of walking through rooms or from building to building will engage the cerebellum.
- Create a collage from recycled materials. This hands-on project allows students to communicate their ideas about real-world issues while expressing themselves artistically.
- Create an advertisement for nutritional eating. Higher-level thinking is engaged as students analyze and decide what information is most important for consumers to know, what will grab their attention, and how to get the message across.
- Make a brochure of your life, school, or community. Who are you? What do you stand for? Choose an audience of peers, parents, teachers, or community. Ask students to discuss how their brochures could change to suit different audiences.
- Teach a lesson in television-talk-show or trivia-game-show format. Students can write questions and keep score. They can also take turns playing host and guests or game participants—and so can you!
- For physical education teachers: Have students design and implement a personal fitness program after assessing personal strength, endurance, and flexibility. Teens will practice setting goals, compete with themselves instead of each other (promoting camaraderie and cooperation), and benefit from improved physical health.
- Research a need in the community, hypothesize a solution, and propose it to the local school board. Not only would students have to think abstractly, they would also have the chance to offer their knowledge to the community. Making a real contribution is a motivator and a true self-esteem builder.

## FEEDBACK: FOOD FOR LEARNING

The brain works via a system of checks and balances. It chooses its next cognitive move on the basis of what it just did (Bangert-Drowns, Kulik, Kulik, & Morgan, 1991). Feedback is required to clarify and correct the information we receive; it allows the brain to readjust and reevaluate what it thinks it knows. Feedback is best when it is corrective in nature, explaining what students did right and wrong. Positive feedback—which can include suggestions about how to improve or change—helps us cope with stress. Our adrenal system goes into overdrive when we are stressed; hearing the words "That's right," "Good job," or "Nice work" keeps us relaxed.

## Secret Revealed

 It's time for teachers to reconsider everything they've thought about giving feedback to students. Teens don't crave feedback because they are insecure about their academic performance or needy for attention—they crave feedback because it helps them finish learning. Learning, the growth of new neurons and the creation of new synaptic connections, is the brain's response to stimulus. Stimulus, response, stimulus, response—responding to environmental stimulus is one of the basic life functions. Externally, we respond to rain by seeking shelter and to hot stoves by pulling our hand away. Internally, we respond to hunger by eating and to germs by activating the immune system—and by restructuring the brain according to knowledge we acquire.

Feedback is one form of stimulus. When the brain gets no stimulus of feedback, it has no reason to respond to information by learning. Feedback is especially important to teenagers because of the changes occurring in their brain. Without information about their performance, their brains won't know what neurons to grow or which ones to prune. Positive feedback actually releases serotonin into the brain, reinforcing feelings of calm and happiness. Feedback, in the classroom and in life, is one of the most important ways you can help teens turn their brains into efficient learning systems.

Feedback is especially important during adolescence, when the brain is undergoing so much building and pruning of synapses. Rarely do students understand things the first time they are presented; the brain learns through trial and error. As their brains take in new information, certain neurons are activated and certain neurons are not. Feedback is just as important as the original information sent to the brain because it completes the cycle of learning. Feedback helps teen brains decide which neurons to turn on and which to turn off, assisting the brain in making adjustments and correcting misinformation. The brain tries one combination and then another until the correct response is learned (and probably does more eliminating than increasing of neuron activity).

Feedback must be timely and specific to be of any use. Consider Lee, who was frustrated and disgusted with his English teacher. "The whole semester we only did one paper, at the beginning of the year, and we didn't get it back until finals. My paper just had one large B on the front—no other comments. It was really stupid. She hardly had anything to grade our writing on, and we never got a chance to improve." Worst-case scenario, sure, but returning work in an untimely fashion is a recurring theme in some classrooms. The assignment that is not returned to the student for weeks loses its impetus, as does the paper that receives only a letter grade with no follow-up comments (Marzano et al., 2001).

Multiple assessment strategies make the failure to grade and hand back assignments much more avoidable. Use a variety of formal and informal assessments to communicate with your students. Distribute slips of brown paper on which students can write questions about the "muddy waters" that obscure their comprehension of the content. Pass quickly around the room having each student contribute one thing they learned in class that day. Keep records on academic and nonacademic achievement, along with portfolios of student work (including photos or videos of work that can't be documented in other ways). At every stage, involve students in the process of their own evaluation and assessment.

## Instructional Strategies

### *Fun With Feedback*

Performance-based assessment counters teacher-made multiple-choice and standardized tests by assessing students during real-world activities, or at least as close to the real world as possible. It emphasizes doing (active participation) and it usually takes places over a long period of time—from a week to even a month. The teacher and students reflect on the work, noting its strengths and weaknesses. Such feedback helps the student strengthen synaptic connections. The possible tools are unlimited:

- Advertisements
- Advice columns
- Autobiographies
- Bedtime stories
- Book jackets
- Campaign speeches
- Data sheets
- Diary entries
- Dramatic presentations

- Editorial writings
- Encyclopedia entries
- Epilogues
- Experiments
- Fairy tales
- Films
- Greeting cards
- Nutrition charts
- Paintings
- Parodies

- Petitions
- Radio programs
- Sales pitches
- Scrapbooks
- Sculptures
- Sequels
- Simulations
- Speeches
- Superstitions
- Tributes
- TV commercials

*(Continued)*

(Continued)

## *Things to Try*

- Before a new lesson, give students a short questionnaire to fill out, or conduct a brief discussion to determine their background knowledge. This formative assessment will help you determine where to start the lesson (and who might need extra attention during the unit).

- Pick an important term or concept from your daily lesson and have students list ideas associated with it. For example, students in a government class might list *Native American, reservation, self-determination, rights,* and *politics* for the word *sovereignty.* Then, have students compare their lists with a partner, noting what items are common to both lists and discussing the items that appear on one list but not the other.

- Distribute empty or partially completed outlines before a class lecture or during a video, and have students fill in the blanks as information is presented. This will focus their attention and help them identify important ideas.

- Have students create a memory matrix based on categories you assign. For instance, you could compare feudalism to mercantilism with the following categories: sources of wealth, generation of wealth, distribution of wealth, and population centers. Students will see immediately what important information they remember and what they need to keep studying.

- Assign a sixty-second paper on what you covered during that day's lesson. One minute is a very small amount of class time to invest in an assignment that will tell you at a glance if students understand the main points of your lesson or are simply focusing on minor and supporting ideas.

- Have students devise a pro-and-con grid for one concept they are learning. Listing advantages and disadvantages requires them to go beyond memorizing facts to analyzing information; it reinforces their decision-making skills.

- Use concept maps—drawings that show the connections between concepts and facts—for insight into how students are thinking about their own thinking.

- Make space in your room to store student portfolios. Annotated portfolios include artifacts from class along with explanations of the significance of the selections. (Often, the relevance of the artifact is explained in terms of classroom goals and content.)

- Let students generate test questions and answers. To write a good question, they must have an understanding of the material and the key points. The quality of their questions can help you assess their weaknesses. Returning these questions to students in the form of a practice test also makes them part of the process, removing them from the role of "innocent bystander" during assessment.

Many of these ideas are from the book *Classroom Assessment Techniques: A Handbook for College Teachers (2nd Edition),* by Thomas A. Angelo and K. Patricia Cross (1998: Jossey-Bass).

## ORGANIZATION ≠ OPPRESSION

The brain stores new information by identifying patterns in it. As it receives fresh material, the brain searches its established neural networks for a background against which it can comprehend the new knowledge. Anything familiar—sensory information (like a remembered scent), a pattern, a relationship—will serve as a connection to information already stored in the brain. If the brain finds nothing on which to build, it abandons the new information. Many study skills and instructional strategies are compatible with the brain's innate desire to decipher patterns. Disheartened middle and high school students make remarks about their homework like "I don't know where to start," "This stuff is so boring," and "One minute I know it, and the next I've forgotten it" because their brains have a difficult time tapping into these patterns.

---

### Secret Revealed

Contrary to popular belief, teens aren't looking to pick fights with the adults in their lives. They aren't arguing about skipping breakfast and borrowing the car because they enjoy the verbal sparring. Parents and teachers who give brooding teens a wide berth to avoid provoking an outburst are going at it all the wrong way. They ought to be looking for ways to guide teenagers instead.

Sound shocking? Prepare yourself for this: Teenagers actually want and need guidance from adults about important life issues like education and work plans (Schneider & Younger, 1996). This emotional support from adults is imperative to adolescents' healthy development. Don't be fooled into backing off just because of a teen's show of resistance to your advice. What may appear to be oppositional behavior is often a desire for personal autonomy. Teens want to choose their own clothes, friends, and hobbies—these things demonstrate their independence and individuality. The search for autonomy is normal; it's the beginning step toward taking on adult responsibilities. Once the argument about homework ends, however, teens are very receptive to suggestions about choosing a college or how to act during a job interview.

---

Help teenagers access these patterns by providing models, organization, and structure to their lives. Every student needs a planner to track assignments; it's hard to accomplish something if you're not sure what you need to do. Hold young teens accountable for keeping their planners up-to-date, and they'll maintain the habit as they grow older. Teach them how to budget their time by deciding what to study and for how long, to take advantage of mental stamina by doing the hard or boring stuff first, to establish a context for studying by always working in the same place—and nag them to get off the Internet!

It's only fair that teachers and parents help teens establish order in their lives; we are the ones who expect them to achieve academically, participate in extracurricular activities, help with many of the household chores, and perhaps hold down a job. Students have never been busier. Many adolescents barely have time to grab a snack or change clothes between activities. They hold up their part of the bargain pretty well but do better when we provide study skills and the support to perfect them.

In class, cue them. Emphasize and repeat important information. Teach students different note-taking methods (Cornell–2-column, SQ3R, outlines, or your personal favorite) and have them practice one style until they can do it automatically while listening to a lecture. Remind them to review their notes within twenty-four hours to improve their retention (and save study time in the long run). The brain remembers images more easily than words, which makes graphic organizers, pictures, charts, and graphs effective tools for organizing patterns.

My personal favorite note-taking style is Double Column notes because they allow the students to encode the information in a variety of ways and are easily modified to meet different students' needs and purposes.

**Figure 2.4**   Double-Column Notes

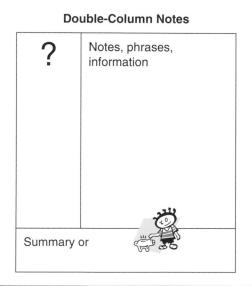

## EVERY GOOD BOY DOES FINE

While we would prefer that all learning be meaningful, in the real world people need to memorize important information that is arbitrary and dull. In classroom situations, students can benefit from mnemonics, techniques for remembering information with images and words (Carney & Levin, 2000). For example, the names of the planets or the number of days in each month are more easily memorized with the help of a mnemonic. Rhymes and acronyms are two common strategies that can be fun for students learning by rote.

A teacher may provide mnemonics, but they are more meaningful when the students construct them. Younger children do better with auditory mnemonics, such as "When two vowels go a-walking, the first one does the talking." Adolescents, with their increased mental capacities, do well with visual or auditory mnemonics like the following examples (Wang & Thomas, 1995):

- PMAT: prophase, metaphase, anaphase, telophase—the four stages of cellular mitosis.
- I Am A Person: Indian, Arctic, Atlantic, Pacific—the four oceans of the world.
- Sober Physicists Don't Find Giraffes In Kitchens: the orbital names for electrons are S, P, D, F, G, I, K.
- Associate each school supply with a particular spot in your bedroom. Imagine your backpack with your desk, band music on the bed, and PE clothes in the drawer. Before leaving for school each morning, mentally walk around the room. Have you remembered all your items? Visualizing your dresser will cue you to bring your P. E. clothes if you've forgotten to pack them.
- To remember that Annapolis is the capital of Maryland, visualize two apples. For St. Paul, Minnesota, imagine a saint sipping a soda.
- To remember the twelve cranial nerves (for a brain-compatible teaching class, of course), just think of the rhyme, "On Old Olympus Towering Tops, A Finn And German Viewed Some Hops": the cranial nerves are the olfactory, optic, occulomotor, trochlear, trigeminal, abducens, facial, auditory, glossopharyngeal, vagus, spinal accessory, and hypoglossal!

Time-management and test-taking strategies also should be taught to teenagers. When students have a framework for remembering information and keeping track of their due dates on calendars, they are much better prepared to cope with the cognitive and structural chaos inside their heads.

Study skills help the brain organize and make connections. Students stop cold if they are overwhelmed by too much to learn in too little time, by not knowing where to start or by not having time to let information sink in. Study strategies can make the difference between academic success and meltdown. Share the following items with your students to help them take charge of their learning.

## Effective Study Strategies

- Take notes. Whether you prefer KWL (What I KNOW, What I WANT to Know, and What I LEARNED), outline, or double columns, pick one and practice it until it becomes second nature.
- Tap into prior knowledge.
- Organize information in notebooks, on note cards, or in a computer.
- Budget study time. Schedule an hour or two each day at a desk in your bedroom or school library, wherever you want. Take a ten-minute brain break every fifty minutes and stick to the plan.
- Summarize in writing what you've learned at the end of each study session.
- Monitor your learning while you study; reflect on what needs more work and what you don't understand.
- Keep an assignment notebook. Break down large assignments into smaller tasks and cross items off your list as you complete them.
- Eliminate distractions, turn off the TV, stop instant messaging, and let voicemail collect your cell phone messages.
- Be positive—as they say, "Change your thoughts, change your life."
- Do the difficult material first, while you are still fresh.

## Secret Revealed

Instant messaging, googling, and downloading songs while attempting to do homework—a good thing or a bad thing? David Meyer, a psychologist who directs the Brain, Cognition, and Action Laboratory at the University of Michigan (www.umich.edu/~bcalab) warns that each interruption requires time for the brain to readjust. A small math or language arts assignment that would normally take thirty minutes, will suddenly take two or three hours if multitasking is involved.

Surprisingly, the more divergent the task, the easier the work is for the brain. If we are trying to pet our dog while we do homework, the brain continues to operate smoothly; however, if we are trying to do two similar jobs with our brain, such as instant messaging and writing a composition, the brain gets stuck on pause.

## Effective Test-Taking Strategies

The pressure to perform on tests is impacting the way teachers instruct, students learn, and parents fret. Providing students with added support in the art of test taking is a requirement for the twenty-first century.

- Test prep should begin on the first day of class (and no, I'm not kidding, high schoolers)—reviews, homework, readings, and attending class, are all important parts of the process. The best way to reduce anxiety is to be prepared.
- Identify your best test-studying strategies—do you study best alone or in a group, with flash cards or highlighting, or is a combination the best?
- Eat before a test; a fully performing brain needs the energy supply food provides.
- Quickly peruse the test when you first get it and catch the general gist.
- Stay positive during the test—if you start to feel anxious, breath deeply, or use other stress-reducing tactics.
- Do the easiest problems first (this is the opposite approach of study strategies, where the most difficult assignments are tackled first).
- Be sure to complete the items with the greatest point value. If something has to give, let it be the one-pointers.
- Students, create a mock test; this requires higher-level thinking and is a good way to review.

## A BETTER DAY STUDENT TEACHING

*"Good morning," the student teacher said to each student as the teenagers shuffled into class. She paused now and then to ask individual students about a dance recital the night before or to compliment them on the tiebreaking goal they scored at the game. The room filled with noisy chatter as the class took their seats. She began class by passing around an empty box and asking students to put something of no real*

*value in it (such as pencils, pieces of paper, or movie ticket stubs). As the box went around the room, she asked the students for examples of storytelling, perhaps from their own families. When the box returned to the front of the room, she told a story about how her great-grandmother had participated in the women's suffrage movement. She punctuated elements of her tale with props from the box—the class was riveted. Afterward, the teacher divided the class and the items from the box into four groups for a cooperative learning assignment. The students told and listened to each other's stories; the signal to clean up at the end of class caught them all by surprise.*

# The Social Brain

Science has demonstrated that emotions strongly impact learning. This is problematic because teens are still learning to balance and manage their emotions. They are also learning how to negotiate their place in the world, from maintaining friendships to practicing the mating dance.

**Did you know that . . .**

- Adolescence is when the brain begins to develop templates for adult relationships
- Teen emotions can easily cement lifelong memories or form powerful learning blocks
- Teens value adult influence even though they complain about it
- Teenagers will climb the moral ladder only as their frontal lobes develop
- Boy brains and girl brains really are different—it's not just socialization

*Senior Prom—the ultimate spring mating ritual. Joseph stood on his porch, arms folded, his face a mixture of happiness and apprehension. His daughter, Sarah, was all dressed up in a full-length, midnight blue evening gown (advertised at the boutique as the "strapless wonder" for obvious reasons). Lex, her date, looked like Prince Charming in a black tuxedo with a white rose boutonniere. The couple cheerfully posed for pictures, waved good-bye, and dashed off in his car. Their anticipation of the night ahead of them was palpable. Joseph watched them drive out of sight and then turned to his wife and said, drolly, "They're all in heat." She agreed immediately.*

## LOVE ON THE BRAIN

Ashley, a bubbly fourteen-year-old, spends most of her time daydreaming about Andy. She watches his every move, wears clothes that are too risqué, and laughs a little too loud, all in hopes of catching his attention. Andy, busy doing his math, is totally oblivious to the fact that the mating dance is about to begin.

Teenagers are very eager to share their thoughts about the opposite sex. You have to prod them to discuss academic subjects, but words just flow when it comes to boyfriends and girlfriends. Boys are consumed with thoughts about girls and girls are consumed with thoughts about boys. Questions such as "Does she like me?" and "Will he ask me out?" hover constantly in their love-afflicted minds; questions about how to solve math equations with double variables are almost never entertained!

Most researchers agree that there are sensitive times for learning certain material. Although the concept of "critical periods" is controversial, clearly there are ideal times to learn to crawl, to talk, and to learn a foreign language (Puckett, Marshall, & Davis, 1999). A number of neuroscientists believe that adolescence is the ideal time to learn the mating ritual. Research by Dr. Martha McClintock shows that boys and girls have their first real crush at age ten (before puberty) and suggests that these crushes spring from connections in their brains that are made during this time (McClintock & Herdt, 1996). During adolescence, teenagers have the opportunity to become involved with their own sexuality and ultimately begin the search to find a mate. The low-slung jeans, pierced belly buttons beneath midriff tops, and macho, fly-by-the-seat-of-your-pants baggy jeans are all attempts to experiment with sexual attractiveness.

### Secret Revealed

To the bewilderment and frustration of teachers and parents, "hangin' around and talkin'" is one of teens' favorite pastimes. Given to their own devices, teenagers can spend a full afternoon mulling over how they will spend the afternoon only to suddenly realize the afternoon is over and it's time to start contemplating the evening. As adults we often view this as time lost, a pure and simple waste of an afternoon, but in actuality this idleness provides a meaningful period of problem solving. It is while they are hangin' and talkin' that they explore, negotiate, and make decisions.

The next time you see them engaged in something that appears to be unproductive during lunch or after school, leave them to their mystifying deliberations. Resist the temptation to offer suggestions (they won't be appreciated) and just walk away knowing they are constructing a new and improved brain.

## THE LEVELS OF LOVE

Anthropologist Dr. Helen Fisher is enamored of the subject of love, in teens and adults alike. She speculates that there are different levels of love, each influenced by a different system in the brain (Fisher, Aron, Mashek, Li, & Brown, 2002). One level is lust—immediate sexual attraction for someone. In this stage, it is accurate to say we have sex on the brain. The male hormone, testosterone, is associated with increasing the sex  drive in both men and women. Because levels of testosterone surge through the teen body during puberty, it is no surprise that teenage thoughts and behaviors focus so often on sexual mates and desire.

Another stage of love is romantic love—think Romeo and Juliet. During this stage, we become obsessed with the person who is the object of our attention. We are unable to think of anyone or anything else. We want to be with this person day and night. This romp with romance can be witnessed in the all-consuming adolescent crush. One high school girl admitted that she spent about ninety percent of her time thinking about her boyfriend. A high school boy said, "I think about girls every three seconds, unless I'm playing Nintendo." Is it any wonder that most girls start dating at fourteen and most boys follow close on their heels six months to a year later? (A girl's interest in dating and being dated usually precedes a boy's for the mere fact that she hits puberty earlier.)

Younger teens are just getting their toes wet in the dating scene. They tend to gravitate toward people who enjoy the same things they do; having fun is usually their goal. When asked to describe his first date in eighth grade, an eleventh grader recalled, "We went to Jeff's house to watch a movie. There were about five of us there—two couples and an extra girl. I thought it was kind of awkward. I'm not sure who asked who out." Another boy said, "My first date was in the seventh grade. We went to the mall with another couple. I had fun. Bought the CD for the Aquabats. She asked me who they were and I said, 'They're awesome.' I can still remember the conversation." A teenage girl recalled, "My first date was in sixth grade. I went to the park with him and a group of kids. We swung on swings and went on the merry-go-round. We didn't talk much but it was fun." Older teens also want fun, but they are beginning to look for more intimacy on dates—someone with whom they can talk openly about their feelings and for whom they feel respect and affection. Of course, until adolescents figure out who they are and develop a self-identity, it's difficult for them to carry on a sustained relationship.

---

**Dating serves a number of purposes for a teenager**

- Provides a form of recreation
- Serves as a source of status and achievement
- Shows independence from the family
- Offers the opportunity to begin to experiment sexually

---

## WHY LOVE FEELS SO GOOD

When we are in love, dopamine is released (and boy do we feel great). Dr. Marian Diamond said that a person in love "is often more creative, has more endurance, more energy and is more focused and less interested in the broad problems of society" (2000, para. 9). The only proof you'll probably need of the veracity of this statement is the memory of the first time you fell in love! And once we are in love, we want to experience this good feeling more and more. Love and pleasure are particularly affected by the chemical dopamine—the all-time feel-good neurotransmitter. At times it seems as if all pleasure is connected to dopamine and dopamine alone. Dopamine's effect on the mind has been compared to the effect of cocaine and other addictive drugs. Our brains interpret love and sex as a reward and actively search for the next fix.

Dopamine and adolescence make a spine-tingling combination. The teen brain seems to be particularly sensitive to dopamine levels and craves the euphoric thrill it brings (Spear, 2002). Curiously, many teenagers equate falling in love with taking a risk, which is another event that increases dopamine levels in the brain. "Hooking up" with that new boy or girl in your chemistry class is a surefire way to get a dopamine rush. Once teens figure that out, the race is on for a date and possible mate. Further complicating matters is the fact that teenagers' lives are filled with action, excitement, and danger—highly aroused states that make them particularly susceptible to falling in love. For some reason, if a teen (or anybody, actually) meets someone at an emotionally charged moment, such as at a football game or during a violent thunderstorm, the chances increase that they'll fall in love. Because teenagers look for novelty and excitement in their lives, they are at risk for finding love in all the wrong places.

As fate would have it, their brain structure increases love's compelling appeal. At University College London, Dr. Semir Zeki and Dr. Andreas Bartels scanned the brains of young adults who had fallen madly in love within the last six months or year and who were looking at photographs of their sweethearts (Bartels & Zeki, 2000). Four regions of the brain lit up like lights on a Christmas tree: the medial insula, which is associated with emotional interpretations—particularly visual ones; the anterior cingulate gyrus, a part of the brain involved in feelings of euphoria; and the putamen and the caudate nuclei, two tiny areas deep within the brain that are related to positive experiences and addiction. Furthermore, love highly stimulates the reticular formation (Diamond, 2000), which is a network in the central core of the brain stem responsible for gathering information from all over the body and for regulating sleep and arousal patterns. Within the reticular formation are neuron groups that run through the lower brain stem and up to the cerebellum, hypothalamus, thalamus, amygdala, and cerebral cortex.

## Secret Revealed

 Stop and compare this piece of new information to what you've always thought: The brain, not the gonads, is what fills teenagers with lust. (Actually, it fills everybody with lust but teens in particular.) Adolescence is when the brain lays down the circuitry that will enable teens to later form adult sexual relationships and reproduce—the main prerogative of the species! Crushes and going steady are just practice, so teens will have it figured out when they are ready for parenthood.

Dr. Semir Zeki and Dr. Andreas Bartels, scientists at University College London, studied love and its expression with MRI technology. They discovered that areas of the brain involved in the feeling of euphoria, emotion, and addiction lit up when people gazed upon photographs of their beloved. Euphoria and addiction—no wonder the teen brain seeks to engage feelings of love over and over again. Add to the mix the fact that teens are still learning to regulate their emotions, and you've got a heady mix of the boy-and-girl-crazies in the classroom!

The more active the reticular formation, the more able we are to focus attention on things outside of us—like a romantic interest. If you see a boy you're attracted to, your amygdala registers pleasure, and your frontal lobes translate it as love. Adolescents have trouble dealing with romantic feelings not only because they have such strong sexual desires but also because their frontal lobes are not yet well developed enough to regulate them. They feel lust, so they make an inappropriate pass at a girl without pausing to think of her reaction. Until age and maturity enable adolescents to better control their desires and focus, learning and responsibility are much lower priorities in their brains.

## Instructional Strategies

### *Sex Versus Social Studies*

It's normal for students to be preoccupied with the opposite sex. Teachers need to accept this fact and get used to it because teens aren't in any hurry to change. Be tolerant of the strange (yet normal) habits and behaviors they exhibit in your classroom (at least, the nondisruptive ones). To attract the opposite sex, teens experiment with hair color, clothes, body piercing, and tattoos (maybe tattoos aren't that normal!). Breakups are traumatic; help them understand that intense feelings are to be expected and that it is acceptable to express them. However, the classroom is a place of learning first and foremost—not a venue to show off spaghetti straps or low-slung jeans. Set limits on sexually explicit clothes. Work with other teachers, parents, and administrators to regulate dress codes and determine what may and may not be worn to school.

Put students in mixed-sex groups to discuss academic issues. Boys and girls who interact in class find common ground that is not based on sex and learn to view each other as more than just future romantic partners. Positive adult role models and mentors are crucial guides for teens as they explore their sexuality. The media portrays casual sex as the rule, not the exception. Young girls in particular draw the conclusion that their sexuality is the most important way to validate themselves and attract a boy's attention. Important adults in their life can balance and channel a teen's energy into other social and academic endeavors. If businesspeople are too busy to act as mentors, ask young adults and college students, senior citizens, or homemakers to contribute. You can also introduce teenagers to books and magazines that don't focus on sex and relationships but rather on hobbies, sports, and educational interests.

## A SENSE OF "ME"

Adolescents' romantic development parallels their cognitive and physical development. Cognitively, the adolescent is able to ponder the future and whip out sarcastic zingers; physically, breasts are budding and limbs are sprouting; and emotionally, a sense of morality and self-concept start to gel (Greenspan & Benderly, 1997).

Adolescence is the time to ponder the question, "Who am I?" Teenagers spend a great deal of time experimenting with various roles—how to look, who to hang out with, what hobbies to adopt—as they form an identity and define themselves as a person. Through constant changes of hairstyles, clothes, music preferences, dating partners, and social grouping, teenagers begin to understand who they are. This is a time-honored tradition of every generation. In the 1950s, teenagers greased their hair, wore leather jackets, and listened to Elvis Presley. In the 1960s, it was go-go boots, long hair, and the Beatles. Today, it's body piercing, crop tops, and Miley Cyrus. (This complements their parents' time-honored tradition of general disapproval and belief that the world was a better place when they were young!) As teens experiment with and identify who they are, they begin to form an image of their strengths and weaknesses.

Our self-concept is the way we view ourselves. "I love playing trumpet; I'm first chair in the band," "Biology is my favorite subject," and "I'm running-back on the varsity football team" are all statements made by students with high self-concepts. In contrast, Will sits at the back of the class, arms folded, silently daring the teacher to ask him a question. He lost interest in this class a long time ago. His reason? "I can't do math." Monica, who constantly talks to her neighbor and glances around the room, has a different reason: "This stuff is impossible to learn. I'm thinking about lunch instead." Both of these students exhibit signs of a low self-concept.

## Secret Revealed

American culture has a long history of not trusting emotions. Instead of appreciating and respecting emotions, our culture tends to devalue them. It is assumed that emotions lead to poor decision making, hysteria, and ultimately chaos. This perspective is particularly pervasive in schools. There, emotions are avoided, not encouraged. They are considered a disruption to learning, not an enhancement. After all, how can teens be attentive and learn if they are emotionally wound up? Fortunately, new neuroscience technology is confirming

*(Continued)*

(Continued)

and legitimizing the dynamic role of emotion. Dr. Antonio Damasio (1994), a primary researcher in this field, has shown that emotions are a key part of cognitive processes.

For educators, this means rethinking the role of emotions and acknowledging emotions not as just a piece of life but rather as a critical part of learning and memory. The logical part of the brain might set goals like acing a serve in tennis or eating nutritionally, but it is the emotional part that makes us passionate about achieving them.

Self-concept is shaped by our past experiences. Positive experiences, such as earning an A in a challenging class, receiving a sincere compliment from a teacher, or having friends who save you a seat at lunch, help build a positive self-concept. Failing a class, being the brunt of a mean-spirited joke, or being humiliated in class reinforce a negative self-concept. All these experiences cause emotional reactions in the amygdala. The amygdala remembers pleasurable experiences and craves more. Likewise, it closes the gate to learning when a remembered emotion is anger or fear. In school, there is a strong correlation between a student's self-concept and academic achievement, motivation, and teacher and peer relationships; the combination puts them in either an upward spin or a downward spiral in school. Students with negative self-concepts are more at risk of dropping out of school, becoming pregnant, or using drugs—scary realities for too many adolescents (Ormrod, 2000).

When academic content is connected to a pleasant experience, we make a pleasant association. The next time we are in a similar situation, the amygdala remembers the pleasant feeling and opens the mental gate to learn more about that particular topic. The amygdala also remembers negative emotions connected to an experience or concept and will be hesitant to pass it on to working memory. If it feels good, we want to learn more; if it does not, we steer clear. We categorize things that make us feel good as our strengths and continue to work on them, further building a positive self-concept in this area. In this way, we continue to positively and negatively reinforce our self-concepts.

Comments like those made by Will and Monica are not-so-subtle clues to problems in math. Teachers react to this by repeating concepts, reteaching at a slower pace, or breaking a large assignment into small steps, but even such basic strategies do not guarantee a student will learn the information. An educator's time would be better spent focusing on a student's emotional feelings about the content. It's very difficult for concepts to override an emotion. Until the student's emotional disposition toward a topic changes, information has little chance of making it into memory. Emotional engagement leads to learning, which leads in yet another way to a positive self-concept.

---

## Instructional Strategies

### Engage Positive Emotions in the Classroom

Middle school students in a family and consumer science class were learning to sew. The teacher spent twenty minutes patiently showing everyone how to thread a bobbin. Finally, after lots of trial and error and some frustration, all the bobbins were threaded. To their dismay, the teacher next told the students to unthread and then rethread the bobbins. This time, all the bobbins were threaded within a few minutes, and everyone was ready to go. To accompany the sound of the sewing machines, the teacher put an Elvis CD on the stereo, and to the tune of "A Hunka' Hunka' Burnin' Love," she told a story of her visit to Graceland and her love of The King. Looking around the room, it was clear that everyone was having fun.

Our emotional experiences always matter when it comes to learning. They affect what we pay attention to, our motivation, reasoning strategies, and our ability to remember. Music can be a powerful memory and emotion builder. It enables us to make personal connections by expressing a variety of emotions, from love, hope, and triumph to fear, anxiety, and despair. It can instill unforgettable fear or create a sense of euphoria. Good manners and a pleasant demeanor evoke positive emotions, as do opportunities for peer interaction. Teachers who encourage healthy expressions of emotions will capitalize on the best of the baffling and boisterous teen outbursts.

### Things to Try

- Share an emotional story like that of a Holocaust survivor or Lance Armstrong's victory over cancer and his subsequent triumphs in the Tour de France.
- Demonstrate your love of learning and enthusiasm for teaching. Not only will you bring emotion into the classroom, you will also act as a role model for lifelong learning.
- Teens find interactive technology like computer animation, multimedia software, or supervised chat rooms fun and exhilarating. Bring it into your lesson plans.
- Celebrate achievement in your class. Go roller-skating on the school blacktop after a week of standardized testing, or watch a movie at the culmination of a unit. Smile in class, be friendly, tell a joke, or play a game. Have fun!
- Show empathy for the problems students encounter by making comments like "I've made that same mistake" and "I can tell you're worried."

*(Continued)*

(Continued)

- Never ridicule a student's questions or comments. If one student verbally ambushes another, model appropriate behavior. Ask the attacking student to express only his or her thoughts instead of abusing another student's ideas.
- During seatwork, allow students to ask a friend or neighbor for help, or establish support groups of three or four students who can turn to each other for assistance.
- Explicitly teach social behaviors, covering everything from keeping your hands and feet to yourself to understanding trigger words for anger and how to diffuse it. Positive peer relationships and the skills to maintain them are particularly important at this age.
- Give students your full attention. Make eye contact, smile, actively listen, and inquire about their state of minds. Remark, "You've got an awfully big grin on your face. Did you get good news?" and "We missed you in class yesterday."
- Communicate honestly to students that you value them. The following comments let students know one adult believes they are important: "I like how you explained that," "I appreciate the effort you put into that project," and "Thank you for helping."
- Play soft music as students enter the room or in the background during an assignment. Music can set any mood and ties into almost any content area: Try "The Planets" by Gustav Holst during science or George Cohan's "Yankee Doodle Dandy" to introduce World War II. Students can also rewrite the lyrics to a song and perform it.

## A MIND OF MY OWN

As adolescents begin to define their self-concept in more meaningful terms, they begin to think about who they are, what they believe in, and where their life is headed. The changes occurring within the adolescent are not happening in a vacuum. They adopt these roles not always for their own sake but because of the influence of the world around them. Parent and peer validation is very important to the formation of identity. The adolescent is emotionally dependent upon supportive parents and accepting peers.

### Secret Revealed

Despite what you may have learned from books and movies, teens don't resist advice and guidelines purely to be ornery (well, not all the time). They are trying to express themselves as unique individuals and are struggling to distinguish their values and interests from other people's. "Question authority" is more than a smart-aleck attitude about following rules—it's an essential stage of a teenager's life!

Swedish scientist Dr. Lena Adamson (Adamson, Hartman, & Lyxell, 1999) specializes in adolescent self-concept formation. Her research team identified teens' need to balance their own wishes and desires in relation to the wishes and desires of others as the most influential factor in developing their own identity. Fitting in with the peer group is one way to strike a balance but so is opposing the adults they know! Ironically, Adamson's research shows that adults are also very important to teenagers as sources of knowledge and experience. (But try getting one to admit it!)

During this stage, adolescents begin to desire emotional autonomy and want to be more independent and self-sufficient. Be aware, there is a significant difference between the autonomy of a younger adolescent and an older adolescent. Seventeen- and eighteen-year-olds are about seventy percent more independent than twelve- and thirteen-year-olds. Perhaps stemming from an instinctive desire to perpetuate the species, teens search outside the family to friends and potential mates. As they gradually (or to the unsuspecting parent, abruptly) shift their interest from parents to their peers, teenagers can appear to be almost indifferent to adults. Mom is someone who puts supper on the table, and Dad keeps the car working—two gray shadows in their friend-filled lives. If asked to choose between spending a night at home with Mom and Dad or going over to a friend's house, the friend wins hands down.

As much as it may appear that teens don't need adults, however, they have a strong need to interact with positive adult role models (Adamson et al., 1999). In these relationships, teens prefer the team approach with all participants on equal footing. In a teen-perfect world, no parents tell them what to do, how to do it, or when. Instead, parents and adolescents make decisions together; if parents lay down the law, they always do so with a thoughtful explanation. Amazingly, that part of what they want is what they need. Teen brains are not satisfied with a "because I said so" response. Their developing frontal lobes prepare them to be involved in the decision-making process and they "get it" when adults explain their decisions.

At the same time that they have a compelling desire for their own space, they desperately want parental guidance and affirmation. Parents need to set limits, hold high expectations, and never let their teenagers see them sweat. It can be a ticklish balancing act for parents, but it is not as big a contradiction as it seems. Parents who use their control to guide the teen and elect to talk through problems when they happen (instead of resorting to other discipline techniques) tend to raise the happiest and healthiest adolescents.

## Common Conflicts Between Teenagers and Parents

- Friends and dates
- Curfews
- Going out
- Going steady
- Hairstyles
- Clothes

- Where they are going
- Household chores
- Spending money responsibly
- Car
- Telephone

- School grades
- Homework
- Behavior at school
- Lack of respect for parents

## Common Conflicts Between Teenagers and Teachers

- Unfinished work
- Bullying
- Tardiness
- Truancy
- Lying
- The question, "Why do I need to know this?"

- Vague directions
- Boring lessons
- Verbal threats of class failure
- Inconsistent limits, rules, and consequences
- Overreactions

- Failure to listen
- The question, "How many times do I have to tell you?"
- Bad attitude
- Disrespect for authority

## CONSCIENCE AND CONSCIOUSNESS

"I'd cheat if I thought I wouldn't get caught." "She got to turn her paper in late! It's not fair!" "I was the one who left the candy wrapper on the music stand."

Moral development in adolescence aligns with cognitive development. As adolescents become able to think abstractly, they climb the moral ladder. Increasing reliance on their developing frontal lobes allows them to realize that moral rules help us maneuver and regulate society. They also learn that, although rules are important, people are more important. The maturing adolescent will change rules and make exceptions and realize  that it will not result in bedlam. Teens learn to take into account personal motivation for people's behavior and understand that it matters why somebody does something (Woolfolk, 2006). The black and white of the world open up first to shades of gray before blossoming into full color. As moral development progresses, adolescent decisions and choices become more rational and thoughtful.

## Secret Revealed

It's too simple to say that teenagers behave better in high school only because they want letters of recommendation for college applications. In fact, teens are in a profound state of moral development and are discovering a conscience! As their frontal lobes gain influence over their behaviors and decisions, they are increasingly aware of the value of social and moral rules and restraints, as well as of how their actions may hurt or help others. Moral development requires a sincere mix of logical and emotional intelligence.

A girl known for her catty remarks in junior high starts ignoring gossip and makes conversation about movies, books, or homework instead. A boy who was famous for his single-minded pursuit of straight A's decides not to cheat on the final exam and accepts the B for the semester grade. Teens begin to learn that silence is golden, not to kiss and tell, and to otherwise exercise discretion and restraint in all facets of social, academic, and personal life. They can imagine how it feels from someone else's point of view and they gain respect and desire for fairness.

As teens mature in their moral thinking, they understand that their lifestyle and culture are neither superior nor inferior to others. They develop a true respect for other ways of life and the value of diversity. Recognizing the importance of caring for others, granting and receiving forgiveness, being honest with themselves and others, and taking responsibility for their actions become a way of life—their lives are no longer just about them. Adolescents often develop an altruistic spirit and the desire to protect other people's rights with their own. Discussions that help students identify their personal values and encourage knowledge, involvement, and contributions to the community build character.

## Instructional Strategies

### Self-Concept and Moral Development

During adolescence, teenagers look inward with questions of "Who am I?" and "What am I worth?" These questions are best explored in an emotionally secure environment. Friends, family, and school form the foundation of that environment. To develop a sense of identity and self-esteem, adolescents look for acceptance and recognition from those people who

*(Continued)*

(Continued)

immediately influence them. Assuming that the school is a physically safe harbor, students are in a position to sift through the rubble in their brain and discover who they are.

### *Things to Try*

- Recognize individual differences. Quality teachers adapt to students' preferred learning styles. Vary the nature, content, and rate of your instruction to appeal to different learners in turn by the minute, the day, or the semester—students' needs and available hours in the day will dictate these changes.
- Cultivate individual student passions and interests. Take time once a month to get to know your students' interests. Showing you value them adds positively to the classroom climate; knowing their interests helps you tailor the curriculum.
- Respect peer pressure. Research shows that its benefits outweigh the disadvantages (Arnett, 2001). Positive influence by friends discourages at-risk behavior and lends that all-important emotional support to troubled or despairing teens.
- Encourage students to look at social issues from a variety of perspectives. Rewrite Cinderella from a stepsister's point of view, act out skits about discrimination, and use the Internet to correspond with people worldwide, always being careful to go only to safe, appropriate sites.
- Let students know you respect and want to hear their opinions; allow them opportunities to speak. Also respect privacy—give them permission to pass if they don't want to share their thoughts on material of a sensitive nature.
- Establish cooperative learning groups and peer-buddy relationships to embed academics in a social setting.
- Teenagers are very social creatures. Social interactions need not always occur in academic settings; sometimes let them socialize just for the sake of it. Give students time to talk about their feelings in large- and small-group discussions.
- Experimentation is a part of identity formation, and adolescents are drawn to fads. They are also preoccupied with sex and spend a great deal of time thinking about each other. Have a sense of humor about it. Understanding these innate and compelling distractions will reduce your frustration levels!
- Present many models for career choices and other roles. Speakers, field trips, and job shadowing will open students' eyes to a world of possibilities.
- Build independence through choice and personal responsibility. Plan some events or assignments together as a class—it is an effective way to tap into individual interests and learning styles. Let them choose a topic to study, such as teenage runaways, drugs, or truancy, and design a performance assessment to complement it—create a video, give an oral report, or present an original brochure or scrapbook.

- Explore current social topics and help students discover where they stand on controversial issues through discussion, debate, and journaling. Participate in worthy causes like a local election, cross-age tutoring, or volunteering at a children's hospital.
- Prod adolescents to examine inconsistencies in their actions and values through friendly discussions. It is not uncommon for teenagers to expound on the value of honesty while boasting that they lied to their parents and attended a party (or for them to emphasize the importance of good nutrition while munching on French fries).
- Establish a caring classroom with moral standards by not tolerating cheating, stealing, or harming others.
- Start a class with "You don't know this about me, but. . . ." Build a relationship with your students; let them get to know you.
- Have students stand on a continuum of Agree and Disagree, and then reflect on why they took their stance.
- Provide class mentors for some students—relationship building leads to positive emotional feelings.
- Write an encouraging note to the athlete before the big game, to the musician before the semester concert, or to the student organizer before their annual service project. Never underestimate the power of your words.

## Secret Revealed

 Twelve thousand high school students were surveyed concerning their sense of belonging. Did they feel liked and valued at school, were they treated fairly by their teachers, were they loved and appreciated at home? Students who felt high levels of connecting and belonging suffered less stress and exhibited fewer at-risk behaviors, such as alcohol abuse, depression, and violence. A spirit of belonging not only makes us feel happy, it adds to our social and emotional well-being (National Longitudinal Study on Adolescent Health, 2008).

## BOYS WILL BE BOYS . . .

Many educators and psychologists attribute to cultural and social factors the gender roles adolescents adopt. Society expects girls to be nurturing and soothing, so they are. Boys are expected to be self-reliant and independent, so they are. It's like all adolescents are acting out roles they learned in some secret Gender School—enrollment mandatory!

The most common examples used to prove society's role in gender preferences are the studies done in the areas of math and science. Boys and girls are equally proficient in these areas until their early teens, when girls begin to lag behind. Nationally, the result of this inequality is that boys outscored girls by forty-five points on the math portion of the SAT in 2006–2007. According to the National Assessment of Educational Progress (NAEP), a higher percentage of boys than girls are proficient in math and science at the eighth- and twelfth-grade levels, though the gap is narrowing. Furthermore, young women take far fewer "hard science" courses in postsecondary education (like physics, engineering, or computer science) than do young men. This disparity in math and science coursework ultimately limits girls' career options and (by extension) future income potential (*Title IX at 30*, 2002). However, girls continue to excel in writing, scoring eighteen points higher than boys at the twelfth-grade level and twenty points at the eighth-grade level (NAEP, 2002).

Discrimination prevailed as the foremost explanation for many years and impacted the decision in the famous 1967 John/Joan case of sexual reassignment (Diamond, 1997). Psychologist Dr. John Money decided to prove this theory in 1965 after a botched circumcision left one male identical twin without a penis. At the urging of psychologists, the infant John's parents allowed doctors to perform sexual reassignment surgery before he was two years old. If gender and gender roles were considered neutral at birth, there was no reason to believe that, with hormonal supplements, the child (newly christened "Joan") could not comfortably grow up female. Nurture would prevail over nature and the baby boy would adjust to life as a girl.

Although the child, his twin brother, and his classmates were never made aware of his birth as a male, he had many problems adjusting to life as a female. Joan fought like a boy, dressed like a boy, and played with dump trucks. When, at fifteen years of age, "Joan" was informed by "her" parents of what had happened, his reaction was of overwhelming relief. He finally understood his life of turmoil and attraction to girls and resumed a male identity immediately—with seemingly few problems, although he committed suicide in 2004 at the age of thirty-eight.

Dr. Milton Diamond, who did much of the later research refuting Money's conclusions from this case, stated, "If all these combined medical, surgical, and social efforts could not succeed in making a child accept a female gender identity, then maybe we really have to think that there is something important in the individual's biological make up; that we don't come to this world neutral; that we come to this world with some degree of maleness and femaleness which will transcend whatever the society wants to put into it" (as cited in Colapinto, 2000, pp. 174–175). Neuroscientists need to examine further the roles that the brain, puberty, and culture play in our gender behavior if they hope to gain a true understanding of it. For example, the brain seems be a powerful determinant of gender roles—as early as the sixth or seventh week of gestation, hormone levels rise in the fetal brain and remain high throughout gestation. This hormone wash contributes to sex differentiation and brain differentiation (Hiort & Holterhus, 2000; Kimura, 2002).

## . . . AND GIRLS WILL BE GIRLS

Brain differences manifest between infant girls and boys shortly after birth. Baby girls look longer at visual stimuli than baby boys do and are also more sensitive to touch, odor, taste, and sound. Boys tend to be better at detecting slight movements in their field of vision and recognizing the passage of time (Kimura, 1992). These differences continue throughout childhood; boys are drawn to cars, blocks, and balls and girls to dolls and playhouses. Boys enjoy roughhousing and girls act out school. (Both, however, seem to enjoy equally the ever-popular "doctor"!)

Gender differences become notably apparent with puberty. Puberty signals dramatic changes in the adolescent's body; estrogen levels increase in girls, and testosterone levels increase in boys; the primary and secondary sex characteristics develop, and first crushes unfold. The increase and decrease of hormones during the menstrual cycle seem to shift girls' performance on certain tasks. High levels of estrogen are associated with poorer spatial ability, better speech, and improved manual-skill tasks, like sewing or making jewelry. Hormones affect boys, too; trivia buffs will enjoy learning that males' spatial ability, ability to visualize objects (an important math skill), and ability to navigate increases in the spring when testosterone levels are lower (does that mean men don't ask for directions only from June to March?) (Kimura, 1996; Ostatnikova, Putz, Celec, & Hodosy, 2002). Researcher Dr. Doreen Kimura recommends further study, however, to find out if there is an evolutionary base for these ability changes during the springtime or if the results were just a fluke.

Research hints that estrogen may play a role in the development of the hippocampus during adolescence (McEwen, 2002). During this time, the hippocampus grows faster in girls than in boys because of the rising level of estrogen during puberty. Scientists speculate that the enlarged hippocampus enables girls to be savvy at coordinating complex social relationships. Girls can size up a social situation and know what to say and what not to say. They are sensitive to others and know when to give a compliment, when to lend emotional support, and when to give someone privacy. They listen well and communicate well, skills that were and are important to our survival.

Of course, there are some downsides to the priority girls give social relationships. Kelsey recounts the following story, "In middle school I was voted 'the most funny.' It was an honor. I was always trying to make the cool girls laugh; sometimes it was easier, sometimes harder. In my heart I always thought they were cooler than me. I remember doing such mean things to stay cool. A nerdy girl I was friends with, but only in German class, put her lunch bag on our lunch table. She thought it would be okay since we were 'friends.' When she went to get a drink I moved her bag to another table. She came back and quietly sat alone. Everyone laughed; I felt bad even then, but I had to publicly reject her to remain cool." Happily, this type of social behavior wanes as social and emotional development progresses.

Just as teenage girls have a more developed hippocampus, teenage boys have a larger amygdala. This helps explain their irritability, anger, and hostility. Binge drinking, driving at warp speeds, and picking a fight with their best friend are all built on illogical, split-second decision making. For instance, one middle school boy, enraged by a "bad" call, tackled his own mom, who was sitting on the sidelines. Needless to say, his coach, teammates, and fans were almost as surprised as his mother. Inappropriate behavior, you bet. Hard to explain, maybe not. The reason for this mystifying behavior can probably be found in his overactive amygdala. Fortunately, boys tend to grow out of this rowdy behavior by age nineteen.

A student teacher who was supervising an afterschool program said he was struck by how insensitive some of the boys could be. "One boy approached a table but it must have been the wrong table because another boy yelled, 'Get the hell out of here,' at him. I couldn't believe how mean he was." Rachel, a bubbly, fun-loving senior has the opposite viewpoint. "Guys are more laid back and girls are more high maintenance. They are way more self-conscious than guys. They care about what their friends will think of their decisions and they are way more dramatic. For instance, if a guy says to another guy, 'Your mom's hot,' he'll just laugh and mess around with him. But if he says it to a girl, she'll get all bent out of shape, say, 'You are so mean!' and try to punch him." Personally, I haven't found girls to be kinder and gentler than boys at this age, either. Research on the hippocampus's involvement with girls' social talents will be interesting to follow in this area.

## YIN AND YANG

Most structures of the brain show no distinction between genders, but there are differences in the hypothalamus, cerebellum, white and gray matter, and the corpus callosum. Some scientists attribute these differences in the brain to evolution. It is thought that the early survival of the species depended on a division of labor; men were responsible for hunting, scavenging, and making and using weapons, and women for gathering food, tending small children and the home, preparing food, and making clothing. A specialization by gender could have allowed for a natural selection process that led to the current differences we see between the male and female brains.

**Figure 3.1**   Human Brain

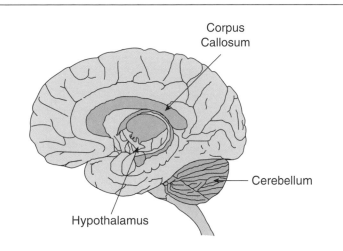

SOURCE: Adapted from Sousa, D. A. (2003), *How the Gifted Brain Learns*, p. 18.

The hypothalamus is the part of the brain responsible for emotions, sexual desire, and controlling the body's thermostat. It controls our biological rhythms. When we overheat, we sweat; when we get a chill, goose bumps appear; when we are thirsty, we get dry mouth—all these involuntary actions are controlled by the hypothalamus. It is involved in the "fight or flight" response and keeps us on our toes when we face danger. The hypothalamus also regulates the release of our sex hormones, maintaining them at low levels during childhood and increasing them during puberty (Kulin, 1991). The hypothalamus is larger and thicker in men than in women. It is hypothesized that this may account for the male's greater sexual desire and aggressive nature (Stoleru et al., 1999). Fifteen-year-old Seth characterizes this drive perfectly. "I love football," he says. "It gives me a chance to hit somebody and not get in any trouble. It's rough but exciting and I feel tough when I play."

## Secret Revealed

 Gender differences are not limited to sex hormones—did you know that the male brain is about eight percent larger than the female brain? That the corpus callosum is larger in females than males? Or that males and females have different ratios of white to gray matter? A bigger brain, however, does not mean more brainpower; males and females perform equally well on intelligence tests. But the differences in brain structure do translate to differences in some cognitive abilities. Boys, in general, have a better spatial awareness; girls, in general, have better verbal skills. Some educators and political activists worry that these generalizations reinforce sexist stereotypes, such as boys can't express their feelings and girls are prone to gossip. Neuroscience, however, puts these fears to rest. Despite differences in how males and females process information, both sexes are capable of learning and remembering as much and as thoroughly. Savvy educators will use information about gender differences for perspective on adolescent behaviors, not to determine what to teach individual teenagers.

The male brain has a greater proportion of white matter than the female brain; the female brain has a greater proportion of gray matter than the male brain. It is speculated that the additional white matter enables men to transfer information easily to all regions of the brain, enhancing their spatial abilities and giving them an advantage in matters of navigation, mathematical problem solving, and aiming at targets (Gur et al., 2000; Yurgelun-Todd, Killgore, & Young, 2002). The abundance of gray matter found in the female brain might allow for more efficiency of thought processes and a greater ability to process information, which perhaps explains the female's strong language skills and the ability to juggle a number of activities at one time. During study hall, a high school girl writes a note to a friend, reviews her chemistry notes, makes a schedule for tennis practice, and flirts with the boy next to her with an ease that puts an efficiency expert to shame. Meanwhile, the high school boy at the next table is concentrating on only one thing: her.

The corpus callosum—the part of the brain that links the two hemispheres—allows information to be transferred back and forth between the left and right sides of the brain. It is another part of the brain that differs by gender. It is larger in females than in males, permitting better communication between the left and right hemispheres. This enhances the ability of women to use both sides of their brain. For instance, while performing verbal activities like chatting, reading, giving a speech, or gossiping, females activate both hemispheres and males activate primarily the left side of their brain—two routes to the same cognitive destination with no effect on either accuracy or speed (Shaywitz et al., 1995). As men age, the corpus callosum begins to shrink (there is almost no shrinkage in women). It was originally hypothesized that this could restrict communication between the two hemispheres, perhaps making it difficult to process information, but no evidence has been found to suggest that occurs. Men are at no cognitive disadvantage to women as they age (Yoder et al., 2001).

There are female professional athletes and male poets, of course—gender does not dictate individual careers or proclivities. It is interesting to note, however, some general brain differences between the sexes (James, 2007). Although the comparisons between the male and female brain suggest differences, they are only group tendencies and can't predict the individual strengths and weaknesses of a male or female.

## Male Brain Advantages and Characteristics

- Performs well at visual spatial activities (visualizing sports positions and plays)
- Adept at aiming at stationary or moving targets (tossing paper into the wastebasket from their seats)
- Adept at throwing and intercepting projectiles (catching a basketball, football, or soccer ball)
- Navigates by distance, spatial cues, and time
- Adept at solving quantitative problems (understanding mean, median, mode, and standard deviation—on the first try)
- Achieves higher scores on multiple-choice tests

*(Continued)*

(Continued)

- Adept at imagining the rotation of an object
- Adept at manipulating an object in a new way (taking apart the classroom pencil sharpener)
- Exhibits more aggression
- Enjoys more rough-and-tumble play (tripping a friend, hurling his hat, or flipping his books)
- Excels in higher levels of math

## Female Brain Advantages and Characteristics

- Demonstrates better verbal abilities (expressing feelings, depicting a social exchange accurately)
- Demonstrates higher ability for memory tasks
- Adept at generating synonyms
- Adept at naming colors (knows the differences between azure, teal, turquoise, navy, cornflower, and blue)
- Adept at listing items beginning with a certain letter
- Adept at organizing (planning a surprise party or pep rally)
- Excels on untimed tests and written tests
- Achieves higher grades in school
- Is more nurturing (first to volunteer to help the teacher)
- Is more attuned to details (has a cover page on everything, remembers the bibliography, adds graphics to computer presentations)
- Navigates by landmarks and experience
- Is more subdued (likes to read, listen, and write—often keeps a journal)
- Adept at interpreting emotions
- Is more intuitive (knows who will ask her to Homecoming)
- Recognizes inferences and hidden meanings (knows from a look or turn of a phrase when she is or is not welcome)
- Adept at language and writing skills (talking to friends, writing notes to friends)

## Instructional Strategies

### Gender-Sensitive Classrooms

Although neither is smarter than the other, boys and girls have different strengths and weaknesses in the classroom, both academic and behavioral. Choose materials in the classroom that portray traditional and nontraditional roles for males and females at home, work, and play. Provide positive role models for both genders. Discuss gender role bias in the media. Have high expectations for all students.

Don't overnurture girls—it encourages dependence. Instead, encourage girls to be active learners. Really involve them in hands-on activities; they tend to be more passive than their male classmates. Balance cooperative and competitive group work in your class; girls prefer cooperative work and boys enjoy the competition.

Boys are under unique pressures of their own, however. Supplement reading and writing activities with action—and let them read from computer screens (when applicable) instead of a book, if that is what they prefer. Right now, boys contribute to ninety percent of behavioral problems and represent eighty percent of ADHD (attention-deficit/hyperactivity disorder) cases in school. Help them out by letting them move and actively involve themselves in their learning—there is nothing wrong with motion in the classroom. The book *Real Boys* by William Pollack (1999) is one source of valuable insight and information about what it is like to be a boy.

### *Things to Try*

- Define and discuss gender bias; constructing a definition gives added meaning to a concept. Use library or Internet resources to examine magazines, newspapers, posters, TV, movies, or music videos for evidence.
- Have students record for one week their personal interactions at school, home, work, and in social situations that counter gender stereotypes. One class period, bring out the lists and let the conversation begin.
- Debate the effects of gender on self-esteem and career opportunities. After the debate, have students research a career from Internet sources and discuss what they found.
- As a class, design a code of ethics that represents gender equity, and keep it posted in the room. Include tenets such as these: Don't interrupt each other, give equal amounts of help, and offer worthy feedback.
- Provide male and female role models: Tiger Woods and Mia Hamm are two famous athletes; Maya Angelou and Allen Ginsberg are two famous poets. Also, include young adult graduates from your high school and middle school who would be willing to meet your class and talk about their lives.
- Boys like competition. Play a trivia game about academic content, or host a contest for the best slogan that describes the current academic unit.
- Girls like cooperation. Don't grade on a competitive curve, and put students into same-sex groups to work sometimes.
- Do you call on boys more than girls? Are you sure? Divide your room into sections and make sure you call on a variety of students from each section throughout the day. Then make sure you're asking girls questions that tap into higher-level thinking and not just the easy, factual questions.
- Stress "safety" concerns as opposed to "dangers"—girls will often back off if they feel there is danger in an activity or lab.

*(Continued)*

(Continued)

- Encourage girls to become active in math and science extracurricular activities.
- Encourage an atmosphere of "effort leads to achievement." Girls tend to credit their achievements to luck rather than to their effort or ability.
- Examine your own biases as a teacher. Talk to an expert, watch a video, or read a book or an article about gender discrimination and bias in school. Discuss your views and findings with your colleagues.

## COOLING OFF THE KIDS AFTER PROM

*Sarah and Lex spent Prom wrapped in each other's arms, dancing to each slow dance and frequently sneaking out to the patio to be alone in the shadows. At midnight, the music stopped and the lights came on. Grinning, they hopped into Lex's car and drove off.*

*When they reached the school gymnasium, they pulled duffel bags with a change of clothes out of the trunk and joined the party that was*

*starting in the all-night "lock-in" inside. Sarah exchanged sexy high heels for canvas sneakers with as much relief as Lex pulled off his bowtie and threw on a sweatshirt. The Prom committee had advertised this event as a not-to-miss party, and it was already living up to its promise. Kids gorged on pizza and chips all night while they played silly games and danced to loud music. Local businesses had donated tee shirts and other prizes for contests and raffles; Sarah won a five-dollar gift card for a fast-food restaurant, but her best friend went home with a DVD player! The chaperoning parents and teachers kept each other awake and kept the junk food coming. This was one evening, at least, when students would worry more about what candy bar to have next than whether they were too high to drive or if they should go all the way.*

# Communication and the Unfinished Brain

Abrupt, mean-spirited comments or a subtle use of irony, symbolism, and sarcasm? No one is ever quite sure what words will come out of a teenager's mouth! The rapidly changing brain is responsible for the adolescent communication gaps and growth. Neuroscientists are finally able to help educators adjust to the highs and lows in teen dialogue.

**Did you know that . . .**

- Adolescence is when language ability and short term memory improve
- The teen brain reacts emotionally instead of logically
- Music is a way to communicate information and emotion
- Teens experience emotions before they can verbally articulate them
- Teenage self-awareness and teenage self-consciousness go hand in hand
- Teens are more vulnerable to stress than adults are

*It was May and time for the final band concert at the middle school. Proud parents, antsy brothers and sisters, and adoring grandparents filed into the auditorium with anticipation. The middle school musicians nervously took their places on the stage, arranged their music, and waited for their band director, Mrs. Hudson, to lift her baton and start the concert. The music filled the air, evidence enough of the students' hard work. They had practiced all semester and it showed; the concert went off without a hitch. After the concert, Mrs. Hudson headed for the band room where students were busy putting their instruments away. As soon as she entered the room, Katie rushed up to her, clearly shaken, and said, "Did you see how I tripped when I was going up on stage?" Mrs. Hudson assured her she hadn't noticed any stumble, nor did she think anyone in the audience noticed. Still, Katie was mortified, certain that everyone had seen her clumsiness.*

## PERENNIALLY TONGUE-TIED

As a mother of four teenagers, I can relate to the communication gap between our generations. My sixteen-year-old daughter pleads with me to let her stay out one extra hour and my thirteen-year-old son insists he doesn't need his coat—even though the temperature outside is below zero! These were the same children who once promised me they'd never act like their older siblings, with emotional flare-ups and temper tantrums. Why did they change so dramatically? Why are we not communicating?

The answer to this question can be found in the temporal lobes of an adolescent's brain. Located below the frontal lobes (right above the ears), the temporal lobes' primary function is to process auditory stimuli. Hearing, language, and auditory memory are all channeled through this part of the brain. Researchers at the UCLA Laboratory of Neuro Imaging found that the temporal lobes do not complete growing gray matter until the age of sixteen, and only then is the brain able to begin the pruning and myelination processes (Thompson et al., 2000)! Although the temporal lobes are delayed in development, once the process begins, they consistently have the highest growth rate of all areas in the brain.

### Secret Revealed

No, teens aren't more articulate than children because they've learned lots more vocabulary words—their brains' language functions are maturing! At UCLA, Dr. Arthur Toga (Thompson et al., 2000) and his colleagues scanned preadolescents, adolescents, and adults and found striking differences in the myelination patterns of their frontal lobes. (Young adults had the most myelination.) More efficient frontal lobes mean a better control of the language; as teens grow up, they are able to communicate and understand elaborate, detailed, high-level information.

Book sales records show that children love whimsical, straightforward stories like *Harry Potter* and the adventures of the *Boxcar Children*. But the older kids get, the more complex the books and movies that they enjoy become. Spy novels and romance sagas show up during silent reading; teens stand in line at the theaters for suspense thrillers and crime dramas. They don't spend their free time playing tag anymore, either. Now they verbally engage with their friends on the telephone and in Internet chat sessions for hours, expressing and analyzing their thoughts, ideas, and feelings.

Wernicke's area, a region in the temporal lobes that is responsible for deciphering our native language and giving meaning to the spoken word, has received particular attention. In cooperation with Broca's area (a part of the brain in the frontal lobes that stores vocabulary, grammar, and syntax), Wernicke's area changes our thoughts into words. Language production is further delineated within these two areas of the brain. For instance, there is a section in the brain for nouns and verbs, with the nouns area further divided into sections for tools and animals. It was once believed that the Wernicke's and Broca's areas solely were responsible for language interpretation and communication—a belief that underestimated the complexities of the brain. Language is not restricted to these two areas; ninety-five percent of our verbal skills reside in the left hemisphere. When we speak, neurons fire all over the frontal cortex.

**Figure 4.1**    Human Brain: Side View

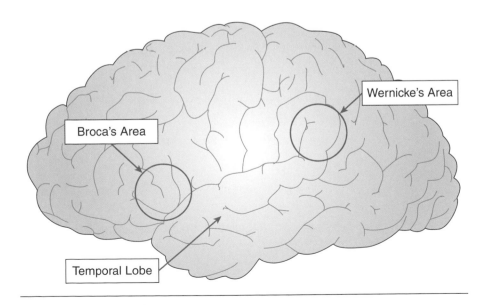

Adolescence is the time when the Wernicke's area begins to be fully connected by myelination in the corpus callosum, which allows communication between the two hemispheres. A number of subskills of most tasks require communication between both hemispheres of the brain. Even uncomplicated activities, such as word identification or singing a song, invoke complex connections between both sides of the brain. The more elaborate the task, the more we need to use both hemispheres, thereby exercising our brain to a fuller capacity (Weissman & Banich, 2000). Without the corpus callosum, the two hemispheres of your brain would not communicate at all. Although the corpus callosum is by no means disconnected before this myelination occurs, it has not yet reached its full potential.

The hippocampus is also located in the temporal lobes. It is the part of the brain that is responsible for short-term memory, primarily for remembering pesky facts and details. During adolescence, the hippocampus changes and develops with the rest of the brain. Finally, teenagers can take pride in how easy it is to memorize the Preamble to the Declaration of Independence and the introduction to the Constitution in an eighth-grade social studies class, or remember long lists of the bones of the human skeleton for a twelfth-grade anatomy lesson. Memorization is a snap—at least in the short term—with the power of the new and improved adolescent hippocampus. The combination of a surge of growth in the temporal lobes' language capabilities and the hippocampus's memory abilities during early adolescence also makes this a favorable time to improve native vocabulary and learn a second language, including sign language. (After puberty, the ability to acquire a second language is greatly diminished, although certainly possible.)

Older teenagers can take their burgeoning temporal lobes a step further. They can interpret, memorize, and comprehend sophisticated literature, such as a poem by T. S. Eliot:

### Lines from *A Dedication to My Wife*

No peevish winter wind shall chill
No sullen tropic sun shall wither
The roses in the rose-garden which is ours and ours only.

To middle school students, the poem is about roses withstanding inclement weather. They understand the words literally. You say what you mean, and you mean what you say. Roses don't go by any other name in seventh grade. High school students, however, are able to view the roses as a metaphor for enduring love because they understand the symbolism. They understand that there is more than one meaning possible in a passage or in the spoken word. Sometimes people speak literally and sometimes they don't; you need to look below the surface of words to understand true meaning. And eleventh graders can.

# Instructional Strategies

## *Knock, Knock. Who's There?*

Where do belly buttons go to college? The Navel Academy.

Immature humor? You bet. Young middle school students will laugh at this joke, but high school students will disdain it. Teens' language skills become more sophisticated as the frontal lobes develop. The older adolescent is able to go beyond a literal meaning to the abstract. They understand subtlety. This increased language ability is one of the most exciting developments we see in school. Humor, sarcasm, irony, symbolism, and satire are an active part of the high school life.

Developing writing and speaking skills is a high priority in our schools. The gold standard for teaching writing emphasizes sentence structure, content, organization, voice, conventions, and word choice. Basic instruction begins in elementary school, where children are taught to structure a sentence or paragraph and make informal presentations. By middle school and high school, adolescents write fiction and nonfiction, news articles, analytical essays, and poetry. They speak in front of their peers in formal and informal situations. Campaigns for school elections, performance on job interviews, and lunchtime conversations reveal their new sophistication.

Journal, compose, and report. Writing prompts us to organize our thoughts and put our spoken and internal thoughts on paper. It is an effective source of ascertaining patterns and helping the brain unravel complex information. It guides our thinking and assists our thought processes. The more we write, the stronger those synapses become, and the better we are at expressing ourselves. Writing is now understood to be an interdisciplinary skill. Teens who practice writing and become skilled at it will develop and strengthen these synapses in their brain.

## *Things to Try*

- Write across the curriculum. Have students keep learning logs as they read *The Scarlet Letter,* write detailed observations of plants exposed to differing degrees of light in biology, and record investigations into the school board's policymaking process for history or civics class.
- Instigate debates. Compel students to look at both sides of relevant issues and frame arguments to substantiate their view. Or for a change of pace, view and analyze political debates on television. (They're constantly broadcast, so take advantage of them.) Ask them to explore a subject in-depth. Assign position papers on opposing views of stem cell research, Alaskan oil, health insurance, or terrorism.
- Spend time brainstorming ideas for writing—how to combat writer's block, suggestions for topics, suggestions about technique, or strategies for revision—and post the list in the classroom.
- Organize student-led book clubs, either with books from the course or for personal reading. Allow them to meet during class time once a week or once a month.
- Teach note-taking skills. There are many different ways to help teenagers formulate their thoughts and ideas quickly into words on the page.

*(Continued)*

(Continued)

- Compare and contrast characters in literature, figures in history, and solutions to mathematical and scientific problems.
- Be creative about the kinds of writing assignments you give. Try original fairy tales, describing dreams and memories, biographies of real people who overcame great odds, stories to explain unusual images or photos of current events, the view through a pair of binoculars, or responses to thought-provoking quotes. What would your students say about this quote from Cliff Fadiman (n.d.): "My Faulkner, of course, is interested in making your mind rather than your flesh creep"?
- Analyze advertisements. How do they look? What are the models and actors wearing? What do they seem to care about? Is this a realistic portrayal of life? What information is missing?
- Trade that journal in for a blog—this interactive site creates a verbal picture of thoughts and experiences.
- Connect to online writing sites, such as fanfiction.com. Write a different ending, introduce a new character, add dialogue, or change the era—fast-forward it into the past or present.

## SCHOOL OF ROCK

Is the song "Crazy Rap Lyrics" by Afroman music to your ears? Probably not, but how about "Honey Honey" by Abba? Two songs, from two different generations, with two different messages and melodies; but both can compel a group (albeit, different groups) to gyrate and shake it up baby. Adults, children, and teenagers all love music. Teenagers, in particular, spend a great deal of time listening, singing, and dancing to their favorite tunes. It calms them, energizes them, and reflects and creates their moods.

Neuroscientists are finding that music impacts both the academic and emotional well-being of teenagers. So what's happening in the brain when we hear that do re mi? Music enters the inner ear, where it begins to ignite numerous areas of the brain. First it travels to the brain stem, then on to the thalamus, and finally to the temporal lobes in both hemispheres of the brain. The various patterns of the beat engage neurons associated with emotions, experiences, and knowledge, allowing us to feel tranquil, invigorated, or just plain happy.

## Instructional Strategies

### *The Positive Influence of Music*

The simple act of listening to music seems to have a positive emotional and intellectual impact, but participating in making music takes everything to a higher level. Research points to active music involvement improving memory, visual-spatial relations (math and science), and self-esteem (Kluball, 2000). In fact, SAT scores in the verbal and math areas improve when music is involved (Americans for the Arts, 2006). It even acts as a protective agent; teenage musicians are less likely to use drugs or engage in other at-risk activities (Costa-Giomi, 1998).

The type of music doesn't seem to make a difference in teenager's academic achievement or put their emotional disposition at risk (depression, aggression), somewhat surprising news. All that matters is that the music is enjoyed. If it's enjoyed, it's a good thing. This finding has implications for concerns about heavy metal music. It seems adult worries are unwarranted; violent and sexual themes in heavy metal music are more a reflection of problems already in a teenager's life than a cause (Copley, 2008). However, music videos that combine music with pictures are a different story. They have a more powerful and detrimental influence.

Lyrics communicate information and blend with the melody, dynamics, and rhythm to express how we feel about information. The potential for learning through this medium is easy on the brain.

### *Things to Try*

- Draw students' attention by starting the class with your own musical talent, such as Jack Black did in *School of Rock*.
- Play soft music as they enter the room to set the mood and quiet the inner beast.
- Create a rap song that reinforces a math theorem, or better yet, let the students create one.
- Bring in musical instruments from other cultures, or if you can't get your hands on the real thing, show visuals. This brings a rich context to the concepts being studied.
- Play music from different periods in history and countries to create an appreciation of our diverse world.
- Assign Internet searches of music and musical instruments as part of a research project.
- Use soothing music as background for journal writing or group work.
- Energize that lethargic mind partway through a lesson with blues, rock, pop, or rap.
- Create your own curriculum lyrics to "The Chicken Dance," and then sing and dance the period away.
- Take rap music (be careful to scrutinize for proper content prior to class) and analyze the message.
- Put the words to "We Didn't Start the Fire" by Billy Joel on an overhead to start a discussion on political responsibility.

Don't leave music in the lone territory of the music teacher; make it a part of your instruction. In the words of Bob Marley, "Music gonna teach dem a lesson."

## Secret Revealed

 Skeptical about the impact of music in our schools? Groundbreaking and inspiring music research out of East Harlem's schools should change your mind. Eighty-seven percent of the student body there was performing below grade level in both reading and in math. It was a demoralizing and frustrating proposition for all concerned. In order to rectify the problem, administrators decided to reinstate their music program. After only eighteen months, seventy-one percent of the students were at grade level, an amazing accomplishment. Administrators attributed the success primarily to the music program (American Music Conference, 2007).

## TEENAGER AHEAD! PROCEED WITH CAUTION

Sincerely trying to help a struggling student, Mrs. Andrews suggested that Tyler come in for extra help after school. The teenager, face red with shame, said to a friend, "She thinks I'm stupid." Beverly and her daughter, Tiffany, enjoyed their day shopping until Tiffany emerged from a dressing room wearing a skintight top. Beverly suggested that Tiffany try the same top in a larger size. Her daughter stared at her in disbelief, deeply insulted, and shrieked, "You think I'm fat! I hate you!" Mariko calls Julia to invite her to the mall, but Julia already has plans with Heather. Mariko is convinced that Julia no longer wants to be her friend.

Teenagers' rooms are messy, they forget to turn in their homework, and don't prepare for college entrance exams until the night before. They burst into tears, fly into rages, and then give you a hug for baking their favorite cookies, all in one afternoon. No wonder adults find their behavior inexplicable! Dr. Charles Nelson, a leader in the field of adolescent brain development and director of the Center for Neurobehavioral Development at the University of Minnesota, was interviewed on "Inside the Teenage Brain," a PBS *Frontline* program (Spinks, 2002). He said, "Teenagers—particularly when they're first becoming teenagers—have every reason to believe and to feel that no one understands them." He believes that teenagers often aren't paying attention, are unorganized, and are unable to multitask. He went on to suggest that they generally understand information quite differently than adults. They hear a disproportionate amount of criticism and rejection, and their reactions to statements that adults would classify as helpful or innocent are overly sensitive and exaggerated.

**Figure 4.2**   Human Brain

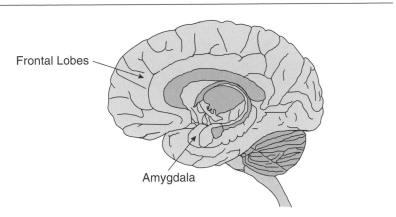

Frontal Lobes

Amygdala

SOURCE: Adapted from Sousa, D. A. (2003), *How the Gifted Brain Learns*, p. 18.

Studies are being conducted on the frontal lobes and amygdala of adolescents to better understand their bewildering behavior. The frontal lobes are the area of the cortex in charge of higher-level thinking skills. Their relationship with the amygdala, the center of emotions, is interesting. Either region could be in the "driver's seat" at any given moment. Do the logical, mature frontal lobes calmly maneuver down the road toward a responsible decision, or does the emotional amygdala floor the gas pedal for a quick joy ride? Even when the amygdala is not at the wheel, it carries on in the background like a jumpy backseat driver.

The amygdala is one inch long, shaped like an almond, and part of the unconscious brain. It is thought to be responsible for our actions when we feel threatened and signals a child to either respond to a bully by running away or fighting back—the "fight or flight" instinct (LeDoux, 2003). Even though the amygdala operates on a lower, more instinctive level as compared to the cortex, its influence should never be underestimated. Damage to the amygdala can be devastating to an individual. In the few reported cases of people who have had their amygdala removed or severely damaged, their quality of life suffered tremendously. Imagination, enthusiasm, and decision making are all drastically affected when the amygdala does not work at full capacity (Damasio, 1994).

Adults depend less on the amygdala than on the frontal lobes of their brain, so they respond rationally to information. Because the frontal lobes of the adult brain have completed their overproduction of synapses and the processes of pruning and myelination, they are ready and willing to take on the added responsibilities of reacting logically and reasonably. Adolescents, on the other hand, tend to rely more on the amygdala, which helps explain their emotional and impulsive behavior. Conversations such as the following are all-too-familiar results of this dependence: A parent makes what he believes is a factual observation to his teenage daughter and tells her, "Your hair is in your eyes." The teenager responds with, "You hate my hair! You've always hated my hair!" and leaves the room in tears (Davies & Rose, 1999).

The reliance on the amygdala goes beyond emotionally charged reactions; it affects how well teens can read body language and facial expressions, too. This ability to interpret someone's affection, agitation, or concern is a learned skill, not something inherently known. Teenagers have not yet mastered the art of body language. To adolescents, interpreting body language is like trying to decipher a foreign tongue. A teacher shakes his head in confusion, and the student explains it as "He hates me." A look of surprise is interpreted as a glare of anger. A teacher cracks a joke, and a teen takes it seriously and finds offense. These misunderstandings and misinterpretations are common occurrences behind much moodiness and temperamental behavior.

At McLean Hospital in Massachusetts, Deborah Yurgelun-Todd's team of researchers used MRI technology to view the brain responses of adults and teenagers as they viewed a series of photographs (Baird et al., 1999). The participants in the study were asked to identify the emotion on the face of a woman. Every adult was able to identify the emotion as fear, compared to only fifty percent of the adolescents. The other fifty percent of the adolescents confused the facial expression with shock or anger. On further inspection, the researchers noted that adolescents and adults used different parts of their brain when interpreting the photos. The adolescents relied on their amygdala, whereas the adults relied on their frontal lobes. At San Diego State University, neuroscientist Robert McGivern made an interesting discovery when he found that children going through puberty decreased in their ability to identify emotions by as much as twenty percent and did not resume normal levels until about age eighteen (McGivern, Andersen, Byrd, Mutter, & Reilly, 2002). Their lack of dependence on the frontal lobes, and subsequent lack of mature thought processes to regulate their emotions, provides insight into an adolescent's emotional state. The adolescent is much more apt to misread another's feelings and may confuse sadness with anger and surprise with fear. No wonder miscommunication is so rampant at this age!

---

### Secret Revealed

 School must be an awfully boring place if teens are so fascinated by sensationalist gossip, right? Why else would they spread and exaggerate rumors about three students dying in a school bus accident that morning (when, in reality, the school bus was empty and the driver wasn't even hurt)? It turns out that a teenager's emotions are regulated by the highly excitable and passionate amygdala. Dr. Charles Nelson (Spinks, 2002), the Director of the Center of Neurobehavioral Development at the University of Minnesota, blames hysterical, knee-jerk overreactions to information on the "emotional lability" (read: instability) of the teenage brain. Adolescents change emotions by the nanosecond, regularly blow situations out of proportion, and find something to be self-conscious about at every turn. Hormones are partly to blame, but mostly he believes it is the still-maturing frontal cortex that is the root of the problem. Until it assumes full executive control of the brain's reactions, the teenage mind will be a volatile place.

---

This apparent obliviousness to the mental states of other people also stems from their newly developing frontal lobes. The teen's ability to understand themselves and others does increase (thanks to the over-production and pruning of synapses and the myelination of the frontal lobes and corpus callosum), but only with growing pains. The frontal lobes and corpus callosum, areas responsible for self-awareness, are maturing, true, but teens lack experience in operating them. Adolescents have trouble distinguishing between their own thoughts and the thoughts of others. They confuse the two. Teens are so busy thinking about themselves that they are sure everyone else is also concentrating on them full-time. Hence, they become more self-conscious. This egocentrism explains why they want to be dropped off five blocks from school, are devastated if laughed at in class, become hysterical over the appearance of a zit, and never, ever want to be seen at a movie with their parents. It's obvious to teens, disgraced as they are by their parents' outrageous behavior, that their peers will notice every embarrassment and make judgments that will linger beyond graduation. I still remember the day my oldest daughter and her friends asked me to duck down below the windows of the car as we passed a group of boys—even though I was the one driving! (The fact that I tried to accommodate them is even more amazing.)

The story doesn't stop there; observing others goes beyond perceptions and interpretations to actual imitation of words, dances, and problem solving. Mirror neurons give the brain the amazing ability to observe another with the sole intention of repeating their actions. Teenagers spend some time observing their parents and teachers for signals and clues, but not surprising they turn primarily to their peers for guidance. Friends are looked to for appropriate behavior, language, and empathy, and what they see they repeat. One could say it's a case of the blind leading the blind (Iacoboni, 2005).

This amazing gift has implications for learning and behavior in school. Instructional strategies such as science demonstrations, conflict resolution, role playing, and modeling math problems are reinforced through mirror neurons. It also lends credence to dealing with inappropriate behaviors quickly and efficiently to avoid imitation.

> I simply told my daughter not to be late getting home.
>
> There was no unkind thought, no accusation, just a statement. All of a sudden, we were in a big argument.
>
> "You don't trust me," she screamed. "I always am being told what to do, nobody trusts me!" The hysteria continued.
>
> Finally, with her hand on the door and her eyes flashing, she yelled, "Just shut the f— up!" Needless to say, that put an end to her evening with friends.
>
> —*Veronica, mother of a teenager*

## WHAT'S (REALLY) UP?

Adolescents' behavior is further complicated because they feel things before they can regulate or articulate them. They feel an emotion but lack the ability to express it in a socially appropriate way, amplifying the frustration between the adolescent and the people who share their world. Parents in particular are often exasperated by their teenager's behavior. They tell a son to clean his room and stop watching TV. He responds by continuing to watch TV. When his parents become angry, the adolescent is genuinely surprised; he hadn't processed the message as a command—it was more like a suggestion, a suggestion he chose not to take. He responds to their anger with a "Screw you." No discussion or reflection about why his parents might be annoyed, just a fiery retort. Something, clearly, has been lost in translation.

## Secret Revealed

It's a classic scene—Lindsey sits in a restaurant pouring her heart out to Matt, who nods mutely, answers her questions with "Uh-huh," and then blurts out something about his brother's car. Immediately, she bursts into tears and stammers incoherently as she tries to explain why her feelings are hurt! No, he isn't insensitive and she isn't high-strung. So how could this conversation go so awry?

This is yet another manifestation of the amygdala's influence on the teen. Not only are the language regions of the brain still maturing in adolescents, they are directed by emotions. When Lindsey finds herself unable to state exactly what is on her mind, what would be mild frustration to an adult she experiences as psychic torture. Furthermore, adults are much better at holding their tongue; adolescents often say the first thing that comes to mind. In a few years, Matt will be able to tell Lindsey how his brother's car relates to her story, and she'll be able to make a joke instead of crying.

At school, Mr. Halstef assigned a writing project to ninth graders on the topic of their choice. They were to research something that interested them and write a five-page paper about it. What could be easier? Anything, it turned out. Students were frustrated and didn't understand what he wanted—they complained that it would never end! Mr. Halstef was frustrated with the quality of work he received. "It was so obvious that most of them had waited until a day or two before the due date to even start it!" he complained. But his teenage students were genuinely perplexed by what he wanted and how to organize it. They put off the dreaded task as long as possible and then did the best that they could. Not one student thought about doing the obvious and asking for clarification; they all trudged along in their own personal misery instead. Once again, the lack of maturation in the frontal lobes left teens prey to the effects of the amygdala (Paus et al., 1999).

Of course, sometimes a teen relying on the amygdala is the right person to communicate with another teen doing the same thing—logic isn't always the best answer among adolescents! Colleen, a freshman tennis player, was mercilessly attacked during games by her doubles partner. Her every shot was criticized, she was to blame for all lost points; the faultfinding went on and on. Understandably, Colleen was dejected and on the verge of quitting the team after only a few matches. She was tired of being verbally beat up but was shy and uncomfortable about confrontation. One of her friends and I intervened to discuss with her how she might best handle the situation.

My reasonable, adult advice was that Colleen should explain to her partner how her remarks were hurting Colleen's feelings and to ask her to please stop. My frontal lobes could clearly see why this girl's behavior was inappropriate and counterproductive to winning the match. Her friend's advice was more direct: "I'd just tell her to shut up." Amygdala versus frontal lobes. This match went to the teen-triggered amygdala. "Shut up" it was. Colleen tried out this succinct phrase the very next day. Her nemesis, shocked, made no more comments for the rest of the season.

## Instructional Strategies

### Discipline Versus Management

We talk, they listen. They talk, we listen. It's a simple concept: orderly classrooms where everyone can talk, think, and work. Who wouldn't want that? Many of our students demonstrate that they do want it—they have mastered self-control and cause no problems—but a disruptive minority of students will be insolent or even aggressive. Your best tactic for handling these outbursts is to look for signs of stress before defiant behavior erupts. Refusals to work, passing notes, slamming books, inattention, huffy voices, and heated gesticulations are all signs of a possible blowup. Circumventing negative behavior with positive discipline strategies will diffuse most potential explosions; when it doesn't, staying calm and acting decisively will help cool tempers down.

Ultimately the purpose of discipline is to develop self-control in our students. The most effective teachers expect that students are capable of high-level work and communicate that expectation to them—a very straightforward, effective strategy.

### Things to Try

- Rather than threatening students who break rules, simply calmly enforce rules. Why prompt another emotional response?
- Track which rules are frequently broken, and rethink those rules and their consequences. Rules are meant to serve a purpose. When they don't, they need to be improved and reconstructed.
- Preempt destruction—desks too near walls and chalkboards become distractions and are prime opportunities for vandalism.
- Use nonverbal actions to redirect behavior. Move closer to a student, make eye contact, hand a noisy student another copy of the class assignment—they'll get the message.

- Create a student-centered classroom where students talk more than you do, creativity is valued, some lessons and assignments are planned together, and courtesy abounds. Setting a positive tone is one way to manage discipline problems proactively (before they even start).
- Ignore fleeting behavior that doesn't really affect others. Identify the difference between your personal peeves and real disruptions. Relationships, even between teachers and students, require give and take. Sometimes it's better to be personally annoyed or distracted if it benefits the dynamics of the group.
- Reprimand gently and in private when necessary. Confronting a student in front of the whole class is disruptive (and could come back to haunt you). Likewise, forcing a student to make a personal apology to you or the rest of the class is humiliating; it's doubtful the apology would be sincere anyway.
- Avoid telling students about your own youthful indiscretions. Rarely will it serve to create a personal bond and more likely will hamper your effect as a positive role model. It may also turn into student rationale for later misbehavior!
- Don't punish everyone for the mistakes of one or two students. Not only is it unfair, it usually results in the entire class being angry with one student and all of them mad at you.
- Don't assign extra work as a punishment. We want to encourage a love of learning, not discourage it!
- Anticipate and prevent problems by paying attention to your students. When a situation is about to sour, often a quiet, calm word will put everyone back on track.
- Speak calmly even when you don't feel calm. Your voice will set a tone and carry the message that you are in charge.
- Immediately involve parents in serious problems; describe an event or behavior with specific details and without commenting on a student's character or personality. This conveys the message that it is the behavior, not the teenager, that you find unacceptable.
- Schedule special student-teacher meetings to enhance communication. Taking time to talk individually to students conveys the message you care about them. It also enables you to build a personal relationship with your students, enhancing the possibility of meeting their needs more effectively and decreasing the chance you'll talk past each other.
- Clarify teacher expectations. Ease anxiety by making your classroom expectations clear to your students on the very first day and then be consistent. Students who understand exactly what behaviors are required from them have a better background against which to evaluate your comments and directions.
- Be careful not to set up fierce competition among students. If winning or losing becomes the top priority, the spirit of working in cooperation will be difficult to establish.

*(Continued)*

(Continued)

- Introduce athletes, scientists, and businesspeople who had frustrations and challenges in their life. Not only are they role models for handling problems, but they show the power of effort and positive risk taking.
- Encourage involvement in sports or extracurriculars. They are the perfect venue to learn how to negotiate on a committee or accept the bad call from the umpire.

## CELL PHONES: CAN YOU HEAR ME NOW?

No one can deny that the age of cell phones is upon us. Everyone wants one, has one, or is wrestling to borrow one. They play an integral part in communication between Hayden, Ella, and Madison and everyone else in the teenager's life. Since they are rarely part of school life and fall more under home domain, a brief word here will suffice.

Most schools have taken a proactive stance and forbidden all cell phones in classrooms. The justification is clear; it opens the door to rampant and unabashed cheating. They make it all too easy and too tempting; after all, you just text a good buddy one row over, and you have your answer. To make it even more inviting, the new phones have Internet features that allow students to surf the Net if a buddy can't come up with the correct answer.

Perhaps just as aggravating is the potential for conversing with friends, letting Hannah know that Jabar is not taking her to the movies, but that Matt is willing to, or even worse, watching *The Dark Knight*—best Batman ever—instead of paying attention and participating in class. No wonder this was a no-brainer for educators.

The other concern with cell phones is the school parking lot. Combining cell phone talking with driving is an accident waiting to happen. Each activity (driving and phone use) draws heavily from different parts of the brain, requiring more multitasking than is humanly possible. The driver and anyone in their path are potentially at risk. In fact, driving abilities tumble so low that it has been compared to drunk driving (Just, Kellera, & Cynkara, 2008). Regrettably, most schools do not have the staff or money to regulate and monitor this effectively. However, some states are taking the initiative and creating legislation to prohibit the use of cell phone use while driving; this certainly helps out schools and everyone on the road.

## ON THE VERGE

Stress. We work to avoid it, attempt to control it, and try to cope with it. Adolescent stress is usually associated with peers, grades, or family dynamics. Susan's mind goes blank during a final exam; she starts to sweat, her stomach hurts, her brain shuts down. Despite all her studying, she is now pumped and primed to fail the exam even though she knows the material perfectly. Micky hates lunch because it's the perfect time for Joe to pick on him. He hasn't eaten his dessert in a month. (Joe, in the meantime, has put on a few extra pounds.) Amanda is convinced that her geometry teacher's only goal is to track down and call on the unprepared; she doesn't hear a single word about equilateral triangles because she is too busy worrying that she'll be the next person to be called on. These are all common stress producers in an ordinary day on a school campus.

Let's face it—school can be a stressful place. Stress may occur between teacher and student, between student and student, or be brought into the classroom from sources outside the school. Students who are ignored by peers or who must babysit younger siblings and make dinner before starting homework show the same signs of stress as students who are intimidated by bullies or who are feeling threatened in other ways (Rice, 2002). Teachers who continually threaten students with detention, lower grades, or loss of privileges also contribute to a stressful atmosphere.

## Secret Revealed

Teens aren't lazy procrastinators. The adolescent brain is very susceptible to stress, and they defensively avoid situations that cause it—like big projects. Have you ever heard yourself snap at a class of stressed-out teenagers when they complained to you about how much work they had to do before finals? "If you'd paid more attention during the semester you wouldn't be worried about exams now!" Try sympathy instead. You may think a history test is nothing compared to your spouse's cancer scare or the mortgage on your house, but a teen perceives it as proof that the sky is falling.

*(Continued)*

(Continued)

The stress hormone, cortisol, can interfere with memory retrieval because of its effects on the hippocampus. Even if they study, some teens can't remember information from the class as they are taking the test. Also, excess cortisol increases the likelihood a teen will make rash decisions, like trying to stay awake all night to study or blowing off a test by going out to a party the night before. Add to the mix all the emphasis placed these days on GPA, and the average adolescent has plenty of reason to be a nervous wreck.

Cortisol is the hormone most associated with stress. It is released from the adrenal glands during moments of physical, academic, emotional, or environmental danger, and it stays in the body a long time. Cortisol depresses immune system function, increasing the likelihood of illness. A prime time for adolescents to experience this particular side effect of prolonged stress is during end-of-semester tests when they are concerned about their grades, sleep deprived, and eating unhealthily and irregularly. They feel stress with a capital S and contract sore throats, colds, and worse. Great numbers of students become ill immediately following this stress-filled week. Scientists from the University of Wisconsin at Madison compared student immune systems before and during finals; they found that immune systems consistently functioned better when they were not under a great deal of stress, like when the student's exams were behind them (Davidson, Coe, Dolski, & Donzella, 1999). Girls are at particular risk for stress because of the hormone progesterone. Children and post-menopausal women have relatively low levels of progesterone, but with the onset of puberty, progesterone levels increase in girls. Progesterone allows cortisol to run rampant. Once the teenage girl becomes stressed, it takes a long time to de-stress.

Mrs. Bartrum, an eleventh-grade English teacher, commented, "Students are under so much stress during finals that it's painful to watch. Once I talked to the class about it and asked how we could reduce some of their stress. They began listing all of their various obligations and assignments; I must admit that even I felt overwhelmed! I ended up extending the timeline for one of my assignments. I felt better, and so did they."

Cortisol also affects the ability to remember and organize thoughts. Elevated levels of prolonged stress (one or two months) can harm cells in the hippocampus (the part of the brain responsible for short-term memory), further impacting a student's ability to retrieve information (Kim & Diamond, 2002). The inability to remember an answer on a test is often stress related. Students may be able to visualize the day and room in which they learned the material, hear the teacher's voice relaying the information but be unable to recall the specific fact. Often, once they finish the test and leave the classroom, stress levels diminish and the answer just pops into their head.

Cortisol in the system increases the likelihood of making rash decisions. Sometimes it is useful to make impromptu decisions before gathering all pertinent information, but it is not a practical habit. The teenager under a great deal of stress overreacts when he misses the shot in a basketball game or forgets to turn in a school assignment. A teenager from a low-income neighborhood doing poorly in academics may choose a more violent solution to a problem than a student who is not experiencing long-term stress. Additionally, psychiatrist Dr. Margaret Altemus from the Weill Cornell Medical Center in New York suggests that higher progesterone levels in girls seem to let cortisol run rampant in their brains, putting them more at risk for stress-related problems than boys (Lurie, 2003). Chapter 6, "The Risk-Taking Brain," further discusses stress and the heavy role it plays in depression and other at-risk behaviors.

---

### Stress Producers for Teenagers

- Failing an exam
- Physical appearance
- Judgment or evaluation by others
- Unrealistic classroom demands
- The future
- Problems with peers
- Problems with a boyfriend or girlfriend
- Any situation that threatens self-esteem
- Disagreements with teachers, parents, or other adults
- Trying to pass between classes in four minutes while stopping at their lockers and visiting the bathroom
- Embarrassing them in front of their peers
- Only one type of assessment in a course
- Not allowing any class discussion
- The pop quiz

---

## Instructional Strategies

### Just Chill

Letizia stood in front of her seventh-grade language arts class giving a speech about Harriet Tubman. She spoke with confidence (despite the fact that speech assignments are undoubtedly stress inducing!). During her summation, however, Letizia informed the class that Harriet Tubman died of pneumonia in 1913. Unfortunately, she pronounced the *p* in pneumonia and the class began to laugh. Not surprisingly, Letizia froze in her tracks, completely unable to remember the rest of her speech.

*(Continued)*

(Continued)

Most people can remember reacting to such an incident in a highly emotional way. Rare is the individual who does not at one point succumb to the overpowering emotional control of the amygdala. If teachers reduce stress and emotional threat in the classroom and help students develop strategies to combat stress, students will learn more. Productive classes are safe and comfortable places.

### *Things to Try*

- Assure students that they are not expected to give all or nothing. Make comments like "You don't have to be able to answer every question today correctly," "It's okay to review your notes in order to remember what we went over yesterday," and "I know talking in front of a group isn't easy."
- Ensure that students have the academic background needed to accomplish their assignments. Frustration and anger can be eliminated if students understand the task ahead and have the knowledge and skills necessary to complete the work.
- Use competition carefully; when there is competition, make sure everyone has a chance at some success.
- Be fair and consistent with evaluation and discipline. Knowing which behaviors are expected and acceptable and believing that equal offenses receive equal consequences reduces stress.
- Offer academic support outside of the classroom with homework helpers and tutors.
- Incorporate full body movement into your lessons with skits, plays, games, and celebrations.
- Before a test, public speaking, or other stressful situations, have students practice tightening and relaxing muscles. Contracted muscles limit blood circulation and oxygenation. Releasing tension from tight muscles allows the mind and body to relax so the brain can perform at its best.
- Look to Howard Gardner's theory of multiple intelligences (Armstrong, 2000). Varied instruction gives everyone a better chance of success by addressing individual preferences and learning needs. Students who may struggle to understand a concept presented in one fashion can take comfort in the fact that you will present it in a different way next.
- Have students rate and chart their personal stress on a scale of one to ten. Quantifying a level of stress can help put it in perspective. Set aside time to journal or talk about the stressors in their lives.
- Encourage students to "play" a favorite song in their heads as a relaxation technique.
- Show a movie of someone who handled a stressful situation well as an inspirational role model.

- Have students role-play appropriate behavior for handling future stress. This can act as a cue when they are in a real life anxiety-producing situation.
- Give students a few minutes to transition to your classroom and its required mind-set, especially if they are under a great deal of stress. A classmate's suicide, bomb threats, and severe illness create different needs in the classroom. Teachers are eager to secure control of the class and not waste a precious moment of teaching time and too often immediately assign a task to students or begin instruction. By giving students a moment at the beginning of class to settle into their new surroundings, their adjustment will be smoother.
- Refer students showing serious signs of stress to a counselor. Students need to realize they are not alone and can take advantage of the many services inside and outside the school that provide support and help.
- Start class with a review, particularly if students are showing signs of frustration.
- Take a break and focus on breathing techniques, one of the most powerful ways to self soothe. Concentrate on breathing for ten breaths, inhale through the nose and exhale through the mouth.
- Allow some choice in content or process; students want/need to do it their way once in a while.
- Incorporate writing: Have students write a letter of frustration and then tear it up; they'll love the chance to vent.

## CALMING DOWN KATIE THE BAND STUDENT

*Trying to convince Katie that her misstep went completely unnoticed would have been impossible—Katie was positive that everyone had seen it. Instead, Mrs. Hudson took a different approach to calm her down. "Even if anyone did see you stumble," she said, acknowledging Katie's concern before redirecting her attention, "I doubt they would remember." Mrs. Hudson shrugged it off casually. "You played great—that's what everyone noticed. I've never heard the French horns sound better. It was obvious how hard you all practiced. Didn't you hear the applause?" Katie nodded and smiled, pleased by the praise. She had heard the applause. Her mortification was forgotten.*

# Self-Concept
# Under Attack

Moodiness, schmoodiness. Adolescence is a time of great fluctuation in the levels of neurotransmitters, the chemical messengers in the axons of neurons that excite and inhibit behaviors. When levels of these chemicals go astray, teens face a variety of mental upheavals such as depression, eating disorders, and shifts in sleep habits.

**Did you know that . . .**

- Testosterone and estrogen are found all over the brain during puberty
- Deficits and excesses of serotonin—the "take it easy" neurotransmitter—contribute to teen depression and eating disorders
- Obesity may have a chemical origin (and that some overweight teens may not lack self-control)
- Melatonin changes the sleep patterns of teenagers

*Eddie slammed Peter up against the lockers and began slugging him. Words like fatty, tank, and tubs stung in his ears; he hated Peter. The other seventh graders circled the two boys, not sure of what to do. One stunned observer said, "I couldn't believe it. Eddie was so mad and he did it right in school. But Peter deserved it—he's really mean." As things heated up, one of the coaches came along, broke up the fight, and marched both boys to the principal's office. Eddie's eyes stung with tears as he recounted the teasing that he'd been suffering. He felt bad enough about his size without having Peter call him names in front of everybody.*

## ON YOUR MARK, GET SET, PUBERTY!

Middle school students are on a roller-coaster ride that won't stop. Forget school—they're dealing with training bras, cracking voices, rampant acne, and underarm hair. They react to these developments with everything from joy and surprise to fear. Jenny's feet are too big for the tennis shoes she bought a month ago; Toby doesn't know if he should pluck the chest hair he found or let it grow. Puberty has found them!

Teachers are daily observers of the nonstop physical transformations of pubescence. A seventh-grade teacher remarked, "I can hardly stand to walk down the corridor during May because the body odor is so strong— I'll do anything to avoid it. We need to have that talk on hygiene again." One physical education teacher noted, "The girls are beating the boys at everything. They can jump farther, run faster. You'd think the boys would be upset but everybody seems oblivious to it."

Neuroscientists believe that the brain, in collaboration with hormones, masterminds the transformations of height, weight, and reproductive function that are the significant physical changes of puberty. Some researchers theorize that it is the pruning of synapses during early adolescence that sets puberty rolling. This rampant pruning prompts the hypothalamus, the part of the brain in charge of pain, pleasure, and sexual appetite, to fire off a message to the pituitary gland. When the pituitary gland receives the message, it increases the production of gonadotropin releasing hormone (GnRH) and then sets in motion an increased release of hormones—androgens in males and estrogen in females. These hormones trigger the further development of the primary sexual characteristics, the testes and ovaries, and secondary sexual characteristics, like breast development and the growth of pubic, facial, and body hair.

The primary sexual characteristics relate directly to reproduction; the testes and ovaries set into motion the processes of sperm production, ovulation, and menstruation. The secondary sexual characteristics are the overt physical changes that distinguish the adolescent from a child: pubic hair and underarm hair grow in both boys and girls; boys grow chest hair and facial hair; skin becomes rougher and more oily and sweat glands increase production, contributing to acne and body odor; voices deepen— especially in boys; bones become denser; boys develop an increased proportion of muscle to fat and wider shoulders; girls develop an increased proportion of fat to muscle, broader hips, a wider mouth with fuller lips, and breasts.

Girls enter puberty around ten or eleven years of age and complete their growth spurt by sixteen. In eighth grade, my own daughter grew six inches, gained fifteen pounds, and went from wearing a child's size twelve shoe to a ladies' size six. In one whirlwind of puberty, she changed from a little girl able to sit on her father's lap to a young woman buying acne cream, deodorant, and tampons. (Menstruation starts when girls have a minimum of seventeen percent body fat and a weight of 106 pounds; most girls meet these criteria in sixth grade; Brooks-Gunn & Paikoff, 1997). A mother of a teenage girl remembers the dramatic highs and lows that accompanied her daughter's period. "After a while, I began tracking her reactions and arguments. After three or four months, I showed them to her. It was the only way I could prove to her how her period was affecting her."

---

## Secret Revealed

 Is puberty really a phenomenon of the brain more than the body? Hormones play an important role in the transformation from child to adult, but the brain sets it all in motion. Furthermore, testosterone and estrogen contribute to more than just development of body hair and deep voices—these sex steroids affect the structures of the brain, too.

Not only does the onset of puberty complicate teenagers' lives by radically changing their bodies as it changes their brains, the timing of puberty can have lasting effects on a teen's mental health, social environment, and attention span. Dr. Julia Graber (Graber, Lewinsohn, Seeley, & Brooks-Gunn, 1997), a professor of psychology at the University of Florida, studies how early and late bloomers handle the experience of puberty. Hardly surprising, being ahead or behind your peers is a mixed blessing. With early physical development often comes pressure to behave as a much older person; late-maturing teens are often not taken seriously by friends or adults. Being aware how the timing of puberty affects adolescents will help parents and teachers interact with them more meaningfully.

---

Boys don't start puberty until they are twelve or thirteen and don't finish their growth spurt until about age eighteen. Throughout the awkwardness of adolescence, girls are about two years ahead of the game. Nothing is a better indication of this lag of physical development than the excruciatingly awkward slow dance in a middle school cafeteria, with boys reaching up to put their arms around their partners' necks. One father of three teenagers said, "I first knew puberty was coming by the physical changes, the bras hanging in the bathroom, my son's cracking voice. They also became more combative—they'd buck the curfew and then argue about it. I don't remember how many times they said, 'I'll be home,' and then they weren't.'"

For a long time, we've known that androgens—the general class of male hormones—and estrogen are associated with the hypothalamus. Only now are we finding these hormones scattered all over the brain, including the cortex and cerebellum (Keefe, 2002). Hormones play an important role in the erratic behavior of teenagers by adding to the commotion of puberty. Testosterone and estrogen are the main culprits. Males and females produce both hormones, but the levels present in the body differ by gender. Males have about ten times as much testosterone (which is associated with sexual interest and aggression) as females; they are jolted by its release about ten times a day! Interestingly, testosterone levels in males have also been shown to rise when they are faced with a fight or are participating in a sporting event. Testosterone can be directed in positive or negative directions; professional athletes, ambitious politicians, and entrepreneurs have all been found to have high levels of estrogen.

Females have about ten times as much estrogen as males. Estrogen stimulates the development of female sexual characteristics and helps maintain the functioning of the uterus and vagina. Higher levels of estrogen have also been linked to girls being more receptive to boys' sexual advances (as compared to lower levels of estrogen). Still, hormones play only a small role in how girls demonstrate their sexuality. The environment, instead, seems to be the greatest determinant of a girl's potentially coy, provocative, spicy, flirtatious, modest, or unassertive behavior. Conversely, testosterone is directly tied to boys' sexuality (Hutchinson, 1995).

Androgens also affect females. Studies have been conducted on girls with congenital adrenal hyperplasia (CAH), a condition where female embryos are exposed to high levels of androgens for the majority of their gestation. Girls with CAH prefer "boy" toys (like guns and cars) to "girl" toys and games (like dolls and playing house). They are also more aggressive than girls with average amounts of androgens and are willing and, at times, eager to fight (Kreeger, 2002).

## TRANSGENDER TEENAGERS

Bobbi is a fifteen-year-old girl trapped in a boy's body. She chooses to express her female identity in her dress and actions. She wears push up-bras, strappy sandals, and short skirts to school. Her makeup includes blush and mascara, and she's a member of the Girl's Club. Today Bobbi is feeling pretty good about herself, but that hasn't always been the case. A few years back, as puberty hit, she became very depressed, hating herself and her peers. She tried morphing herself into a male-female blended identity; it didn't work. Feelings of hopelessness and being lost permeated her mind. To add to her pain, kids would ask her hurtful questions like "Are you a boy or a girl?" Fortunately, through therapy, family support, and a few good friends, Bobbi has learned to accept herself just as she is.

Some of the most solid research has emerged connecting transgender with the brain. Transgender is the state of believing you were born in a body that does not match your true gender identity. A female feels she is trapped in the body of a man or vice versa. Now neuroscientists have found concrete evidence that supports these convictions. For example, transgender males have a significantly smaller hypothalamus, the part of the brain associated with sexual interest, than their heterosexual counterparts. This research may support why transgender individuals feel they really are trapped in the wrong body (Zhou, Hofman, Gooren, & Swaab, 1995).

Puberty holds painful challenges for these students. Identity formation, in particular, is difficult because they are conflicting in a very basic way with society's expectations. As a result depression often follows.

Suggestions for dealing with transgender students:

- Examine your own prejudices and bias; talk to a counselor if you think you will have difficulty treating this student in a way that will benefit their positive identity formation.
- Use the name they prefer and the desired pronoun, *he* or *she.*
- Provide private restrooms.
- Arrange a private locker room for physical education.
- Keep their biological gender confidential if they desire.
- Respect their clothing choices.
- Refer them to a counselor or other professional if needed.
- Suggest transgender support groups.
- Forbid harassment from their peers or other staff.

## "DO THESE JEANS MAKE ME LOOK FAT?"

"Am I hot?" "Am I a dog?" Adolescents spend a lot of time in the mirror searching for answers to these questions. The physical and mental changes of puberty affect the way teenagers look at themselves. Body image is your perception of your body and the level of satisfaction (or dissatisfaction) you have with your looks. It is considered an important part of our self-esteem. It is estimated that about twenty-five percent of how much we like or dislike ourselves is determined by our physical appearance. Taken to the extreme, a poor body image coupled with immature coping skills and life stresses may even lead as far as the development of an eating disorder, depression, or suicide attempt.

The timing of puberty is key to how we view teens and how they view themselves. Late bloomers and early bloomers can have very different self-concepts. Consider Matt, an eighth grader with a mustache. To say he sticks out in a sea of hairless faces is an understatement. A fine baseball athlete, Matt is a skilled infielder and has a powerful swing. Early maturing boys have a distinct advantage over their peers because they embody everything our society values: masculinity, attractiveness, and competence. They have an athletic edge and are often chosen as leaders. Early maturing boys enjoy a positive body image (Alsaker, 1992), but as with most things, early onset of puberty has a downside: Society places high expectations on early maturing boys and pressures them to make lifelong decisions on things like career, religion, and political affiliation at an early age. As a result, they tend to be more somber and serious than their age-mates.

On the other hand, the late-maturing boys are routinely seen as less mature because of their childlike appearance—regardless of their actions. They look like children and are treated like children. Like a self-fulfilling prophecy, they live up to these expectations and behave immaturely. If given the choice, teachers and parents (and people in general) give them fewer important responsibilities; girls are less likely to view them as dating material, and they are typically the last people chosen for an athletic team, partly because they are seen as less capable (and possibly because they are still growing and developing coordination). Not surprisingly, they are less self-assured, more restless, more talkative, and less popular (Laitinen-Krispijn, Van der Ende, Hazebroek-Kampschreur, & Verhulst, 1999). Fortunately, they also feel few pressures to grow up fast and enjoy their teen years without the stresses of the adult world looming menacingly ahead of them.

David is a late-maturing boy on Matt's baseball team. Not only does he look much younger than his teammates, he is a staggering eight to ten inches shorter than they are! While it is often difficult from the bleachers to identify boys in their uniforms, parents always know where David is, when he is batting, and what position he's playing—he's the short one (fondly dubbed the "Mini-Me" of the team). Everybody likes David, but he isn't always taken seriously. He talks too much without saying enough and jumps up and down in a frenzy to get anyone's attention. His juvenile tactics mean he is usually ignored.

Late-maturing girls experience a prolonged childhood with few of the negative experiences of late-maturing boys. They physically develop about the same time the average boy does. They may have a few worries at the outset about acquiring full femininity, but once they physically catch up with their peers, they quickly come to terms with their newfound womanhood (Magnusson, Stattin, & Allen, 1986). Mary Pat didn't start her period until she turned fifteen, long after all of her friends. Relieved at the proof that nothing was wrong with her after all, she rode her bicycle to her friend's house shouting, "I'm a woman! I'm a woman!" the whole way.

Early maturing girls have the most difficult time adjusting to their rate of physical development. They can mature two to three years ahead of girls their age and five to six years ahead of boys. In the scheme of their lives, this is a big age difference. Furthermore, not only are their bodies growing quicker, so are their brains! They tend to be ahead of their peers in interests and abilities. Further complicating matters is the fact that these girls are treated as old as they look; many of these girls start hanging out with an older crowd of friends. Older boys lust after them, which leads to early sexual experimentation. They seek more independence from parental control and have more problems in school with grades and behavior. The laundry list goes on and on. They are more likely to smoke, drink alcohol, be depressed, or suffer from an eating disorder than their on-schedule peers (Kaltiala-Heino, Marttunen, Rantanen, & Rimpela, 2003). Although their brains and bodies are developing at turbo speed, they lack the life experience to deal with the above-age pressures. Fortunately, once they become comfortable with their bodies, they have the confidence and ability to responsibly enjoy their popularity in older adolescence.

In general, boys have more positive body images than girls. Girls tend to be very critical of their attributes and complain about hair being too curly, thighs too fat, and eyelashes too short. Girls usually think they are less attractive than they are. In contrast, boys rate themselves pretty well, wishing only to be a little more muscular (a wish that naturally comes true soon enough). The right friends (captain of the football team, president of the senior class, and homecoming queen) and appearance (usually elements of physical attractiveness such as having fine features, flowing hair, and a creamy complexion) also weigh into the mix. A sense of belonging and having friends further reinforces positive self-esteem (and vice versa). On a side note, appealing looks indirectly influence self-esteem because attractive people have a better chance of being accepted into a group of peers; they benefit from their good looks.

In both genders, however, body image is strongly tied to self-esteem. The more attractive teens believe they are and the more accepting they are of their looks, the higher their self-esteem—and vice versa. Adolescents' bodies are constantly changing, so it is easy for them to have a distorted image of themselves. If they sometimes feel like they are all arms, legs, and nose, it is because they often are.

# Instructional Strategies

## You're OK (But Am I OK?)

Most students enter puberty together and develop at the same rate. They are all beginning to sprout and bloom at about the same time. These students find comfort in numbers and feel normal (as normal as possible) because they are sharing this experience with their friends. Because the physical changes of puberty affect teen friendships, self-esteem, and (ultimately) academic achievement, the teacher who understands this process of transformation can better meet their school needs.

## Things to Try

- Steer clear of calling attention to physical differences, particularly height or weight. The students who are shorter don't always want to stand in the front row. Don't allow nicknames based on physical characteristics such as "Shorty" or "Ribs."
- Work information on physical development into your subject area. Chart growth rates in math, journal about physical changes in English, examine how standards of attractiveness differ between developing and developed countries in social studies. The power of eating cauliflower and staying in motion are perfect topics for health, PE, and life and consumer science. Support the physical education program in your school.
- Furnish opportunities for group work and other social interaction. Independent work is fine (even essential to some parts of learning), but it is important to make students part of a group at times. It's reassuring to be one of many, especially when all their physical changes make teenagers feel like they are the only ones experiencing them.
- Give students models of successful adults who do not meet the standard body image. Abraham Lincoln was tall and scrawny, Stephen Hawking is in a wheelchair, and Queen Latifah and Oprah are overweight, but all are famous for their ideas and actions rather than their looks.
- Examine the media's role in physical expectations. Analyze popular TV shows, critique teen magazines, and discuss music videos.

- Compliment students on their abilities rather than their looks. Be a good role model—avoid criticizing your own body.
- Learn your school's policy of discussing physical concerns like menstruation and obesity with a student. If a student has a question, should the teacher respond or refer them to the nurse or guidance counselor?

## "I HATE MYSELF, I HATE MYSELF."

Keith was a late bloomer, puberty didn't hit until late in his junior year of high school. During ninth and tenth grade, he was the butt of everyone's jokes and suffered merciless teasing, all because of his physical stature. Brad, an athlete and probably the last person anyone in the school would have expected, felt compassion for Keith and made a point of getting to know him. Brad said, "It seemed so ridiculous, he was getting picked on for something he had no control over." Years later, Keith told Brad that he had been considering suicide during high school, and the only thing that stopped him was Brad's friendship. The power of one cannot be denied.

As many as one in twelve teens suffer from clinical depression. Between 1990 and 2003 there was an actual decline in teen suicide, but alarmingly 2003–2004 saw an eight percent increase; it's the third leading cause of teen death, following motor vehicle accidents (#1) and homicide (#2). During high school, seventeen percent seriously consider ending their lives (Center for Disease Control and Prevention, 2007). Strangely, the method has changed; in the past, firearms were the weapon of choice for both boys and girls, but now girls are choosing hanging and suffocation. It is not  unusual for a teen to feel blue (in fact, teenagers have a more negative disposition than adults or children—this ends about age eighteen), but a constant lament of gloom, moodiness, and drooping energy is a sign of true depression. The causes of teen depression are complex. Most professionals believe depression is a combination of genetics, environment, and biology. A genetic link is suggested by the documentation of families with a history of this illness running through aunts, uncles, cousins, and parents. An environment of physical and mental abuse during childhood has been associated with depression. Academics, unrealistic family expectations, and problems with friends can also lead to feelings of rejection, which are related to depression—teens are subject to overreact to any and all of these situations, putting them at greater risk for depression. Getting kicked off the football team, breaking up with a boyfriend, or receiving a D in a class may signal the end of the world to a teen, that they have nothing left to live for and that the shame and pain of this humiliation is impossible to bear.

---

## Secret Revealed

 It's not true that teens have nothing to complain about. No, they don't pay rent or buy food, and yes, they get to go to school and see their friends, but life is just as stressful to them as to adults. Breakups, sports losses, homework, and arguments with friends are just a few of the ordinary events that contribute to adolescent anxiety and depression. Even in a perfect life at a perfect school, however, a teenager would succumb to periods of depression—the teenage brain is vulnerable!

Serotonin, the neurotransmitter that makes us feel calm and at peace, is at a natural low during adolescence. Additionally, because the frontal lobes are in the process of maturing, the amygdala has more control over the brain of a teen than of an adult. As a result, the emotionally reactive, often negative amygdala gets more input than the calm, cool, collected cerebral cortex. To some teenagers, being subjected to the dramatic highs and lows of assessing everything as a possible threat makes it seem like everything in life is bad. With less calming serotonin and more negative impulses, life can be demoralizing and scary. No wonder rates of teen depression are dramatically high.

---

Then there's the role of biology. Researchers from the National Institute of Health studied the connection between puberty and depression. They found the rate of major depression correlates with how far along a child is in puberty as opposed to his or her chronological age. It seems that as we develop physically during puberty, the chances of depression increase (Walkup et al., 2001).

The teen years are marked by low levels of the neurotransmitter, serotonin. Serotonin manages a multitude of jobs in the body spanning from head to toe; it regulates temperature, blood pressure, blood clotting, immunity, pain, digestion, and sleep. It also plays an important role in our emotions as a calming agent. In the properly functioning brain, serotonin inhibits the firing of neurons, making us feel relaxed. It counteracts the emotional amygdala. The decrease of serotonin during adolescence is natural. During the pruning stage, serotonin neurons are selectively eliminated. This normal process does not cause problems for most teens.

But for the others . . . ? Two theories exist about why serotonin levels may cause depression in some teenagers: Either their brains are unable to properly use the serotonin that is there (they have enough serotonin but can't take advantage of it), or their levels of serotonin are so low that the brain is unable to run smoothly. These two educated hunches have spawned the use of medications with a serotonin base to treat depression, which has proven effective in some cases.

**Figure 5.1**   Human Brain

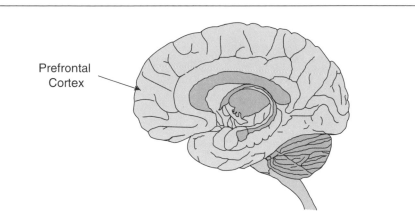

SOURCE: Adapted from Sousa, D. A. (2003), *How the Gifted Brain Learns*, p. 18.

But serotonin is not the only influence on feelings and emotions. The right prefrontal cortex is activated by negative feelings, and the left prefrontal cortex controls positive feelings. The two usually work in sync, keeping our emotions in balance. The left prefrontal cortex is the side that receives and filters emotional information from the amygdala. If the amygdala signals danger, the left prefrontal cortex processes the information and then relays its interpretation of the information back to the amygdala: "Yes, this is a problem" or "Calm down, everything's okay." If the left side decreases in activity (a sure sign it isn't working properly), the amygdala runs wild. Feelings of helplessness, despair, and anxiety run amok. This inactivity in the left prefrontal cortex results in the dominance of the right prefrontal cortex—the controller of negative feelings—and may explain why people with depression tend to remember negative memories rather than pleasant ones. As a person comes out of a depression, the activity in the left prefrontal cortex increases. Which is the cause and which is the effect is not known, but the link between depression and the left prefrontal cortex is clear.

Stress is also related to adolescent depression. Although school, friends, and family are all sources of potential support to teens, they are also potential stressors. Teenagers suffering from depression are more likely to drop out of school or start abusing drugs and alcohol. They are at high risk for committing suicide. Ignoring teenage depression and assuming that "they'll snap out of it" are mistakes no one can afford. Teachers are in the perfect position to spot two of the early warning signs: increased absenteeism and a drop in achievement (an A or B student may suddenly struggle to maintain Cs and Ds). The sooner an adolescent with depression is identified, the better. Letting teens know that there are people willing to help and educating them about the available support systems at their school and in their community can make a real difference in an adolescent's life.

Depression has more than emotional repercussions; it also affects the hippocampus, which influences short-term memory and our ability to process emotion and information. The hippocampus actually decreases in volume during episodes of chronic depression because its neurons wither and die. Fortunately, the hippocampus is resilient and grows new synaptic connections when the depression lifts (Thomas & Peterson, 2003).

## WASTING AWAY

Shawna was a well-adjusted high school student, confident and well liked by her peers. Sophomore year she tried out for the cheerleading squad and made the team. It changed her social life overnight. "Suddenly I went from being accepted to being really popular. Everyone noticed what I was wearing and what I looked like. I liked the feeling, but I also felt a little uncomfortable, like it was all out of control. People were giving me a lot of attention, but I wasn't sure if they really liked me. Sometimes it seemed like they didn't even know me.

"With the extra cheerleading workouts I dropped about ten pounds, and I began to get more compliments. That's when my obsession with food began. I started to watch everything I ate. I wanted to lose weight, but then it got out of control. At one point I was barely eating, maybe having just a diet soda and a cigarette." When five-foot-six-inch Shawna dropped in weight to ninety-five pounds, she was hospitalized. After a six-week treatment program, she returned to school, quit cheerleading, and spent all her energy on regaining her health. Each morning she was weighed; if she had lost weight, she wasn't allowed to attend school that day. Shawna has since graduated from high school but still struggles to maintain a healthy lifestyle. If she follows the course of most recovering anorexics, she will likely struggle for the rest of her life to lead a normal existence in terms of food.

Perhaps up to ten percent of all Americans suffer from some kind of an eating disorder, of whom the vast majority afflicted are females (Spearing, 2001). Although this problem persists into adulthood, its origins are in adolescence. Eighty-sixty percent of adults with an eating disorder say it started before they were twenty years old. This is definitely a teenage problem (Paxton et al., 1991). Rates of anorexia nervosa and bulimia—two of the most common eating disorders—are on the rise with teenage girls in America. In fact, the numbers have doubled since 1960 (Ice, 2003). Anorexia and bulimia have the highest mortality rate of any mental illness—up to twenty percent of those afflicted die. Fortunately, this figure of twenty percent reflects relatively small numbers; only about one percent of the population is anorexic, and only three percent bulimic.

Anorexia nervosa is self-starvation characterized by excessive weight loss. Though people with anorexia avoid eating, they have an intense interest in food. It's not unusual for them to set a formal place for themselves at the dinner table, replete with place mat, silverware, and plate. Anyone walking into the dining room would think they were ready to sit down and enjoy a hearty meal. Instead, their meal would consist of a small amount of low-calorie food, which is cut into small pieces and slowly eaten. Symptoms of anorexia often include noticeable weight loss, the consumption of large amounts of water or noncaloric beverages, always feeling cold, and developing a fine downy hair over the entire body. Individuals with bulimia, in contrast, turn toward food to cope. They often eat large quantities of food, but with the help of purging, suppositories, and laxatives they are able to rid the body of unwanted calories. This cycle of binge eating and purging causes weight fluctuation. Symptoms of bulimia include deterioration of tooth enamel, chronic constipation, and depression. Complications from either of these eating disorders may include kidney failure, loss of menstruation, impaired thinking, and ultimately death.

## Secret Revealed

Teenagers with eating disorders are not necessarily gluttonous or vain. Pathological issues with body weight—manifested in anorexia nervosa or obesity—have significant impact on teens, partially due to changes in their brains. Serotonin and leptin are two brain chemicals currently under scrutiny for their contributions to obsessive eating behaviors. Twenty

*(Continued)*

(Continued)

percent of anorexic people die, making it the most lethal mental illness (Ice, 2003); eighty percent of teenagers who are obese will become adults who are obese and will then suffer from the myriad of health problems that accompany obesity, from heart disease and diabetes to muscular problems. Although it is certain that many other factors besides neurotransmitters contribute to the desire to over- or undereat, science is hoping that finding the causes in the brain will help heal teens with these conditions.

The media and societal expectations have taken the brunt of the blame for our obsession with weight. The message they send is simple: Unless you weigh one hundred pounds and wear size two jeans, you are not making the grade. Although this message is pervasive and harmful, neuroscientists believe that changes in the brain during puberty make their own contributions to eating disorders. Serotonin is thought to impact obsessive, anxious behavior (Barbarich, 2002); girls with eating disorders such as anorexia and bulimia have higher levels of serotonin than girls of average weight (Aguilera, Selgas, Codoceo, & Bajo, 2000). With the increased serotonin levels in these girls' brains, they become obsessed with their weight and with food. Complicating the situation is the fact that food contains elements necessary for the body to manufacture serotonin. By not eating, the body of an anorexic or bulimic is unable to produce serotonin. As these girls starve themselves, they reduce their serotonin levels. This eventually enables them to reduce their own obsessive behavior and feel calmer, but the price they pay is high—irregular heart rate, osteoporosis, kidney failure, and ultimately death can be the consequence of an eating disorder. It is estimated that three thousand young women die each year from eating disorders.

## "WOULD YOU LIKE FRIES WITH THAT?"

Obesity is starting to be classified as another type of eating disorder, one as tied up in body-image issues as anorexia nervosa and bulimia are (Heller, 2003). For people suffering from obesity, food is an obsession with physical repercussions. Obesity has no gender bias; males and females are equally plagued. It's not easy to be obese in our thin-obsessed society. Adolescents with obesity deal with more teasing, fatigue, and lower self-esteem than their friends of normal weight—and the problems don't stop there. Adolescents are heavier than ever before, and we are beginning to see them contract Type 2 diabetes at an alarming rate. (Ninety percent of all cases of diabetes fall into the Type 2 category.) Individuals with diabetes either do not produce enough insulin to control their glucose levels or else their cells do not respond to the insulin in their bloodstream. Obesity is a major contributor to this disease because excess fat blocks insulin from moving glucose into the body's cells to give them energy. As adolescents who are obese enter adulthood, health issues such as heart disease and cancer develop at an alarming pace.

There is no doubt that obesity is a growing problem in the United States. The U.S. Department of Health and Human Services reported that fifteen percent of school-age children are overweight, triple what it was twenty years ago (Dietz, 2002). Health patterns established in adolescence are highly associated with obesity in adulthood—eighty percent of obese adolescents eventually become obese adults (Manisses, 2003). Traditionally we've looked at genetics, eating habits, exercise, and metabolism to understand the overweight body, but the time has come to look at the brain's role.

It takes ten minutes after eating for the brain of a person of normal weight to get the information that the stomach is full—the hormone leptin is released from fat cells and informs the brain that you've had enough to eat. The delay is longer in people who are obese. Research shows that individuals who are obese are not receiving signals to the brain that tell them to quit eating. Their brains  don't seem to get the message. Researchers hypothesize that the message is not received in their brain because either leptin is being transported improperly or the brain is misinterpreting the information (Banks, 2003).

As a result of not getting the signal to stop eating, it is speculated that people who are obese go into a frenzy to get the signal moving to the brain. They eat more and more, hoping to produce a surge of leptin and send the necessary message to the brain. Their internal logic is correct—in the person who is normal weight, this eating would have the intended effect. Unfortunately, for the person who is overweight, the reverse happens. Obesity prevents the signal from getting to the brain, so their overeating is an act of futility. Now the vicious cycle has begun. The less leptin received by the brain, the more obese they become. They eat more in an attempt to break the brain's barrier to leptin and get the signal.

Nor do the brain differences between the obese and normal-weight person stop there. The U.S. Department of Energy's Brookhaven National Laboratory showed that obese people have fewer brain receptors for dopamine (a neurotransmitter that creates feelings of pleasure and calm) than normal-weight people. When a person eats, he or she is rewarded with a rush of feel-good dopamine. (We've all had that satisfied feeling after consuming a hearty meal.) Regrettably, the person who is obese has fewer dopamine receptors and so needs to overeat to release the same amount of dopamine. Much like the addict who anticipates the craved pleasure or the numbing that accompanies the drug, the person who is overweight craves food to achieve that satisfied feeling (Wang, Volkow, & Fowler, 2002).

The impending health factors are not the only problems. The teen with obesity worries about body image and social acceptance like any adolescent, but unlike normal-weight teens, teens with obesity may also worry that they don't "measure up" in adult society's eyes. Poor self-esteem and rejection can lead to depression; depression can negatively affect academic performance. The domino effect is irrefutable (Manisses, 2003). Just being overweight can indirectly start the toppling—the first to fall is body image, then self-esteem, followed by depression and difficulty in school.

Explanations for the rise in anorexia nervosa, bulimia, and depression are not forthcoming. It is possible that the rates are the same as they have always been but we keep better records or that the stigma associated with these diseases has lessened so more people seek treatment. Some people blame the changing standards of beauty and attractiveness in the media and the availability of cosmetic surgery for putting pressure on individuals to strive for unattainable perfection. Dr. Elizabeth Young, professor of psychiatry and research scientist at the University of Michigan Mental Health Research Institute, speculates that teenagers are under just as much pressure and feel just as much stress as their parents do (Lurie, 2003). They are juggling boyfriends and girlfriends, schoolwork, jobs, parents—all of which are complications to life and commonly considered sources of depression.

## Instructional Strategies

### *Educate Teens About the Issues That Affect Them*

Eating disorders and depression are the leading internal issues facing teens today, and all these conditions are on the rise at alarming rates. But why now? Why are today's teens more at risk for these dangers than the teens of fifty years ago? Obesity perhaps has the clearest explanation. The caloric intake of the average American has increased by twenty percent since 1982, and sugar intake has grown by twenty percent (Putnam, Allshouse, & Kantor, 2002). Physical activity is on the decline, and girls in particular become less active during adolescence. Teenagers watch more television than they used to—forty-three percent watch more than two hours a day! They also spend more time playing sedentary computer and video games. Trying to explain why eating disorders are on the rise may not solve the problem, but it does give us a place to start looking for answers.

### Things to Try

- Involve teens with their peers. Healthy personal relationships improve self-esteem and are fun.
- Encourage students to participate in sports, find an afterschool job, or join extracurricular activities. If their minds are occupied with external activities, they will be less likely to focus on destructive internal issues.
- Focus on the positive in class. Wearing a smile actually helps your disposition and may directly contribute to a student's happy thoughts and good mood.
- Arrange help for students who are afflicted by depression or eating disorders. Refer them to the guidance counselor or proper school personnel.
- Greet students at the door each day, and get to know them as individuals. This personal attention may give an isolated teen a sense of belonging; friendly rapport with your students will put you in a better position to note changes in behavior that may signal depression.
- Internet Web sites can offer support for specific issues that teens face (of course discretion is advised).
- If a teen confesses an eating disorder, depression, or other problem, validate his or her feelings. You don't have to approve of the behavior, but you do need to acknowledge that it's okay to feel upset, overwhelmed, or depressed.
- Signs of depression or an eating disorder that persist longer than two weeks should be taken seriously.

## THE NEED TO SLEEP

It's noon at my house, and two teenagers are curled up under the covers, snoozing away. "Never wake a baby or a teenager" is a rule I live by. And boy, do teenagers love to sleep! The complaints from parents about it sound so much alike. "My son will fight tooth and nail to watch another half hour of sports at night and then drags the next morning." "No matter what time she goes to sleep, Sandra cannot stay awake in church." "Going to bed early means 1:00 a.m.! They'll sleep as late as I let them and even then can't focus on what they are doing." "During their sports season, my teens are irritable, short-tempered, and disrespectful." It is not uncommon for adults to think teenagers are lazy. After all, sixteen-year-olds sleep until noon, walk around the house in a daze, and then shuffle into the shower—where they spend the next thirty minutes. What happened to the child who woke up early, hungry for a bowl of cereal, and eager to watch cartoons? In a word, puberty!

Puberty changes the sleep patterns of the adolescent. During puberty, the body secretes melatonin (a hormone associated with sleep) at a different time than during childhood or adulthood, significantly altering their

sleep cycle. This change causes the teenager to fall asleep much later at night and wake up later in the day. Children who fell asleep at 9:00 or 9:30 p.m. now find themselves wide-awake at midnight. Besides the change in sleep patterns, teenagers also need more sleep than adults do. It's thought the average adult needs eight and one-quarter hours of sleep, while the average teen needs nine and one-quarter hours. This change may be ascribed to the fact that the body is trying to encourage their sexual development—the hormones necessary for sexual development are mainly released while you sleep. (There is no proof, however, that losing sleep derails the release of these hormones; Carskadon, 2002.)

Teenagers themselves are painfully cognizant of their new sleeping and waking cycles. "In the summer I sleep way too much, and during the school year, not nearly enough. On weekends, I get up at noon and I'm still tired." "At night I never get tired and don't know how much sleep I need until the next morning. During marching band season, I have to get up at six in the morning every day. I'll reset my alarm for five more minutes and then reset it again until I have about five minutes before it's time to go! Sleep is the most important thing in my life." "During free time in class I lay my head down and sleep. If I could stay awake, I'd read or talk to a friend."

## Secret Revealed

Although it certainly seems so, teens don't sleep in on Saturday morning just to shirk chores. Adolescence has completely altered their daily sleep and wake patterns! Dr. Mary Carskadon (2002) from Brown University has been studying teens and their sleep schedules and has discovered that they need more sleep than their parents but not as much as their younger siblings.

And not only do they need more sleep—they get sleepy later than ever. Even teens who try to go to bed early find themselves awake and restless until close to midnight. Complicating matters is the early start time of most secondary schools. Instead of being tucked into bed at 8:00 a.m., finishing up a dream, students are already on their way to their second class. That's hardly good for learning. It's not very good for teacher-student conflicts either—notice how snappy and touchy you get when you are tired. Imagine what a teenager (still learning to manage emotions) feels like!

Dr. Mary Carskadon from Brown University is an expert on understanding adolescent sleep patterns. She found that the majority of high school students were sleep deprived, resulting in twenty percent of high school students falling asleep in school. Perhaps even more interesting was that she found forcing them to go to bed earlier did not solve the problem (Carskadon, 2002). Not surprisingly, most high school students get less than eight hours of sleep and one-third get less than seven. School schedules only complicate the situation. Schools start early, some as early as 7:15 or 7:30 a.m. On the weekends, motivated by aggravation or misguided efforts to produce an industrious child, parents wake teenagers out of a sound sleep. This leaves them starting their day tired and run down. We have a flock of sleep-deprived individuals trying to maneuver their way through adolescence.

There are significant differences between those students who get enough sleep versus those who do not. Sleep deprivation makes it more difficult for most students to learn, remember, and think creatively. Research studies show that high school students not receiving enough sleep suffer in grades and overall school success. Emotions are also harder to control when adolescents are sleep deprived. Normal mood swings that accompany hormone changes increase, as do irritability and depression. The immune system is negatively affected, leaving a student at risk of catching a cold or developing a sore throat. Most disturbing is the increase in aggressive behavior in students who are sleep deprived (Carskadon, 2002).

Minnesotans have been particularly concerned about the impact of sleep on high school students. Many districts have moved their school start time from 7:20 to 8:30 a.m. Grades improved and discipline problems decreased at these schools with a later start time (Reiss, 1998). School systems, however, are reluctant to change school start times. Bus schedules and extracurricular activities make it a complicated venture. The best we can do is encourage teenagers to get plenty of sleep. Verbally acknowledging and reinforcing the fact that they actually do need more sleep then adults gives them "permission" to indulge their desire to sleep (after school, of course!).

If adolescents are tired, listless, and only thinking about their next nap, it is not easy to get their attention in school. Sleep impacts memory and creativity. That extensive list of defined biology terms and the fanciful memoir will both be of higher quality if the teenager does them when awake and refreshed. Likewise, sleep affects our emotions. When teens are tired, they are more likely to be irritable and have mood swings. The student who would amicably agree to work in a teacher-chosen group when well rested may become upset and even belligerent about it when tired.

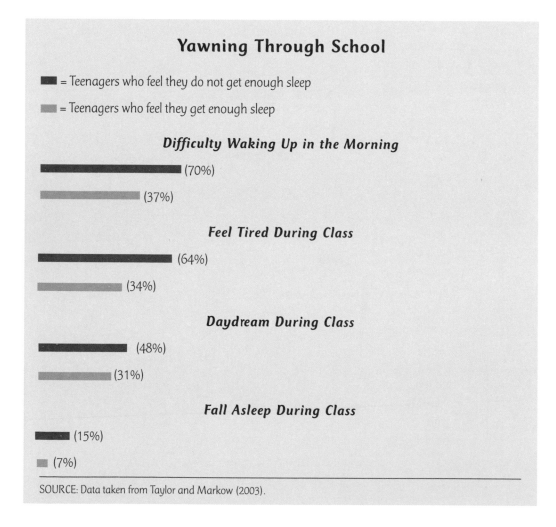

# Yawning Through School

■■ = Teenagers who feel they do not get enough sleep

■■ = Teenagers who feel they get enough sleep

### Difficulty Waking Up in the Morning

(70%)

(37%)

### Feel Tired During Class

(64%)

(34%)

### Daydream During Class

(48%)

(31%)

### Fall Asleep During Class

(15%)

(7%)

SOURCE: Data taken from Taylor and Markow (2003).

# Instructional Strategies

## *Accommodate Sleep and Wake Patterns*

Imagine all your students coming to class wide-awake—what a lovely dream! Sleep is one process that affects both behavior and achievement over which teachers have little or no control. No wonder we are so frustrated when we see a student sleeping through class time—teenagers and their parents are the only people with the power to change this situation. Your best bet for ameliorating student sleepiness is with a relentless informational campaign. Use school newsletters and parent-teacher conferences to educate them on the importance of sleep to the teenager, or take your message to the entire community by writing a letter to the editor or a small article for your local newspaper.

## *Things to Try*

- Let indoors imitate outdoors as much as possible. Keep lights low in the evening and open a curtain in the morning. (Light helps reset the biological clock.)
- Introduce the issue of starting high school later to the school board. If biology and puberty do not seem like sufficient reasons, remind them that the change of schedule could also help reduce teenage crime and pregnancy—rates of each peak between the hours of 3:30 and 5:00 p.m., when teens are often without supervision. (*After School for America's Teens*, 2001)
- Encourage parents to allow teens to sleep until at least 9:00 a.m. on weekends and later if possible.
- Educate teenagers on the importance of sleep to their physical well-being. Design a two- or three-day unit on the importance of sleep, or assign a research paper or project on this topic. Knowledge is power; most teens probably walk around too tired to wonder why their energy is so low and would be relieved to have an answer for it.
- Stay away from stimulants such as caffeine and nicotine because they interfere with the body's natural sleep processes.
- Avoid stimulating activities before bed, such as heavy studying or computer games. Energizing activities arouse the brain, making it difficult to prepare the body for a good night's sleep. But do exercise during the day; a minimum of thirty minutes per day will help tire you out and prepare you for a good night's sleep.
- Eliminate late-night arguments. Encourage parents to save it until morning. Confrontation raises the heart rate and blood pressure, which also stimulates the brain and makes it more difficult to fall asleep.
- Start a worry book—unload all your worries into a worry book and then let your mind relax. This will reduce adrenaline production.

*(Continued)*

(Continued)

- Create a sleeping habit—wake up and go to sleep at similar times each day (this recommendation is made with the realization that most teens like to burn the midnight oil on weekends—and so it may not be a realistic option).
- Don't sleep with a pet—they are frequently sleep disturbers.
- Resist the temptation to look at the clock (It's 2:00 a.m. and I'm not asleep—aaaaah!); seeing the time tends to create more anxiety.
- Keep the temperature cool, no higher than sixty-eight degrees for optimal sleeping.

## HELPING EDDIE HANDLE HIS AGGRESSION

*The principal spoke to Eddie and Peter separately about the fight. With both boys he calmly discussed the motivation for the fight and suggested appropriate ways to handle their anger. "Next time," he gently chided Eddie, "find a teacher or just walk away." Eddie nodded the whole time. He already knew he should respond to teasing without fighting, but cracks about his weight hit too close to home.*

*Mr. Wyatt, Eddie's teacher, wasn't really surprised that Peter's taunts finally had this effect. When Eddie resumed classes, Mr. Wyatt took him aside a few moments during lunch to talk not about the fight but about starting a club. The two of them had something in common, he said—they were both collectors. Eddie collected stamps, he collected American memorabilia . . . did he know any other collectors who would like to join? The project caught Eddie's interest and he started asking around. Within a month, he'd rallied enough interest to organize one. Focusing on the club's activities gave him more to think about than his weight; Peter's name-calling lost its sting after a while. Later, when Mr. Wyatt and Eddie talked about walking for thirty minutes a day instead of spending the time watching television, Eddie took the advice as wisdom rather than as an insult.*

# The Risk-Taking Brain

The teen years have always been risk-taking years but not because adolescence is boring. Teenagers don't drive too fast and smoke cigarettes behind the gym out of youthful exuberance. Neuroscientists are shedding light on the brain's significant role in reckless behaviors, suggesting that mistakes teens make now can have lasting physiological effects.

**Did you know that . . .**

- Teens are very susceptible to the dopamine rushes that come with taking risks
- Teens have trouble anticipating the consequences of their behavior because they rely more on the emotional amygdala than the rational frontal lobes
- Teens are extremely vulnerable to addiction and that adolescent addictions are harder to break
- Violent video games reinforce violent behavior in boys
- Cutting releases endorphins into the body, creating feelings of pleasure

*With much enthusiasm, eighth-grader Scott detailed how he, his father, and his uncle took mountain bikes down Vail Pass, a trail with an extremely steep grade. Scott felt excited and confident as they approached the top of the path. His uncle planned to pace his descent at twenty-five miles an hour and had brought a speedometer to control it. Scott rolled his eyes and told his father how weird and dorky that was.*

*Scott set a fast pace for his own ride down the mountain and found it fun. "I thought I could handle it because it was paved and well traveled," he said. "A lot of people ride this trail. So could I." He rapidly picked up speed and took a curve too quickly. His bike skidded and he was thrown over the handlebars, arms and legs flailing. The result? Bloody elbows and knees, a serious case of road rash, and a very bruised ego.*

*The rest of his ride down the mountain was uneventful. "I was cautious. I took slow turns, slow everything. I got nervous when someone passed me. I kept thinking, at least I'm OK, no broken bones." When asked if he was surprised that he had fallen, he said, "I didn't really think it would happen."*

## RISKY BUSINESS

We know a lot about what makes a teenager an "at-risk" teenager; poverty, violence, substance abuse, neglect, and sexual assault just begin the list. Adolescents living under these conditions have a greater chance of dropping out of school, becoming pregnant, or turning to drugs. Even the "safe" end of the at-risk continuum includes smoking a cigarette, sipping a beer, and driving too fast—tantalizing and dicey adventures for the teenager.

The statistics are alarming:

- Seventeen percent of high school students seriously consider suicide; it's the third leading cause of death among teenagers (Center for Disease Control and Prevention, 2007).
- Seventy-seven percent of the calls to the National Runaway Switchboard (2008) are females, and the primary reason they give for running away is family dynamics.
- Nearly twelve percent of teenagers have used an illicit drug in the past month (compared to just over eight percent of the national population) (U.S. Department of Health and Human Services, 2002).
- Nearly fifty percent of high school seniors drink alcohol at least once a month (Johnston, O'Malley, & Bachman, 2003).
- About twenty-five percent of males are arrested before the age of eighteen (Ortiz, 2003).

Fortunately, not all teens face deprivation and abuse—most experience the world as a safe and secure place. But the changes brewing in the adolescent brain put them all at risk for making unhealthy decisions with somber consequences. Teenagers, in general, travel a dangerous road; reflecting back on your own adolescence will possibly evoke some ill thought out decisions and activities.

## TECHNOLOGY MEETS THE TEENAGE BRAIN

"I swear at the computer game." "I want to karate chop my littler brother." "I'd like to punch somebody." These are all quotes from teens expressing their feelings while playing violent video games. As surprising as their remarks are, the real surprise came when I went into a classroom and asked who played violent video games, and three-quarters of the class unashamedly raised their hands.

There is no doubt that teenagers love video games; ninety percent play them regularly. They are the new generation's recreation of choice. As is true in so many things in life, there is an upside and a downside to this pastime.

Torkel Klingberg (Fernandez & Klingberg, 2006) found the upside. He conducted an intriguing study involving memory training through computer games. His research showed that some computer games were able to increase attention and reduce hyperactivity in middle schoolers with ADHD (attention-deficit/hyperactivity disorder). The more the game simulated real life, the more effectively it strengthened attention. To add further excitement to his discovery, memory and creativity also improved.

The downside to this technology comes in the form of violent video games. They are a prime example of an element introduced into the environment that counters everything the teen brain is working to overcome. Teenagers are trying to become more reflective and exhibit fewer knee-jerk reactions, but computer games play on their reflexive responses, encouraging them to make faster and faster decisions. Quickly they learn that blasting and exploding their way to the next level is the way to win.

There is no doubt the lack of impulse control is computer-game induced—frontal lobes actually become less active while playing violent video games and continue to remain so for a period of time. In addition, higher levels of testosterone are released into the system, further agitating the amygdala. The emotional amygdala is reinforced, and the reflective frontal lobes are neglected. The teen is now ripe to take this behavior out of the computer and into the classroom.

Neuroscientists also found that older adolescents who frequently played violent video games had less empathy. When shown real-life violent crimes, they underreacted. In effect, they become numb to others' pain and bloodshed.

Mirror neurons, the neurons that allow us to learn from observation, bring an interesting piece to the puzzle on violent video games. Cutting-edge research conducted by Marco Iacoboni (2008) led to speculation that playing violent video games (and watching violent movies) influenced imitative violence. The teenager who "kills" for hours on a video game is then more likely to become violent in real life. Frighteningly, in this context, neuroscientists found that individuals were often unaware and powerless when it came to producing or inhibiting the automatic imitations found in mirror neurons; it was beyond their control. The more subjects observed, the more they imitated. Hence, extensive playing of violent video games may put teenagers (and children and adults) at risk for aggressive and cruel violence.

In addition, Iacoboni's research team found that what a person brings to the game is more important than the game content. An adolescent who has a sense of what normal behavior is will recognize unhealthy behavior and not want to imitate it. Conversely, an adolescent who has experienced violence and aggression in life may view the violence in video games as normal behavior (Iacoboni, 2008).

Cell phones are another source of concern. Initially, the combination of driving and cell phone chats were thought to be brain possible. The multitasking required by this twosome calls for different parts of the brain to ignite, something the brain finds easy to do compared to two similar tasks. (For instance, it's simpler for the brain to listen to music and read than it is to write and speak at the same time.) However, researchers found that driving abilities were reduced by thirty-seven percent when talking on a cell phone, making it more likely to not stop at the red light and more likely to swerve into the next lane (Spice, 2008). Indeed, there seem to be limits on how far we can stretch the brain's multitasking abilities. Dangerous and deadly, cell phone use and driving are not brain compatible.

The Internet is another source of technology with multiple positive and negative possibilities. In one short decade, the Internet has redefined the term friendship. Web sites like My Space and Facebook enable teens to recover their long-lost friends, share thoughts instantaneously (no reflection necessary, discretion to the wind), and then back up their comments with personal pictures to ensure everyone has a visual. Teenagers are flocking to them like bees to honey; in their mind it's the perfect blend of friendship and technology. (Personally, thanks to his Facebook I just found out my son and his girlfriend broke up—he's now registered as "single.")

Surfing the Internet makes it possible for them to connect with chat rooms and blogs that share their common interests and activities 24/7. The support and camaraderie they find add to their social and emotional development. The adolescent fighting bulimia, the athlete considering steroids, or the student who just had a fight with a teacher can find a soul mate any day, anytime. Used properly, this type of technology can enrich lives and act as a techno safety-net.

The Internet also supplies us with a huge amount of information; for educators, this means the library doors expand the globe, increasing the growth of dendrites and synaptic connections. This has created a boon of knowledge, a school dream come true. As educators we walk the tightrope of enthusiastically embedding technology into our classrooms while vigilantly monitoring it's every click. This visionary technology, for all its promise, can cause loss of reputation, safety, and job. Cyberstalkers are eager to prey on the young and naïve. Teens too frequently disclose personal information that puts them at risk for becoming someone's victim. School and parental supervision are necessary for children and teenagers in this ever-expanding techno-world.

## Instructional Strategies

### *Things to Try: Technology Rules!*

- Collaboratively set up rules for working on computers at school. Rules might include the following:
  - o Don't alter the hard or soft drive.
  - o Stay on your assignment; computer work must be related to schoolwork.
  - o Do not surf the Internet or check e-mail unless you have permission.
  - o Print only the pages necessary—be Green.
  - o Cite the URLs used for assignments; remember copyright laws.
  - o Don't eat or drink near computers.
  - o Share computer time with your peers, and limit your time if someone is waiting.
  - o Report any problems (malfunctions, inappropriate sites) to the teacher.

- Allow all students access to technology. Be sensitive to homework that requires a computer—students may not have home access.
- Directly instruct students on how to determine if a source is credible or not. Then let them select a topic related to your content and send them surfing to find two legitimate and two shady sources.

*(Continued)*

(Continued)

- Discuss cybercrimes such as downloading games and music, hacking, and plagiarism. Then draw connections between the real world and the cyberworld; for example, pose these questions: Is it legal to go into a store and take a DVD without paying for it? Does this differ from downloading music without paying?
- Give students the benefit of the doubt at the outset; many don't realize that downloading and hacking are illegal. Consider it an honest mistake; then set up the expectation that now that they know better, they will do better.
- Permit pairs to work on computers; this becomes a true learning trifecta: socializing, subject content, and technology.

## Secret Revealed

Neuroscientists compared the brains of individuals playing Nintendo with those doing simple arithmetic problems. Considering the flash and flair found in Nintendo, they expected to find the same kind of dynamic drama going on in the brain. Instead, they found the computer game stimulated a few meager areas of the brain, primarily vision and movement, while the basic arithmetic problems engaged the frontal lobes in both hemispheres of the brain.

## CUTTING

Katie appears to be an average middle schooler; her father is a physician and her mom stays at home to care for the family, but in Katie's words, "my mom has issues." When Mom is in one of her ugly moods, it is not uncommon for her to call Katie a "whore," "worthless," and "stupid." Needless to say, their relationship is dysfunctional. During eighth grade, Katie began hanging out with older kids; she liked their company, and they seemed to have a lot in common. One night she went to a party; drinking was involved and before the night was over, she had been sexually assaulted by multiple boys; that's when she began cutting. With every cut, a little pressure was relieved; in her words, "It's a way to cope."

It has been said that boys explode and girls implode. Cutting, along with eating disorders and depression, is one of the chosen forms for teenage girls to implode. This form of self-harm is particularly prevalent in young adolescents. It stems primarily from environmental issues that exist outside the school walls. Sexual and physical abuse and neglect are the primary culprits, but the brain also plays a role.

Every cut acts as reinforcement for further cutting. As girls cut themselves, endorphins are released into their body, generating feelings of satisfaction and calming their wounded soul. At the same time, serotonin, the great pacifier, is not effectively used in their brains (Schwarz, 2006).

Cutting tends to occur during young adolescence, making middle school teachers the first line of defense. Be on the lookout for girls who always wears long sleeves to school, no matter how hot the weather. Once identified, these girls need to learn alternative, healthy coping skills with the help of professional counselors.

## VIOLENCE AND AGGRESSION

The gym was reduced to a barroom brawl; punches were thrown, lips were split, and eyes were swollen shut. It was the ultimate fight: football players against wrestlers. No one knew how it started, and no one cared. It took ten teachers and three administrators to end the chaos. Once things calmed down, one of the rebels, Bruno, had the following to say, "The fight was between football players and wrestlers; it didn't matter who he was, if he was a football player, I was punching him. It was out of control."

Violence and aggression increase during the teenage years, particularly for males. The environment plays a large role in explaining this turbulent behavior, as does the search for autonomy (parents have less control than in childhood), but the brain is also a culprit. Neuroscientists are adding to the body of knowledge provided by psychologists and sociologists on this confrontational and cantankerous behavior during adolescence.

Serotonin levels have been linked to aggression and violence. Unfortunately for the teen, levels of serotonin in the prefrontal cortex are especially low, reducing its ability to control the emotional amygdala. There are also lower levels of glucose metabolism, an energy source, in the prefrontal cortex and higher levels in the amygdala, hippocampus, thalamus, and other emotional areas of the brain. As a result, we find less energy in the decision-making, logical part of the brain and more energy in the emotional areas of the brain (Dahl, 2003). Not the balance needed for healthy choices.

## Secret Revealed

 Teens are acutely susceptible to stress, peer pressure, and other negative forces. Controlling their lives is a struggle for most of them, and for some, violence becomes their means of taking charge. Interestingly, teens begin showing violence toward others around the age of sixteen, but as the brain develops they seem to grow out of it. If they haven't committed a violent crime by nineteen, they probably won't.

The uniqueness of the adolescent brain propelled Laurence Steinberg, a Temple University psychology professor, to prepare the legal brief for the U.S. Supreme Court from the American Psychological Association (Beckman, 2004). A case was made to differentiate juvenile criminals from adult criminals. In essence, they successfully argued that juveniles' brains are not fully developed (this does not mean they aren't responsible for their actions).

## WHY NICE KIDS DO STUPID THINGS

Andy is fourteen years old and taller than most of his classmates. He is a quintessential class leader, liked by students and teachers equally. It is not uncommon for a group of kids to gather around Andy's desk as he tells funny stories about football practice—he can make anyone laugh and puts everyone at ease. He knows how to handle his popularity and is a responsible person. Still, he has some serious lapses of judgment. Last week, for instance, he was caught driving without an adult in the car. When asked why he was driving without a license or training, he simply replied, "I don't know."

Why do nice kids do stupid things? This is not a rhetorical question—adults want an answer. How can we explain the crazy behavior of teens and their decisions to try things even a child wouldn't risk? Blame their inherent cravings for novelty. Teen brains are drawn to rowdy and foolhardy acts, more so than children or adult brains. Novelty, especially when attached to the thrill of danger, is very attractive to adolescents because it produces intense feelings of pleasure that tempt even cautious and prudent teens to engage in dangerous experimentation. In the brain, novelty stimulates dopamine, which makes you feel good. It is believed the same neurons are affected by novelty as those affected by drugs such as cocaine. Reckless behavior provides the same rush. To complicate matters, levels of serotonin (the calming neurotransmitter) seem to decline during adolescence, further jeopardizing their stability and the likelihood of impulsive behavior (Chugani et al., 1999).

## Secret Revealed

When two teenage drivers race along the road, darting through traffic in order to get ahead of each other, it's not because they think they are still on the sports field. They are doing it partly because of the risk and danger involved—risk and danger reward the brain because they trigger the very pleasurable dopamine. At this stage of life, risk and danger are fun!

Adolescents' attraction to novelty is in part responsible for their reckless behavior. Most educators think of novelty only in terms of livening up the classroom, but teens look for it in every facet of life. No wonder they flock to amusement parks to ride roller coasters and free-falling attractions—high speeds, fast corners, and turning upside down are not usually experienced on the school bus. When life seems too predictable, wild excitement can seem like a perfectly reasonable pursuit.

Neuroscience is shedding light on the wild side of the adolescent brain, too. Findings suggest the volatility of adolescent behavior is, in part, caused by the lack of emotional regulation in the frontal cortex (Spinks, 2002). Furthermore, the frontal lobes are not always functioning fully in teenagers, which suggests that they do not think through the potential consequences of the impulsive behaviors prompted by their amygdalas.

This imbalance between amygdala and frontal-lobe control in their brains may explain their minor and major at-risk behaviors, from arguing over a homework assignment to drug experimentation and unprotected sex. Think of a teacher-student confrontation. In each person, the frontal lobes consciously and logically analyze the information from the event, evaluate it, and decide upon a reaction (Siegel, 2001). Perhaps the frontal lobes in the adult and the adolescent identify accompanying emotions as fear and anger. The teacher, with fully developed frontal lobes, will probably get the mental signal to calm down because fighting with a student is inappropriate. The teenage student, however, is at the mercy of the amygdala and will likely react explosively by accusing the teacher of unfairness, calling the class stupid, or slamming books around.

Interestingly, increases in testosterone levels in males during puberty cause an enlarged growth in the amygdala. As a result, boys' amygdalas are much bigger than girls' (Giedd, Castellanos, Rajapakse, Vaituzis, & Rapoport, 1997). This proportional difference is thought to explain aggressiveness and greater at-risk behavior by boys. Still, this does not mean that all boys experience increased aggression just because their testosterone levels rise. Whether a boy reacts reflectively or impulsively to aggression depends on his disposition (Sylwester, 2000).

## BAD THINGS HAPPEN TO OTHER PEOPLE

With her dark, curly hair swept neatly into a scrunchie on top of her head, tennis racket in hand, and shy demeanor, Jennifer hardly looked the risk-taking type. As she put it, "I'm generally a good kid."

But Saturday night, she and a friend sneaked out of the house to walk to an all-night convenience store. As teenage luck would have it, her dad walked past her closed bedroom door and noticed a slight draft. Curious, he gently knocked. There was no answer. After numerous attempts to awaken his daughter, he opened the door and discovered the empty bedroom and open window. When Jennifer returned, her father, in a tone mixed with anger and relief, asked simply, "Why?" Her response? "We wanted to. It seemed fun. Nothing was going to happen—it was just two blocks away." When reminded that her mother had specifically forbidden them to walk to the convenience store after dark, she said, "I thought Mom was being pointless and overprotective."

The teen brain is unaccustomed to relying on its frontal lobes. There are still lots of rough edges to smooth out before it becomes a fine-tuned thinking machine. Synapses are generating, pruning is liquidating cells, myelin is spreading—the changes literally boggle the mind. One of these rough edges is teens' belief that they are indestructible. As adolescents adjust to the frontal lobes' new capabilities of abstract thinking, symbolism, and logical reasoning, they become totally absorbed with themselves—naturally assuming that everyone else is, too! The next conclusion that adolescents draw is that they are pretty darn special. (Why else would everyone be so interested?) From their sense of their own uniqueness comes the frustration and loneliness of believing that no one could possibly understand them. With a condescending tone and a perfectly straight face, they can tell their parents, "You don't know what it's like to be in love!"

This belief in their unique place in the world promotes the belief they are invulnerable and nothing can hurt them, which leads them to take chances. They can walk alone at night without tempting fate. They can drive drunk, have unprotected sex, and experiment with drugs and face no serious consequences. Bad things happen to other people, not them (Rice & Dolgin, 2002). Their inability to determine the consequences of their behavior contributes to their mistaken view that they are indestructible. It also gives them permission to take risks because they don't fully comprehend the ramifications of the choices they make.

# Instructional Strategies

## *Mr. Toad's Wild Ride*

Three middle school boys were running down the street with a computer chair. One would sit on the chair while the other two pushed him down a hill—backwards. Mystified, I observed them for a few minutes before asking them what they were doing. One boy spoke up for the group and said, "We were bored. There's nothing better to do and it's really fun when the chair flips."

I, an adult, stood perplexed by their behavior. The hazards were obvious to me and certainly not worth the second or two of excitement riding a chair down the street provided! None of my friends would think it was fun. Even small children would think it was a harebrained, dangerous idea. But these boys decided, without hesitation, that it was perfectly safe. Teens seem to go out of their way to find thrills and chills. If you can bring the emotions of riding a roller coaster into your classroom, students will find learning (if not exactly thrilling) very exciting.

## *Things to Try*

- Place less emphasis on textbooks and more on projects. Take away sedentary seat time and actively involve them in learning.
- Individualize the members of your class rather than always treating them as a group. Get to know each student's abilities, talents, and interests. Knowing who your students are and what they like is a first step in offering a curriculum that they can relate to and get enthused about.
- Play up problem-solving skills. Don't provide all the answers—let students discover solutions. The process of solving problems is what is important anyway, not necessarily having the correct answer. The ability to think abstractly, engage in reflective thought, hone critical reasoning skills, and develop alternative solutions to frustrating situations will create challenges and allow teens to take the risk of being original.
- Teach a thinking curriculum—content and process. Process will help students learn how to make decisions. Being skilled at a process is as powerful as having knowledge.
- Give students plenty of opportunities for success. Victory is a thrilling sensation, especially after a serious challenge. You don't always have to pit students against each other—pit cooperative groups against a difficult problem or help individual students master a task they've been struggling with.
- Encourage reasonable risk taking. Ask students to try something they've never done before, like inventing a game, composing and performing a song, learning a new sport, or designing a cartoon.
- Advocate involvement in extracurricular activities. An encouraging word can make the difference between taking the risk of personal involvement and sitting on the sidelines.

*(Continued)*

(Continued)

- Support afterschool programs for middle school students who are unsupervised after school. Middle school (and high school!) students left totally alone on a daily basis for long periods of time make poor choices. Adult supervision is a much-needed and well-deserved safety net.
- Scaffold, create that firm foundation for learning. Start with the concrete and get creative: Show a clip of modern dancers, and have students identify the geometric shapes in their movements.
- Encourage participation in sports. Running for the touchdown, kicking the winning goal, or securing the final match—it's hard to beat sports for healthy risk taking. In sports, effort is rewarded by achieving goals and gaining recognition, motivating the athlete to continue. Dopamine is in high swing, reinforcing every thrill. Additionally, preliminary research shows that participation in sports may reduce other types of risk-taking behavior (Bloom, Beal, & Kupfer, 2006).
- Rethink your school discipline policy; is punishment overused? In some schools, students are given detention for going to the restroom during class (it doesn't matter that your period just started), for not having their bottom completely on their chair, and for not having a pen in class (ignoring the fact that the pen ran out of ink while taking class notes). If this sounds like your school, it's time to reconsider the rules.

## DECISIONS, DECISIONS

Adolescents face difficult decisions every day: to smoke or not to smoke, who to date, when to do homework, and where to go with friends. Research by educational psychologists parallels the information neuroscience reveals: Young adolescents demonstrate a lack of thought when they make decisions. Making decisions is a complicated process that involves searching for options, tapping into prior knowledge, problem solving, creativity, and evaluation. It's unrealistic to expect teenagers to organize information and make decisions with the same skill level as an adult.

A significant difference has been found between the ability of young adolescents and older adolescents to make decisions. For instance, when young adolescents consider careers, they may choose to be a professional athlete, movie star, or rock musician. To them, no career choice is

Three boys were arrested for breaking curfew. When the officer couldn't reach any of their parents, he told them they could make one phone call. Half an hour later a man showed up at the police station. The officer asked, "Are you their lawyer?" The man said, "No, I'm delivering the pizza they ordered."

—One teacher's joke about teenagers

unrealistic or impossible. It's simple—make a decision based on what interests you: "I want to be a lawyer, politician, chiropractor, or fashion designer." The increased brainpower of later adolescence, however, identifies more options, consults more experts, and anticipates future consequences of decisions (Friedman & Mann, 1993). Older adolescents weigh their personal interests with their values and capabilities, thereby making more realistic decisions: "I decided to be a biologist because I saw a pamphlet on it and it seemed fun. I'd done well in biology classes and thought they were interesting."

## Secret Revealed

Why should teenagers worry? Parents and teachers already worry too much about what they're up to, so they don't bother. Actually, teens forge blindly ahead with whatever they want to do because they can't imagine all the things that could go wrong with the same clarity as an adult. Adolescents live for the moment and are under the notion that they are indestructible: They are not accustomed to letting their rational frontal lobes control their decisions. The excitable amygdala is having fun, so they go along. Until they learn to put emotional impulses in context and develop a sense of how the world affects them, teens are oblivious to the dangers that accompany jumping off the roof into the swimming pool (as well as to the problems of choosing a college based on where their girlfriend is going).

Teens tend to focus on the immediate future—right now—when they make choices. This is a severe limitation on the quality of their decisions—decisions they may have to live with for a week, month, or even a lifetime. Teachers, parents, and mentors can soften the potential blows of poor decision making by allowing teenagers to make age-appropriate decisions but structuring the larger, life-impacting decisions for them. For instance, choosing where they want to apply for a job, decorating their bedroom, and (in most cases) deciding what friends to hang around with are all age-appropriate decisions. Deciding to stay out all night, ditching school, or experimenting with drugs have long-lasting repercussions.

Friends carry a lot of influence when adolescents have to make decisions. If their friends think something is a good idea, teens are easily persuaded that it is. Sometimes their friends direct them down a solid path to a worthy decision. But beware. A teenager's well-intentioned friends are still teenagers themselves! They don't have the life experience to always

make thoughtful decisions. And unpredictable teenage emotions complicate any matter; a teenager in a good mood will ignore a snotty remark,
but that same teen in a bad mood might think starting a fight is the best response. Adolescents can benefit from direct instruction on the decision-making process. Peers and the emotion of the moment are powerful influences at the point of making decisions; having a backup plan to rely on can make the difference between teenage fun and teenage disaster.

---

**Directly teach
decision-making skills**

- Make a goal.
- Identify obstacles to realizing the goal.
- Find alternatives for overcoming each obstacle.
- Rank the alternatives.
- Choose the best alternative.

---

## TEENS IN TROUBLE

*October, 2003, in Sioux Falls, SD:* A high school senior is charged and booked for possession of drugs and resisting arrest.

*May, 2003, in Northbrook, IL:* Twelfth-grade girls haze younger classmates by covering them in feces and hitting and kicking them.

*October, 2002, in Virginia and Washington, DC:* A sixteen-year-old boy and his surrogate father embark upon a sharp-shooting spree, leaving ten people dead in less than three weeks.

Sometimes adolescents make bad decisions that break not just school rules but also the law. These stories make headlines too often to be ignored. Adolescent crime is particularly unsettling; we see teens as children in many ways and have a difficult time comprehending how a child could commit an act so egregious. Much controversy surrounds the question of the legal culpability of minors. Advocates for adolescents agree that they should be held responsible for their actions, but not to the same degree as adults. They argue that the dramatic hormonal, emotional, and physical brain changes occurring during adolescence would benefit from a corrective, as opposed to punitive, stance (or sentence). No one thinks that teenagers are exempt from criminal sanctions, but many people wonder if incarceration is truly a solution. Our current juvenile correction programs have high recidivism rates, particularly at the larger facilities—once an adolescent enters the correctional system, it is difficult to break out.

## GROUP IDENTITY

Teenagers want to be liked by their peers and be part of a group. Not only does belonging serve as a form of social validation (it is a benchmark against which they can measure themselves), it has the added bonus of being fun. Members of groups often share the qualities of age, race, and socioeconomic status, and among younger teens, they are of the same sex. These groups, the social cliques so often portrayed in movies and on television, take on distinct personalities: the preppies, the motorheads, the jocks, the nerds, the activists . . . the list goes on and on.

School is the perfect staging area for teenage groups. Because kids are required to attend school, they can always count on finding friends to eat lunch with, sit next to in class, or gossip with in the hallways. Within these gregarious groups are even tighter alliances; teens (as do adults) find a few people with whom they are extremely close—people they can count on for help and loyalty. From "She won't talk behind my back when I leave practice" and "I know he'll stand up for me in a fight" to "He'll bring home my schoolwork when I get sick," these intimate relationships form the foundation for positive self-esteem and social adjustment.

Gangs are the antithesis of friendly peer groups, although teens join them for many of the same reasons that their peers hang with the chess club or form an arts group: companionship, protection, and fun. Ironically, gangs reflect the positive cultural values of courage, heroism, masculinity, and physical strength; gang members express these values, however, through illegal and particularly violent acts. They provide security and protection to fellow members, but in antisocial ways—gangs directly challenge family, school, and police. A positive classroom environment can go a long way toward fulfilling the sense of belonging that so many students seek in dangerous places. From establishing a warm and inclusive classroom dynamic to building opportunities for productive social interaction into their lesson plans, teachers can make a difference in a lonely student's life.

### Instructional Strategies

#### Working With At-Risk Kids

Derrick seems to cause problems wherever he goes. He purposely pushes other students in the hallways and instigates fights. Twice he's been suspended from school for fighting; one more incident and he'll be expelled. He is rude and defiant to teachers. He typically comes to class

*(Continued)*

(Continued)

late, sits at the back of the room, and falls asleep. He is belligerent and does not hesitate to yell profanities. He refuses to participate in class activities, doesn't complete assignments, and resists all efforts by the teachers to give help. He seems to be counting the days until he can drop out of school.

In the best-case scenario, students like Derrick are at risk of failing to take full advantage of the benefits of a high school education and in the worst-case scenario of dropping out altogether. Without a high school diploma, the adult workforce is one long, dead-end road. "Stay in school" isn't just a public service announcement cliché; it is an economic lifeline.

## *Things to Try*

- Identify "at-risk" students as soon as possible. Early intervention plays a key role in setting them on the right track to academic success.
- Create a sense of hope by acknowledging that all students have a right to participate, and establish a community of fairness with clear rules that apply to everyone equally.
- Set clear, consistent boundaries. Involve students in determining class rules and consequences.
- Develop students' feelings of security with their peers. Promote noncompetitive group activities, and set challenges that are positive. Make sure that leader and supporting roles rotate among the students. Within group activities, help students concentrate on their similarities rather than their differences. (Just committing to work together on a project lays the foundation for one set of experiences they can share.)
- By concentrating on students' assets, you'll be able to better see and teach to their potential. Find ways for them to use their unique backgrounds to make positive contributions to the class. Helping others builds self-esteem; helping to build self-esteem and providing a caring environment are two effective ways to serve at-risk kids.
- Teach life skills like cooking, balancing a checkbook, or filling out a job application. Possessing the skills needed to maneuver through life reinforces a teen's sense of self-sufficiency and self-esteem.
- Vary your instruction by teaching to a range of learning styles and multiple intelligences. Include multicultural content. Let students know that you value all the classes taught at the school, from art and PE to music and community service opportunities.
- Ask students to assess (with a ten-point scale or simple rubric) how they feel at the beginning and end of the day. Discuss ways to cope with feelings.
- Have students write a personal mission statement to stimulate their thinking and help them set goals. Setting goals can make the difference between dropping out of school or walking across the auditorium to pick up a diploma.
- Do not eliminate repetitive practice, but do reduce it. Drill and routine can seem boring and meaningless; you'll lose student engagement eventually.
- Do keep unsupervised seatwork to a minimum. Adolescents too easily become distracted. They lack self-control and will benefit from your guidance.

- Do not rely on tracking—tracking is particularly damaging to low-achieving students because it has been abused too often to evoke confidence in its benefits. Rather than educating students more effectively, it has tended to merely separate them from each other. Offering help before or after school or arranging for a tutor or a mentor are better ways to provide academic assistance.

- Alter the assessment landscape with portfolio assessments, self-examination journals, and creative artwork.
- Encourage students to attend conflict-resolution and anger-management classes to increase their coping skills. Some schools offer these classes during the school day in an attempt to better serve their students; more options are probably offered through the community.
- Facilitate their involvement in extracurricular programs, community service, and after-school jobs. Not only do they provide opportunities to belong and succeed outside of academics, but they also allow the teenager to put their problem-solving skills to work in meaningful ways.
- Ask your school board, administrators, counselors, and fellow teachers if all students have the opportunity to take college prep courses. If the answer is no, consider it the perfect opportunity to become active in a worthy cause.

## IT'S HARD TO JUST SAY NO

Walk into any hospital emergency room and you'll see some patients suffering from life-threatening conditions, like heart attacks or strokes, and other patients sporting relatively minor cuts and bruises. Everyone needs help, but for some patients, it's a matter of life or death. The same is true of adolescents—any teen is vulnerable to the temptation of having a drink or smoking a cigarette, but they aren't all equally at risk of becoming addicted to alcohol or nicotine.

Words like *adventurous, novelty seeker,* and *impulsive* are used to profile people with the highest risk of developing addictions (to anything), according to Dr. Alan Leshner, the director of the National Institute on Drug Abuse, who was interviewed on the NPR (National Public Radio) program *Gray Matters: Alcohol, Drugs and the Brain* (Kirchner & Gunther, 2000). These words also describe an adolescent! Is it any wonder that so many teens are at such a high risk for addiction? At the same time, it would be unfair to say all teenagers are "at-risk"—most are just transitioning between childhood and adulthood, trying to form an identity while facing childhood insecurities. It's a complex time of life.

The environment, genetics, and stages of brain development all make their contributions to the development of addictions. One of the more dramatic sociocultural studies was of Vietnam veterans in the late 1960s and early 1970s (Kirchner & Gunther, 2000). An unusually high number of soldiers were returning home addicted to heroin; eleven percent were using heroin on a regular basis—an alarming figure by anyone's account. The army was greatly concerned; this drug use threatened not only the military but also the stability of our homeland as these soldiers returned to their normal places in society. Curiously, within one year of returning to their normal lives, ninety-nine percent of the veterans that had been addicted were no longer using heroin. Once they were removed from the war environment, they found no reason to use the drug. A wartime Vietnam was perhaps more tolerable within the haze of a drug-induced cloud; the peacetime United States could be endured and even enjoyed with mental faculties intact. On an ordinary scale, teenagers who belong to certain groups of friends may find more "reasons" to indulge in alcohol and drug use than do teenagers who belong to a more sensible (or protective) crowd.

The genetic connection to alcoholism is also well researched. A few years ago, scientists excitedly believed they had identified an actual alcoholism gene (this was later disproved); the current genetic explanation is much more complex. It is now thought that a combination of genes creates a predisposition for alcoholism. Interestingly, individuals with a family history of alcoholism are less sensitive to the effects of alcohol. In other words, they can hold their liquor. A genetic predisposition to alcohol is only a predisposition, however. You may be at greater risk of developing a behavior, but you have a choice about your destiny. To drink or not to drink? Some people who are genetically predisposed never become alcoholics. The ones who do become alcoholics fight an uphill battle for recovery.

## THE "DEADLY PLEASURE"

Approximately fifty percent of high school seniors drink once a month, more than a third of eighth graders have been drunk one or more times, and girls are particularly susceptible to alcohol addiction (Johnston et al., 2003). Alcohol kills brain cells, impairs the decision-making process, and spurs impulsive behavior. Girls put themselves in unsafe sexual situations, boys recklessly speed while driving, and both escape to the pleasant stupor found within a bottle of beer rather than addressing the problems that arise from living in the world. Habitual drinking begins as a voluntary activity within our control. Once we are hooked, however, the habit is unyielding and ruthless. Thoughts of alcohol permeate your consciousness. One recovering alcoholic admitted, "I thought about drinking constantly. I even dreamed about it."

Teenage drinking is a constant and clear problem (White, 2003), partly because alcohol modifies the brain. Typically, we feel a natural high when we hand in an excruciatingly long research paper or successfully give a speech in front of the class. Alcohol short-circuits the brain's ability to generate the natural high and leaves the brain demanding more alcohol for itself instead. (Alcohol is such an easy way to trigger the high that some people start to rely on it as a shortcut.) Research confirms the power of pleasurable experiences. Experiments in the 1950s and 1960s found that rats were so motivated by pleasure that they were willing to scamper across a hot griddle, run themselves to exhaustion, or go without food in order to press a lever that was connected to electrodes stimulating the pleasure area of their brain. Although humans may not be willing to walk across hot coals or starve to death for pleasure, it is a powerful motivator. A middle school principal told the story of a girl who always seemed to have a bad attitude in school; she put forth little effort academically or socially. One day her teacher casually complimented her on the pretty sweater she was wearing. For the next week the girl wore that same sweater every day to school. A simple compliment meant more to the girl than the teacher had ever dreamed.

## ON SHAKY GROUND

Andrew Chambers, MD, at Yale School of Medicine believes that although society and genetics play a role in alcoholism, they fail to fully explain it. He was a member of a research team at Yale that studied the role of the brain, especially the adolescent brain, in the development of this disease. Using magnetic resonance imaging (MRI) technology, he found that adolescents are particularly susceptible to addictions like alcohol, nicotine, and drugs. The very regions that are rapidly changing within a teenager's brain—the frontal lobes and hippocampus—are also the ones associated with addiction. This fact may explain the rapid onset and endurance of addictions that begin in adolescence (Chambers, Taylor, & Potenza, 2003).

## Secret Revealed

Why are teenage parties always represented with cigarette smoke in the air and alcohol flowing from kegs? Many assume that teens are impatient for the onset of adulthood and enjoy some of the privileges a few years early. Adults consider adolescents' binges as an unfortunate phase that will pass when they graduate from high school and college and can legally enjoy those substances. The work of Dr. Aaron White (2003) at Duke University, however, reveals that the rapid changes occurring in the adolescent brain—susceptibility to the rewards of dopamine, a decrease in serotonin levels, a disrupted sleeping cycle, and an attraction to danger—render teens vulnerable to addiction.

Not only are teens attracted to the altered states that accompany substance use, they are also in danger of building a dependence on the substance into the circuitry of their brain! An adult who drinks heavily may take five to fifteen years to become fully dependent on alcohol, but the adolescent may become addicted in less than eighteen months (Bloom, Beal, & Kupfer, 2006). Sadly, for many adolescents who succumb to the temptation of nicotine, alcohol, and other drugs, the developing processes in their brains will make it very easy to become addicted and very hard to kick the habit when they are older.

The adolescent hippocampus is especially sensitive to the adverse effects of alcohol (De Bellis et al., 2000). Alcohol interferes with new memories (rather than long-term, stored memories) by selectively shutting down the activity of cells it comes into contact with. In the best of circumstances it is easy to forget the name of people you just met, but under the influence of alcohol, you may not only forget their names but also forget even meeting them! The more you drink, the more the hippocampal circuitry is disrupted. Teenagers who drink suffer in cognitive performance—especially memory (Brown, Tapert, Granholm, & Delis, 2000). That history exam or list of Spanish vocabulary words is much more difficult to recall for teens who live life under the influence. Binge drinking (often defined as five drinks in a row for men and four for women) may result in a complete blackout with absolutely no memory of the event. In fact, memory may be affected for up to a month after a single binge-drinking episode. The hippocampus is generally very resilient—when drinking stops, it usually returns to normal cell structure and size—but MRIs show the hippocampus is smaller in adolescents who abuse alcohol on a regular basis. Preliminary research shows that if this brain structure is continually exposed to alcohol, it will suffer permanent damage (Uekermann, Daum, Schlebusch, Wiebel, & Trenckmann, 2003).

Alcohol also disrupts the workings of the prefrontal cortex, which is instrumental in making good decisions. Even if judgment and physical coordination are impaired, drunk teenagers still believe they are in control. From this perspective, those few shots of tequila have nothing to do with the ability to drive home (Lyvers, 2000). Alcohol also tends to reduce inhibitions in the subcortical regions of the brain that are responsible for sex, eating, and the "fight or flight" response, like the basal ganglia and cerebellum (both involved in movement) and the hypothalamus and amygdala (Zhu, Volkow, Ma, Fowler, & Wang, 2004). After a few too many drinks, the mild-mannered boy becomes irate if someone looks at his girlfriend or steps on his feet. The usually reserved girl sheds her clothes and skinny dips with strangers. Mary, a sophomore, remembers a time when a group of drunk guys decided to beat up a boy because they thought he was a loser; they were so drunk, they attacked one of their own friends. None of these things would happen under normal circumstances, but alcohol changes the rules of the game.

## A HARD HABIT TO BREAK

As was explained in Chapter 4, "Communication and the Unfinished Brain," preliminary research points to the teenage brain being particularly sensitive to stress, which puts them at further risk for alcohol and drug abuse (substance abuse). Alcohol is a depressant that interferes with glutamate, the neurotransmitter that keeps us alert. Teens under a great deal of stress may turn to alcohol to reduce anxiety and tension because as they drink, they relax. If they drink enough, they will fall asleep.

Remember that the feelings of pleasure triggered by dopamine can be addictive. Some scientists believe that the alcoholic's brain doesn't release dopamine in normal amounts with the effect that there is a reduced feeling of natural pleasure; drinking more and more alcohol is required to reach the "stoned" zone (Volkow, Fowler, Wang, & Goldstein, 2002). Others believe that dopamine receptors in the brain do not function correctly, rendering the individual more vulnerable to addiction (Dagher et al., 2001). In either case, by drinking larger quantities, alcoholics can achieve extreme pleasure and so are seduced into drinking more and more.

The problem of addiction doesn't stop with alcohol. Nicotine is another legal drug chosen by teenagers. Just like the adolescent susceptibility to alcohol, people who begin smoking in their teens are particularly vulnerable to nicotine addiction because the region of the brain that governs impulse and motivation is not fully formed. Not only that, because of neural development and plasticity, a still-growing brain sculpts itself around the nicotine addiction, hard-wiring addiction into its very structure. Ninety percent of smokers had their first cigarette before the age of twenty-one; five percent of eighth graders and nearly twenty percent of high school seniors smoke regularly (*Adolescent Smoking Statistics,* 2003). Tobacco smoking, associated with lung cancer, cardiovascular disease, and emphysema, is the single largest identifiable cause of death in the United States. Perhaps this is because nicotine is one of the most addictive substances on earth—it causes dopamine to spike in the body and feeds the brain a steady stream of satisfaction afterward.

The teen brain is susceptible to other addictions, too, like cocaine, crack, marijuana, and heroin. Heroin use is at its highest in twenty-five years; ecstasy use nearly doubled from six percent of the population in 1996 to eleven percent in 2000. Like many aspects of technology, drug manufacturing has improved; drugs produced now are of a higher grade and more powerful than they used to be. Because of the changes occurring in the brain during adolescence, teens who use drugs risk permanently damaging their brains (Chambers et al., 2003).

Marco Iacoboni's (2008) groundbreaking research on mirror neurons has important implications. He specifically conducted research on smokers and found that when past smokers observed someone smoking, mirror neurons were automatically activated. They struck the lighter, inhaled the smoke, and then exhaled—vicariously enjoying every puff. This put them at greater risk of a smoking relapse. Iacoboni speculates that this has consequences for all addictive substances: alcohol, cocaine, and meth. The social nature of teenagers puts them particularly at risk when trying to break an addiction. They may find it intolerable to break the habit while at the same time remaining in the company of friends that have the bad habit.

## Secret Revealed

"It was the summer after sixth grade; we were at the back of the city swimming pool, where a lot of bad things went down. Somebody that smoked let us all take a puff. I didn't really want to, but I did want to try." Obviously, this sixth grader, almost seventh grader, has mixed feelings about smoking, but push comes to shove and she gave it a try, a pretty typical choice for her age.

Warning for pregnant women: Smoking during pregnancy seems to rewire the infant brain making their future teenager susceptible to cigarette addiction. Teenagers whose mothers smoked during pregnancy showed signs of addiction after just five cigarettes. And for the skeptics in the crowd, these mothers did not smoke after pregnancy, eliminating the chance of it being the result of role modeling.

## Instructional Strategies

### Drugs, Alcohol, and Sex Education

As fourteen-year-old Amanda says, "It's not like when you're little and you think there's going to be this person in an alley saying, 'Do you wanna smoke?' It's so casual. A friend is smoking and they just say, 'Oh, would you like one?' It makes it easier and harder to say no." Antismoking and drinking programs have been met with mixed reviews. Even if they have increased public awareness to the problem, their impact on curbing drug or tobacco use is constantly up for debate. There is no simple solution to combating addiction and substance abuse in teens (or for that matter, eliminating risky behavior), but that doesn't mean schools shouldn't try.

### Things to Try

- Encourage resilience by providing opportunities for meaningful participation. Once students have gained a skill, give them chances to use it. Act like a coach rather than a teacher, and let students work. If one attempt fails, encourage them to try again until they reach success.
- Introduce students to mentors. Gary Sykes, an expert on mentoring, pointed out that "a personality, rather than a technique, a skill or knowledge, was most important in touching the lives of students" (Taylor-Dunlop & Norton, 1997, p. 275). Someone with life experience can help teens expand their horizons and put possibilities like college, jobs, and extracurricular activities on their radar screen. Mentors can also encourage adolescents to pursue their goals, examine their belief system, listen to troubles and triumphs, and offer opportunities to assume responsibility. Whether a mentor is an older adolescent, a caring member from the community, or a recovered addict, he or she can still lend a hand. Despite their skepticism of adults and their ways, teens consider them very important.
- Develop character by having teens examine the people in their lives who inspire them, someone they want to emulate, a hero. Barack Obama? Hillary Clinton? Their teacher? Role models are examples we live by; watching how one person adapts to challenges in life gives guidance to how we can tackle the problems in our own.

*(Continued)*

(Continued)

- Bond, bond, and bond. Teens need to feel like they belong, and they need adults in their life who are interested in their well-being. Do as much as you can to reassure them that you want them to succeed and are willing to help.
- Divorcing parents, romantic breakups, and added responsibilities outside of school (like contributing to family finances and babysitting younger siblings) all contribute to stress in students' lives. Be aware of these important life changes and be sensitive to requests from students for accommodations. Feeling overwhelmed and powerless to cope with sudden changes is one reason many teens turn to drugs, alcohol, or reckless behavior in the first place.
- There are also many support groups on the Web; once checked out by a responsible adult, they can give twenty-four-hour-a-day support.

## SCOTT THE MOUNTAIN BIKER: THE NEXT RIDE

*Last week, Scott and his friend John hit a local bike trail. The two boys picked up speed and passed cyclist after cyclist on the path. With their heads down, they pushed forward harder and harder. No sooner had they whisked by a pair of "slowpokes" than came two other riders barreling from the opposite direction. The hair rose on their necks as they narrowly avoided a collision. "We made it!" John called, laughing and darting ahead at breakneck speed. But Scott slowed down with thoughts whirling in his mind. He'd already had one too-close-for-comfort call on his bicycle. Then he remembered a checklist his teacher had given them about staying safe and avoiding accidents. Pedaling more thoughtfully, he mentally checked off items on the list as he pedaled more carefully to catch up with his friend.*

# Reaching and Teaching Today's Adolescents— Tomorrow!

Our new understanding of the teenage brain and its unique characteristics should be reflected in how we run our schools and our classrooms. Now that educators and scientists are aware of what really drives teen cognition and behavior, middle schools and high schools need to reexamine how they are structured and how they can better help their adolescent population.

**Make school a place that . . .**

- Eases the transition from child brain to adolescent brain and appeals to teenagers' innate interest in the world around them
- Feels more like a community than an institution and nurtures teens' burgeoning sense of empathy and compassion
- Allows teens to explore and develop a self-identity and express themselves as individuals
- Provides the support and structure teens need to productively channel and invest their energy and enthusiasm

*A Montreal community was drowning in poverty. More than a third of its residents were homeless or unemployed throughout their lifetime. The situation was grim. Social scientists had tracked the neighborhood for generations searching for an explanation for the high levels of violence and the low levels of education. In hopes of breaking the poverty cycle, they searched for common threads among the small number to reach middle class and found one: Miss A, a first-grade teacher. Miss A was a teacher who constantly reinforced the idea that school was important and could improve their lives, who spent extra time helping students who needed it, and who believed absolutely that every student was capable of learning. Amazingly, not one of Miss A's former students was homeless or unemployed. This one teacher made a life-altering difference to each and every one of her students (Fallon, 2002; Pedersen, Faucher, & Eaton, 1978). Her life and work is eloquent proof that teachers do matter to students and really can affect their lives.*

## TEACHERS MATTER

Working with adolescents can be both frustrating and rewarding. Teachers are dedicated to meeting the unique needs of the teenage brain but often find their efforts to tailor their curriculum unproductive. It's not easy to design a course that appeals to the unpredictable teen personality—they are simultaneously restless, self-conscious, impatient, and idealistic. The power of the primitive amygdala is partly to blame; adolescence is when the frontal lobes are just beginning to assert themselves and myelin just starting to coat the areas of the brain that improve higher-level reasoning and abstract thought. Teens aren't quite in full control of their rational faculties!

Educators are not innocent bystanders merely witnessing this transformation of the teenage brain. We either promote neural growth or stunt it depending on the kind of classrooms we set up. Our job is to figure out how to create classrooms that will foster learning, support emotional and social growth in our students' brains, and ease the transition from childhood to adulthood. However daunting this task appears at first glance, it is nonetheless very doable upon closer inspection. Teens come to school wanting to learn, wanting to form relationships with classmates and faculty, wanting the chance to express themselves as individuals, and wanting (however secretly) the guidance and advice teachers and administrators can give them. To meet these desires, all we have to do is adjust our schedules and routines in small ways that will nonetheless make a huge difference in the effectiveness of educational programs.

## MAINTAINING THE DESIRE TO LEARN

In the last decade, a lot of time and money has been spent on determining what students need to learn. State governments have created the long lists of standards that give form to our curriculum. Their enthusiasm perhaps has taken them so far that students' personal interests—a very important part of the equation—have been overlooked. When we take student interest into consideration, we help guarantee that the standardized content can be applied to real life. This interplay between knowledge and application is critical to motivating students.

Just because the teen brain is becoming mature enough to understand the value of having information that may not be immediately appealing doesn't mean that everything a teen learns has to be presented in a dry and abstract manner. Too often we hear teenagers expressing their skepticism of academic content with a perplexed "Why do I need to know this?" (As one senior boy resignedly said, "The only thing I'm ever going to need calculus for is another math class.") Relevance is the key to gaining student attention and prompting motivation. Relating content to real life is imperative for learning to occur. It's difficult for students to find meaning and purpose from worksheets. Filling in the blanks with measurement units and matching fraction questions and answers can seem pointless; however, you'd be hard-pressed to find a student who isn't intrigued about applying these same skills to plan and build instrument storage cabinets for the band room or a gazebo for the school campus.

Despite observations to the contrary, teenagers are passionate beings. It is evident in their enthusiasm for sports, music, technology, and friends. The student who is bored by Marco Polo's travels to China may have memorized everything there is to know about the history of Middle Earth (the hobbit stuff); the student who skips math class may have spent the weekend programming computer software to enhance the play of a favorite video game; the student who spaces out in English class may have planned an elaborate surprise birthday party for a friend, complete with handmade invitations and party favors. These passions can be brought into the classroom if you sustain teens' natural curiosity.

## Another Perspective

Adolescents are not merely proto-adults getting ready to enter the workforce. Rather, they're cognitive, physical, social, emotional, and spiritual beings. Students come to school to learn and grow; they prefer to be active participants in the process rather than passive recipients of knowledge. Their engagement is strengthened when they are involved in activities that stress thinking about what they are doing (as opposed to mimicking a technique or reciting information by rote). The development of abstract thinking skills and the analytical and

*(Continued)*

(Continued)

physical coordination skills made possible by the maturing frontal lobes, parietal lobes, and cerebellum means that teens are more capable than ever of understanding meaty, detailed information at greater depth. Provide opportunities for them to enjoy it!

Tap into adolescent interests by shifting your instructional strategies and content to appeal to your students, and you'll have a classroom full of self-motivated learners. Be adventurous; incorporate topics like animals, oceanography, basketball, World War I, chemicals, movies, politics, and finances into your prescribed curriculum. Besides, if students already have interesting background knowledge when they embark upon a new unit or lesson, their personal mastery of that subject doesn't seem like an arbitrary or remote possibility.

Students who believe that they have the chance to be successful are intrinsically motivated to learn; students who constantly face failure and criticism quickly define themselves as inadequate (Brendtro, Brokenleg, & Van Bockern, 2002). An educator's task is to curb feelings of inadequacy and promote a sense of mastery in our students. Because the brain is naturally social and collaborative, providing opportunities for personal interaction will engage students in the learning process and give them incentive to keep participating.

Offering choices to students is a wonderful way to encourage them to develop ownership of their learning. Identifying subtopics within a required unit is just one way to give students options. For instance, if you were studying communities, you could give students the choice of researching local government, hospitals, cemeteries, senior citizen centers, newspapers, or transportation. Not only will the variety motivate students to study an issue because it personally interests them, they will get practice making decisions and taking responsibility for the time they spend in your classroom. Like a sponge, the brain can soak up the material it encounters and still thirst for more.

## Secret Revealed

 A few years ago, neuroscientists found monkeys' brain signals could control a robotic arm reaching for objects and grasping for food. The world was amazed. This research has now been expanded, taking a particularly exciting tangent. Duke University (2008) studied the ability of a monkey's brain in the United States to control a robot's actions in Japan.

Electrodes were attached to the monkey's brain as he walked backward and forward on a treadmill. All the time, the electrodes were collecting information from the neurons. Researchers recorded the brain activity, made speculations concerning the pattern of the movements, and forwarded the commands to the robot. The robot walked.

The implications of this study reach beyond the ability to fascinate us. Researchers hope this discovery will lead to robotic leg braces for severely paralyzed people, allowing them to walk again and forever change their lives.

## ADOLESCENTS ARE NOT ALL ALIKE

A recent visit to a middle school presented this all-too-familiar scene: A frustrated sixth grader stood with his head against his locker, staring into space, exhausted by his attempts to open the combination lock. According to the sympathetic, eighth-grade witness, he'd been standing like that for half an hour. It is easy for adults to forget what an anxious time these years can be!

Like high school students, middle school students struggle with puberty, the desire for independence, peer influence, and their interest in love and dating. Unlike high school students, they are struggling with a fundamental change in the way they are educated at the very same time. Middle school students go from being part of an established group with a single teacher in an elementary classroom to one of many students with a mix of teachers in a variety of classrooms. To top this off, they also suffer the loss of status as they go from being the top dogs at elementary school to occupying the lowest rung of the social ladder at middle school. No wonder these students and their parents pass more than a few sleepless nights in the days leading up to the change.

A smooth transition from elementary to secondary school cannot be made with one ceremonial tour of the building. The switch is better managed with a gradual exposure to the complex environment of lockers, hallways, and multiple teachers (versus the self-contained classroom and personalized cubbyholes to store class materials). Visiting the middle school well before school starts helps. Students need chances to find classrooms and practice opening a locker—that universal nemesis—with the full support of teachers, administrators, and other school staff. Query parents, administrators, and other teachers about ways to better accommodate new students at middle school

(or even high school!). Relieving incoming students from the stress of imagined terrors awaiting them on a new campus will benefit everyone during the first few weeks of the school year.

Realize, too, that middle school students have different needs than high school students. Great differences exist in the brains of older and younger adolescents. Older adolescents have a better reliance on their frontal lobes; they are more logical and less emotional, make better decisions, and think abstractly with ease. Younger adolescents are more reactionary, impulsive, and curious and are still trying to figure themselves out. Exploratory programs at the middle school level are an excellent way to expose them to a range of academic subjects like foreign languages, personal finance, music composition, and creative writing and to interests such as technology, student government, community service, and art as well as to recreational pastimes like intramural sports and clubs. Wondering and seeking information helps them form their identity.

Still, middle school students welcome some familiar vestiges of their elementary school days. Interdisciplinary team teaching, or assigning a core of teachers to the same group of students, not only offers some of the security of a smaller group of classmates within a larger school setting, but it allows for much academic flexibility. When teams are in place, thematic units are possible. Teachers are often criticized for curriculum that is a mile wide and an inch thick; thematic units allow in-depth study, with richer learning. Thematic units do much more than integrate subjects—they encourage young teens to seek answers, dream, struggle, argue, and love the act of learning. A thematic unit on rivers, for example, provides chances to measure water levels, track animals, journal, determine power sources, research the history of the river, design maps and graphs, study local ecology, and maybe incorporate some travel. In-depth study of a subject requires a great deal of cooperation and work from the interdisciplinary team teachers, but despite its initial messiness, the effort pays off in the long run.

Middle schools can offer added support to young teens and their families by providing an afterschool program. The majority of adolescents have mothers and fathers who work outside the home, and the time gap between parents' schedules and school schedules can amount to more than twenty hours per week of unsupervised time. Afterschool programs provide safety for these kids and the communities they live in as well as a fun place to socialize with friends and enjoy some unstructured time after a day of school. But they don't have to be supervised parties; some programs use the time to teach kids the skills usually taught in organizations like 4-H and Girl Scouts. As a result, students develop a sense of self and build social relationships. The positive social and emotional effects of an afterschool program spill into other aspects of the middle school student's life, including academic performance.

## Making It Work

Adolescence is when the brain starts to "think outside the body" and see the world from a broader perspective. Teens value novel experiences and appreciate the chance to exert their new cognitive and abstract thinking skills. Teachers and school administrators often perceive teens' goals to be at variance with their curriculum requirements and testing obligations, but student interests do not have to be suppressed in favor of instructional efficiency.

*Federal and state legislation have put so many requirements on our school! How can we teach to proficiency on all these academic topics and still have time to incorporate students' personal interests?*

Exploring students' personal interests by combining them with content leads to proficiency and achievement. Actively involving them in real-world projects, role-playing situations, writing, and physical activities will engage their brains, tap into their new cognitive strengths, and interest them in the next lesson.

*If I hear "Why do I need to know this?" or "I'm never going to use this!" one more time, I'll scream. How can I help my students see the importance of what they are learning?*

As frustrating as they can be, these exasperating questions really are legitimate concerns. The teen brain is so full of stimulus here and changes there, all of which are hard enough to keep track of. Teens want to be sure that teachers aren't wasting their time when their lives are already complicated. Help students see the connection between what they are learning and how to apply it to their lives by giving them real-world context for the subjects they study. If they can see how it will immediately benefit them to know something, you bet they'll pay attention! If you can't easily make a connection between academic concepts and practical application, investigate why those concepts are in the curriculum.

*(Continued)*

(Continued)

*Middle school students start the year eager and optimistic about changing classes and learning "older" subjects, but by the end of the year they are listless and bored. What can we do to maintain their curiosity and expand their horizons?*

Young teens are still learning where their interests lie. Choosing one elective class at the beginning of the semester is not enough opportunity to explore all the things that are out there! Chances to explore new turf within the classes they have—and through intramural clubs and activities—open their eyes to exciting possibilities. The more they learn about themselves, the more they'll want to know. We also need to be aware of what we are emphasizing. Scientists and psychologists have worried that our middle schools require too much multitasking and quick decision making. These tasks are emphasized at the expense of skills such as planning and reflection, important lifelong skills (Bloom, Beal, & Kupfer, 2006).

*Those poor sixth graders who start school here! The look of fear on their faces is so pathetic. If they weren't so scared, I think some of them might actually enjoy the experience of middle school. Is there any way to make the transition easier?*

Have you gone to elementary schools to ask fifth graders what makes them nervous about middle school? Addressing the specific fears and anxieties about what awaits them at their new school will go a long way to ease the transition. Recruit seventh and eighth graders to act as "buddies" for new sixth graders so students start the year with an older and wiser friend on campus. Invite parents to visit the school and learn what routines are in place (like how to handle absences or what kind of food the cafeteria offers). If students don't feel like complete strangers to the student body and the school system, they might actually anticipate (rather than dread) the change.

## THE SPIRIT OF BELONGING

Belonging is a basic human need. Young children find belonging when they have someone to hold them, feed them, protect them, and otherwise assure them that the world is a safe and caring place. For adolescents, a sense of belonging comes with friends and family they can depend on and who respect, support, and validate them. Unfortunately, too many students live in the world without feeling like they belong there; they experience a world where neither the home nor community nor school meets their needs. Some desperate students form bonds with gangs or cults rather than live a life of loneliness and isolation. Although schools cannot completely fill the gap left by absent or disengaged parents, teachers have within their power the ability to make the six or seven hours students spend there warm and friendly.

But read the responses of a group of high school students asked to describe their school! "It's all about the worksheets—fill in the blanks or busy work." "There are a lot of rules. The teacher talks and we just sit; it's a long day." "Even the good kids get in trouble sometimes." These first impressions are harsh. Too many students regard school as an obligation, some unpleasant reality. Teachers are frustrated, too. We've all seen students who are physically, but not psychologically, present in the classroom. We spend the class talking, doing, and encouraging, but students are barely there, staring into space, oblivious to any and all of our efforts. They equate learning with negative feelings and have no plans to invest in the experience. To make matters more challenging, the abundance of testing and documentation that is required by state and federal mandates often overshadows the job of teaching. How can we meet the external dictates while still fostering the emotional and social growth of our students?

A supportive classroom environment starts with the teacher-student relationship. Make personal connections in small, sincere ways. Talk informally with your students, attend their extracurricular activities, and single out a few when you cross the lunchroom, and they will receive your message that you care about them. They appreciate it. One student commented, "Mr. Halsted always said 'hi' to us; even if we were far away, he'd yell our name and say 'hi.'" Another student said, "Mrs. Sorenson told funny stores about herself, like the first time she went skiing. Everyone there had perfect matching gear and she was dressed in blue ski pants, pink hat, red jacket, and brown mittens. She didn't know how to stop and crashed into a group of skiers all decked out in color-coordinated ski gear!" No wonder these students enjoy their teachers—Mr. Halsted and Mrs. Sorenson are considerate and fun loving.

Since teenagers face such pressure inside and outside of school, a caring teacher-student relationship is a protective factor against their stress-filled lives. If teachers can't completely protect their students from experiencing stress (and they can't), they can at least not add to it. Stress hurts. Mild forms of classroom stress come from teachers who are too controlling. "They always think they're right," one student said about such teachers. "You can't discuss anything with them. You tell them they missed a step and they say, 'No. The subject is closed.'" Higher levels of stress from constant yelling or threats like "At this rate you'll never graduate" not only negatively impact the individual student but the class as a whole. Students who may not be able to escape physically from stressful classrooms do so mentally. If they feel powerless or at the mercy of others, they may become aggressive or submissive just to cope.

In fact, creating a sense of belonging will reduce student stress. Teachers who give students a voice, pay attention to their interests, and make themselves available and approachable run less stressful classrooms. Accommodate students in this way by conferring with them and asking for their input—what do they think is a reasonable way to approach this assignment or that classroom rule? Each semester, give students one or two "late tickets" for assignments to turn in after a deadline without any penalties (the mere fact of knowing they could turn in an assignment late reduces anxiety). Set up an e-mail account for corresponding with students and check it regularly (even put assignments on a Web page). Finally, remind students when important events or deadlines are forthcoming—that common courtesy would be appreciated by anyone.

## DEVELOPING A CONSCIENCE

Human beings find safety and comfort within the boundaries of a caring community, but accepting these benefits obligates the individual to give back to the community in return. Codes of ethics and morality exist to address the needs of communities to have an agreed-upon set of values and customs that makes living within a group as beneficial to everyone as possible. Moral character, however, does not develop naturally—it has to be encouraged and challenged. Teenagers, as members of many communities, deserve schools that promote moral sensitivity and character. These ideas can be taught through character education, sensitivity training, moral dilemmas, and community service or can be embedded in the curriculum. Morality and ethics discussions help students see their place in a larger community and understand the positive and negative consequences of their actions. Having students consider relevant questions, like whether or not truancy should be punished with suspension or whether one student should turn in another for cheating, are good starting places that can be accommodated in any class. School and life experiences that support moral character foster individuals with high self-esteem who are capable and willing to give back to others.

Teaching morality can be a dicey business. Take the character education programs at the middle school level—some teachers and students find them very meaningful, but others criticize them for having a "flavor of the week" approach (if it's Wednesday, it must be "Respect" day). High school moral education is often a free-for-all by individual teachers with no schoolwide efforts. Sure, values and cooperation are taught pervasively, but too indirectly. A concerted plan for moral education is necessary to real progress in this skill.

Moral education begins with realizing the importance and power of communication. It's through communication that we relay our thoughts and begin to understand someone else's. Understanding how other people's words affect you and how your words affect them increases our sensitivity. The eleventh grader who says, "That is the stupidest thing I've ever heard," "Who cares?" or "Do you ever shut up?" may be expressing an honest response but needs to know how that choice of words affects her peers.

Knowing that we have a variety of choices available when we make decisions and then making the correct choice advances us up the moral ladder. It isn't until we develop abstract thought that we realize the multitude of possibilities and the probable consequences of most situations. Making decisions is more than deciding "What works for me?" Mature and sensitive people take into account the effect their behavior has on others. Adolescents are finally in a position to understand that they have options about what actions to take. Teenagers start to realize that they can control what they do in advance of an event: "I'm going to drink at the party," "I'm going to the party, but I'm not going to drink," or "I'm not going to the party; I'll find something else to do." They ponder how their choices will affect themselves and their friends, teachers, and parents before making a decision.

## Another Perspective

Teenagers who always choose the party or the television program over dinner with family or algebra homework need to be challenged in their thoughts—what's really important and why? Morally motivated individuals are capable of prioritizing personal values such as school, friends, work, and pleasures. Setting priorities lets us reflect on what is important and what is peripheral to our lives. Teenagers who only value partying until dawn, using the TV clicker adeptly, and ordering fast food efficiently are going to face some serious disadvantages when they embark upon adult moral terrain. If they are unable to engage in the normal give-and-take of personal interactions while still under the protection of their parents and teachers, how are they going to navigate through life when they have job responsibilities and landlords?

Individuals with moral character live up to the strength of their convictions. They are able to persist in the face of fatigue, discouragement, or distractions. This takes work. Too often it's easier to go along with the crowd instead of taking a stand or fighting the good fight because it seems like too much effort to bother. To overcome challenges, we set goals and exhibit self-discipline. And age has nothing to do with the ability to instill positive change. Teenagers start charity drives, do community fundraising, and take up the cause of political candidates. Their actions belie their moral convictions.

## THROUGH ANOTHER'S EYES

As adolescents begin to see from the perspectives of other people, they acquire empathy. From empathy develops altruistic behavior. A spirit of generosity is based in unselfish and giving behavior. Children are egocentric by nature—it's beyond their mental capabilities to realize that other people have different feelings and experiences. They perceive the world by how it affects them; if they are happy, everyone must be happy! Adopting an alternate perspective is the first step towards becoming less egocentric. Seeing the world through another person's eyes enhances your ability to be empathetic. As the adolescent brain develops, the world broadens and teens are able to look at matters from the perspective of others (Brendtro et al., 2002; Woolfolk, 2006).

Service learning is an effective way for teenagers to develop a spirit of generosity. More than just volunteering, service learning invigorates the traditional classroom by incorporating students' educational backgrounds into service. Students profit from the feelings of empathy and altruism they develop through this experience, and the community profits from their meaningful contributions (Witmer & Anderson, 1994). High school students who mentor at a middle school afterschool program or track water levels for a local environmental agency benefit themselves and others.

Classrooms that nurture a spirit of generosity and encourage morality create an atmosphere where all individuals know they are worthy because everyone is needed to sustain and enrich the community. As individuals grow, the group is strengthened. The aim is for all to reach their full potential, not just a select few. Only in this way will all benefit and will the group flourish. Altruistic behavior may begin in the classroom, but it expands to the community, family, future coworkers, and possibly the nation. Adolescents who learn how to make contributions to the world around them will live satisfying lives and come that much closer to self-actualization.

# Making It Work

The brain's instinct is to flock to social groups, and teens are usually enthusiastic about the chance to pal around with each other, especially during class. Teamwork and community involvement also help adolescents learn to appreciate the strengths and talents other people possess, as well as instill in them a sense of pride when they can lend their strengths and talents to help another person. Focus their attention and energy on ways they can contribute and you'll find yourself in a class of willing participants.

*Besides the fact that they live within the same school boundaries, my students are too diverse to make a community. Some work after school, some play sports, some are just biding time until graduation. . . . They have nothing in common outside of school.*

No matter what teenagers spend their free time doing, they all need and want a place to belong. The fact that they spend seven or eight hours a day together is sufficient reason to make school a community in which everyone is an important member. They share classrooms, lunch yards, and other school facilities—they have plenty of commonalities to act as starting points for them to develop new interests together.

*I have great students, but if I spent time every day talking to them, we'd never get any work done!*

Teachers are the focal point of the classroom community, not because they have the most author-ity but because the teacher is the one constant in a class that may have students transferring in and out as schedules change or families move. It takes only a few minutes a day for a teacher to greet students at the door and ask individual students about personal milestones or struggles. A smile every day to the class and a kind word to an individual student once in a while go a long way toward making teens feel as though they are valued within the community.

*Once teens start talking to each other, it's hard to get them to stop! Won't mixing socialization and academics be too much of a distraction in class?*

Socializing is an important part of adolescence. Teenagers are compelled to seek out each other's company. Combining socialization with academics will probably reduce their distractibility during class time because the opportunity to interact constructively has been provided for them. Cooperative groups, peer tutoring, and support teams are just a few ways to meet their need to socialize and your need to deliver content.

*(Continued)*

(Continued)

*I am a moral person, but I have no business foisting my beliefs on anyone else. Besides, shouldn't public schools stay out of the morality business?*

Morality is not solely the province of religion. Giving adolescents the tools to make thoughtful decisions, communicate effectively, understand other people's viewpoints, respect diversity, and actively contribute to the world they live in is an obligation of every adult in their lives. Moral development in school is as useful as cognitive development, and teens will benefit from it just as much.

## LENDING A HELPING HAND

Puberty and adolescence can be a very lonely time for some teenagers. Their bodies and brains are changing so rapidly that they often do not know if they are coming or going. They surprise themselves by what they say and often overreact to what other people say to them. More than a few adolescents become so unsettled that they develop an unhealthy fixation on themselves and their problems. They appreciate the attention and assistance a concerned adult can give them, but they desperately need the company of peers, too—peers who can empathize with them because they are also in a state of rapid biological and cognitive change.

## Another Perspective

The success of a peer-tutoring program depends on how it is presented to participating teens. Enforce the idea that it is a partnership with no passive roles. The tutor is not the person doing all the work—the tutee must be willing to express his or her thoughts on the subject, ask questions, and take risks. If peers don't communicate their feelings and ideas about the subject matter, then there is no way of knowing if knowledge is being shared and developed.

With sufficient preparation and the right attitude, adolescents can benefit from peer-tutoring relationships in ways that would not be achieved in an adult tutor relationship. Interaction is more balanced and lively between peers, which contributes to positive emotions. Because peer tutoring usually occurs on campus—within a class period, during study hall, or before and after school— it takes place in a familiar environment. Finally, it's far more likely that a tutee will get the chance to return the favor later by tutoring a peer tutor in another subject. Both participants benefit.

Frequently, putting aside one's own problems to help other people with theirs is therapeutic. Peer tutoring—one student helping another student (at the same grade level) with a skill or concept—is one particularly useful arrangement for teenagers struggling with this stage of life. Not only have successful peer-tutoring programs been found to improve the tutee's academics, social interactions, classroom discipline, and peer relations but also to benefit the other individuals involved (Thomas, 1993; Kalkowski, 1995).

The enjoyment tutors find while helping a peer is obvious: They get to be a font of knowledge and information, which builds confidence; and they reap the internal benefits of altruism. The tutee is perhaps in a more precarious position. On the one hand, some students find it difficult to accept help from anyone, especially from someone their age. On the other hand, the tutee benefits from personalized attention in an era when schools are overcrowded and teachers are overextended. A peer-tutoring program, formal or informal, that is structured to put everyone at some point in the roles of tutee and tutor (after all, everyone has some expertise to share) is much more likely to be welcomed by students. It is even better if the teacher or adviser spends time at the beginning training students on how to be successful tutors; one class period is usually sufficient. A mind-set in which students relate to each other and understand that it is important for everyone to learn makes peer tutoring a rewarding experience for all participants.

## TO EACH HIS OWN

Another way to help adolescents confused by the changes they experience is to acknowledge that the changes are happening. Yes, it's normal to hang out with a new group of friends; yes, it's normal to change your mind about what you want to do in the future. By adolescence, each teen has a unique set of background experiences, personal interests, aptitudes, and curiosities that combine to create an environment of many different individual needs. Even the most rigid standards of curriculum can be expanded to address this diversity of learning needs and desires. Furthermore, the use of cooperative learning groups allows students to teach each other. With more "instructors" in the classroom, content delivery and performance will be that much more diverse.

Differentiated instruction is one method of reaching a multitude of interests at once. It is based on two premises: (1) There are multiple paths to learning for different abilities. (2) Every brain is unique. Content is presented in ways that address personal interests and different styles of learning. Teachers can differentiate instruction through the content choices, delivery processes, learning products and outcomes, and individual learning styles. Furthermore, varying experiences help student brains remember what they've learned. Problem-solving assignments give students multiple ways to arrive at the same solution. Cooperative learning groups, hands-on and student-centered activities, and flexible scheduling are all ways to address students' questions, focus on real life, actively engage learning, and emphasize collaboration and community between peers.

## MEANINGFUL ASSESSMENT

"I did not get along well with my French teacher, so I was surprised when I was chosen to take a prestigious exam; it was an honor. I had to go everyday for two weeks for tutoring before the exam. I had to be there on time—exactly. I kept dreaming about it every night; it just kept running through my mind. I woke up once, thought it was time to take the test, woke up my mom, she showered, we ate breakfast, and then realized it was still dark outside—it was 4:00 a.m. It was so stressful!"

As teens' interests and passions develop, so do their talents. Discovering an aptitude for a certain skill or task frequently encourages a student to apply it in other ways—like with an enthusiastic demonstration to the teacher! Teens practically burst with excitement when they finally solve a problem or comprehend an idea that has been eluding them. They are eager and proud to show off their newfound knowledge. Many classrooms, however, have no provisions for incorporating these spontaneous demonstrations into formal assessments.

The responsibility of educating our youth is filled with more and more objectives and guidelines, and the proof required of schools and teachers is overwhelmingly in the form of standardized tests. Politicians and administrators emphasize assessment with the best of intentions—to improve education in our schools—but their insistence on evaluating students by statistics and numbers has forced educators to concentrate on memorized facts and to define students by test scores. Not to mention the fact that divergent, creative thinking goes out the window in favor of the one correct answer required in standardized tests. The ability to think divergently, to problem solve, would serve them better in real life.

One teacher commented, "There is more emphasis on finding out what students don't know than what they do know." This overemphasis on traditional assessment establishes an atmosphere of stress and competition within the classroom. The message to work against one another, as opposed to working with each other, is the one most heard by students (and it is heard loudly). Although some students thrive in this competitive atmosphere, many develop feelings of inferiority.

The focus on assessment needs to shift from who made the grade and who did not to making good decisions in the best interest of our students. Meaningful assessment accounts for individual differences in style, attitudes, and interests. Ongoing records, discussions, anecdotal notes, portfolio entries, conferences, and observations are all means by which we can informally assess students and develop a picture of their individual progress. Formal assessments, often the preferred way to determine what students have learned, can take the traditional form of a paper-and-pencil test, or they can include personalized, performance-based assessments in the form of portfolios, presentations, projects, science experiments, written reports, and short investigations. Before selecting any type of assessment, consider your purpose and the student you are assessing, and match that to an appropriate assessment tool.

Although multiple-choice tests are quick to grade (and therefore cheap!) and easy to compare against students from other districts or other nations, they are not the best way to get a complete picture of what a student has accomplished during a course. Furthermore, they are mentally exhausting and minimally inspiring. Learning where your score falls against the national percentile is not nearly as rewarding as hearing the applause for giving a great oral presentation or seeing your annotated diagram of how space dust becomes a solar system hanging in the front office.

## Making It Work

The physical and mental experience of adolescence is trying enough, even without the stress of succeeding in a school where uniformity is the primary experience. When students are asked to excel at the same subjects and demonstrate knowledge in the same way, is it any wonder that some teens criticize themselves as never being able to fit in? Offering variety in content, instruction style, and assessment methods reinforces the idea that teens don't have to be the same. Rather than worrying about whether their term papers are as good as everyone else's, teens—given the freedom to pursue their interests and talents—focus instead on what they are good at.

***I feel like my students are completely overtested, but I have no control over the federal and district mandates that require the testing. What can I do to ensure that what we are testing is meaningful to the students?***

Students do take a lot of tests these days, but assessments have potential to help students and teachers. Change the way you perceive them. Explain to students that testing is just another form

*(Continued)*

(Continued)

of feedback that helps them see what they did correctly and what they need to fix. Use your class scores to identify points of mastery and holes in the group's knowledge when you design your lesson plans.

### How can I meet the individual needs of my students and at the same time deal with a classroom full of thirty students?

Although no one will tell you it is easy to individualize curriculum to meet students' personal interest and academic levels, the payoff is tremendous. Differentiated instruction and teaching to the multiple intelligences helps every student reach his or her potential. But you don't have to write several different lesson plans for each day of class—build flexibility into your instruction. Offer students choices about how they would like to present work or about what subtopics they'd like to study more.

### My students hate cooperative groups and so do I.
### One or two people end up doing all the work,
### and the other kids in the group get credit for them.
### Why should I waste any more class time with them?

Working cooperatively in groups doesn't come naturally to teens—you will have to teach them how. But using cooperative groups in the classroom doesn't come naturally to teachers. It's a skill that needs to be learned and practiced. If there are no staff development opportunities available for you to learn how to structure and manage a cooperative group, find a book about it. Many titles are available that address cooperative learning in a variety of situations; *Cooperative Learning* by Spencer Kagan (1994) is an excellent start.

In general, start with small groups doing short assignments (perhaps pairs of students analyzing a poem). Gradually expand to more complex projects and larger groups. Diversity within the groups promotes a better exchange of ideas (and therefore better learning); sometimes mix boys and girls and high achievers and low achievers to achieve a heterogeneous mix. If your first attempt at using cooperative groups in your classroom is less than successful, don't give up. Most things worthwhile don't come easy.

## FRIENDLY ADULTS

Peer interaction is not enough to help teenagers become healthy adults. Even the nicest friends are subject to the upheaval of the teen brain, too! Left alone, responsible teenagers frequently engage in risky activities for the simple reason that it seemed like a good idea at the time. Running an idea by an adult first often averts disaster. It's not that easy, however, for some students to find adults to talk to. Parents often work two jobs, neighbors often don't know each other, and teachers and administrators are stretched thin at crowded schools. Chances to interact with adults on a personal level are usually hit or miss. Some students are fortunate enough to have a relationship with a coach or extracurricular adviser, but many are not. Time scheduled during the school day for students to share their interests and concerns with dedicated adults will support their social and emotional growth.

An advisory program can be a veritable lifeline. It guarantees the opportunity for a student to interact meaningfully with peers and an adult. It also creates a sense of belonging in the classroom. More than a reincarnation of the traditional homeroom class (where nothing happened but taking attendance and making announcements), advisory programs build close relationships between students and adults. Relatively small groups of students, ideally fewer than twenty, are assigned during one period to a caring teacher, administrator, or other staff member to form a safe haven in which advisers and advisees communicate abut issues near and dear to the teenage heart. Topics of discussion may range from becoming an oceanographer or a nurse to why your mother makes you wear a coat or do chores. Programs like this contribute to a better school climate and develop student self-concept (Coleman, 1996).

## Another Perspective

Even though the definition of family is changing, one thing is not—students need their parents or guardians involved in their life. Caring teachers, coaches, and mentors can enhance the security families provide, but they can never replace it. You may have to extend special efforts to involve some families in school activities. Single parents, grandparents acting as parents, and guardians are often struggling with issues that the traditional family does not face. Shortage of time and financial strains may further impact any family's ability to interact with the school. Immigrant parents may have limited experiences in classrooms and find schools foreboding and unwelcoming places. Illiteracy or the inability to speak English may prompt further separation. Unconditional acceptance and realistic expectations will foster their involvement.

Mentoring programs that introduce caring adults in the community to teenagers serve many of the same purposes as advisory programs, although they are not centered in the classroom. Mentoring is a one-on-one relationship between an adult and teen based on trust. The teen learns to rely on a mentor as a constant presence in his or her life. Their commitment to each other is long term; rather than a semester or school year, mentor friendships can last a lifetime. Because mentors are usually older and more experienced than the mentee, they guide and nurture the adolescent's growth, giving structure to the tumultuous teenage life.

Mentors provide support in a variety of ways to the teenager. They care just as much about band practice and Friday-night parties as academic achievement. ("Finally!" you can hear teenagers sigh in collective relief, "somebody cares about the same things we care about!") This caring adult provides a friendly forum for examining and communicating thoughts and views. Opinions like "I think we should lower the drinking age" and indignant questions like "Why can't we drive at fifteen?" are bantered in a casual atmosphere. The typical adult (parents or teachers) may be tempted to use these openings for a lecture on what the teen should and shouldn't do—the choices are clear, after all, to them. The savvy mentor knows that it is far more productive to withhold judgment and encourage the teen to explore their thoughts with a responsible adult rather than limiting such discussions to their age-mates. Mentors, like teachers, also serve as important academic role models. They can demonstrate professional skills, such as how to be an effective writer or researcher, or personal skills, such as how to be a gracious winner or loser.

## READY, SET, GOAL

As adults, it's easy to understand why students need to understand this or memorize that. Communicating the reason to teenagers is where the challenge comes. Secondary education—splintered across many subjects and rampant with rules about what classes to take when and requirements for graduation—can be so overwhelming that success seems unattainable. Goals, which motivate people to act, are a way to connect the student with the curriculum. Goals also direct our attention to what we still need to accomplish to achieve our desires. Teenagers become engaged in learning when they see a practical application for a course. Showing them how learning algebra will help them finance a car or how writing with correct grammar will help them get a job (to pay for the car loan!) will increase their motivation to succeed.

Goals are motivators because they are personal challenges. (Objectives that are too easy to accomplish have little meaning.) Difficult, but not impossible, goals inspire us to work just a little harder and more creatively to achieve them. If something in our strategy for reaching a difficult goal goes awry, we devise alternate strategies to succeed. If we want to make the varsity dance team and don't, we try for the junior varsity team or work harder in other dance classes. On the other hand, aspirations that are unreachable are very easy to abandon. Many middle schools and high schools actively teach and promote reasonable goal setting. One school district has students write their goals for each course and share them with their parents at conferences. Not only does the writing of goals give students some direction for success in a course, the goals serve as an excellent communication tool between school and home.

Setting goals also grounds students in realism. If they can say, "I want a high school diploma" or "I plan to paint houses when I finish school," most likely those things will happen. Sadly, many adolescents don't understand what goals are and answer the question "What are your goals for after high school?" with responses like "Skateboarding," "Modeling," "Either be a scientist or beautician," and "Play for the NFL" (this from a boy who had never joined the football team!). Not that skateboarding and modeling aren't possible careers—but if the only plans they've made to attain them are to assume that they will be discovered by talent scouts while walking down the street, they are not likely to realize these dreams. A student who can't decide between scientist and beautician has made no differentiation between the educational demands and requirements of the two careers. Students need goals that are realistic and attainable, not fantasies, and we should teach our students how to create them.

Setting short-term goals reduces the likelihood that students will become distracted by other goals. A seventh-grade teacher who only promotes setting goals for how to live life after college will find that students have trouble staying focused on events so far away. It has been said that to the middle school mind the future is 3:00 p.m., or whatever time they get out of school. Even high school seems like a lifetime away. (Hardly a coincidence, a sense of time and future doesn't develop until about age fifteen or sixteen, when the frontal lobes take on more responsibility.) Work with students to establish goals that are worth accomplishing (personally meaningful), and follow up with their progress.

## Ways to Practice Setting Goals

- Project completion timelines
- Explore careers
- Establish study habits
- Prioritize amounts and types of social involvement
- Personalize unit goals
- Share goals with friends
- Brainstorm ways to achieve goals

## Goals to Set

- Apply to college
- Solo in chorus
- Earn a part in a play
- Achieve in sports
- Attain an advanced seat in band or orchestra
- Run for class office for extracurricular activities
- Accumulate volunteer hours
- Choose a behavior to improve
- Commit to beneficial exercise habits
- Eat healthier

## Making It Work

Apprenticeships are as old as industry itself. The best way to learn to be a silversmith is to train with one. Learning to be an adult is no different. Teens who are left to their own devices or who spend most of their time in the company of friends enter adulthood without the same wisdom and perspective that many of their peers have. Schools need to give teens the chance to interact with adults as individuals so they can thrive and eventually make productive contributions to society.

*More than seventy percent of the students at our school qualify for free or reduced lunch, and the majority are from single-parent homes. What meaningful support could we possibly offer to these adolescents?*

Time during the day to discuss life's triumphs and difficulties, like during an advisory period, goes some distance toward supplementing the attention they get from their family. Advisers are also in a position to identify kids who might be at risk so that they can get the immediate intervention that they need. Establishing a relationship with a mentor also gives the student the chance to interact with an adult who does not need his or her help as a babysitter or wage earner—during the time they spend together, the teen is free to meet his or her own needs first.

*Parents in our neighborhood are just so busy.*
*How can we get them involved if they don't have the time?*

Most parents come to open house, and many are willing to help but don't know how. Take the initiative and communicate—through a school Web site or with a newsletter—specific ways they can participate. Besides chaperoning field trips, businesspeople can open their office to student interns, and crafty parents can help make costumes for the drama department; other parents can staff homework centers or act as translators for parents who may not speak English well. Identify what you would like from parents and then ask for it.

*How can I teach goal setting when class time is*
*already filled trying to get through all the standards?*

Goal setting isn't something you spend a day or week on and then hope students do it themselves for the rest of the year. Goal setting should be incorporated into every single lesson plan of every subject. It takes mere seconds to do. Ask students to write down what they hope to accomplish during a science project, or ask them to make a checkoff list for tasks they need to complete before finishing a term paper. Teachers already have students keep assignment books and homework logs—goals are just another element to include.

# Conclusion

## *Secrets of the Teenage Brain—Revealed!*

No one has a more challenging job than teachers and school administrators who work with teens on a daily basis. Until recently, we've had only our personal experiences and our preservice college classes to guide us down the rocky path of instructing adolescents (and we've done amazingly well). Now, discoveries about the brain and how it changes provide clues to help us solve the mystery about why teenagers behave the way they do. Even information that confirms what we already suspected sheds light on the motivations and desires of these students.

Any book on education risks overwhelming the reader. Idea after idea is put forth—far too many to implement at once. So start small. Take from this book one or two suggestions that have the most meaning for you, and work them into your classroom routine. That way you won't bury yourself in unrealistic expectations but will rather grow new dendrites in your own brain as you strive to make your classroom adolescent friendly.

Adolescence is a pivotal time in a person's development. The changes teens experience determine much about who they are—their work ethic, interests, self-esteem, morality—and who they will become. This, in turn, shapes our society; teachers play a critical role in determining the kinds of people who will lead us into the future. Educating teenagers is not an easy job, but it is a rewarding one. As the world becomes "smaller" and our activities more global, teachers quite literally are changing the world— one teenager at a time.

# In Summary

## CHAPTER 1. TEEN BRAIN: UNDER CONSTRUCTION

Teen brains resemble blueprints more than they resemble skyscrapers. Instead of thinking about a teenage mind as an empty house that needs furnishings, understand it as the framing of a house that still needs walls, wiring, and a roof.

### You've learned that . . .

- The brain, not hormones, is to blame for the inexplicable behavior of teens
- Short-term memory increases by about thirty percent during adolescence
- The activities teens invest their time and energy in influence what activities they'll invest in as adults
- Teens are ruled far more by their emotions than by logic

## CHAPTER 2. TEEN COGNITION AND LEARNING

Teenagers are not incoherent, clumsy, sex-crazed, unpredictable, irrational monsters who can't be reasoned with—they are intelligent creatures not yet accustomed to their (unevenly) burgeoning mental strengths and capabilities. Adolescence is a time of startling growth and streamlining in the brain, enabling teens to think abstractly, speak expressively, and move gracefully.

### You've learned that . . .

- The teen brain is particularly susceptible to novelty
- The burst of growth in the frontal lobes means that teens overcomplicate problems, idealize the world, and say one thing while doing another

- The development of the parietal lobes helps teen athletes improve their pace and teen musicians improve their beat
- Physical movement helps the cerebellum develop, thereby helping teens improve their cognitive processing skills
- Feedback improves the brain's efficiency
- Teens crave structure and organization in spite of their attraction to novelty
- Brains of individuals with ADHD differ from those without it

## CHAPTER 3. THE SOCIAL BRAIN

Emotions strongly impact learning, which is problematic because teens are still learning how to balance and manage their emotions. They are also learning how to negotiate their place in the world, from maintaining friendships to practicing the mating dance.

### You've learned that . . .

- Adolescence is when the brain begins to develop templates for adult relationships
- Teen emotions can easily cement lifelong memories or form powerful learning blocks
- Teenagers value adult influence even though they complain about it
- Teens will climb the moral ladder only as their frontal lobes develop
- Boy brains and girl brains really are different—it's not just socialization

## CHAPTER 4. COMMUNICATION AND THE UNFINISHED BRAIN

The rapidly changing brain is responsible for the adolescent communication gaps and growth. Neuroscientists are finally able to help educators adjust to the highs and lows of teen dialogue.

### You've learned that . . .

- Adolescence is when language ability and short-term memory improve
- The teen brain relies more on the amygdala than on the frontal lobes, setting the stage for emotional outbursts
- Teens experience emotions before they can verbally articulate them

- Teenage self-awareness and teenage self-consciousness go hand in hand
- Teens are more vulnerable to stress than adults are

## CHAPTER 5. SELF-CONCEPT UNDER ATTACK

Adolescence is a time of great fluctuation in the levels of neurotransmitters, the chemical messengers in the axons of neurons that excite and inhibit behaviors. When levels of these chemicals go astray, teens face a variety of mental upheavals such as depression, eating disorders, and shifts in sleep habits.

### You've learned that . . .

- Testosterone and estrogen are found all over the brain during puberty
- Deficits and excesses of serotonin—the "take it easy" neurotransmitter—contribute to teen depression and eating disorders
- Obesity may have a chemical origin (and that some overweight teens may not lack self-control)
- Melatonin changes the sleep patterns of teenagers
- Transgender has its roots in the brain, not in the genitals

## CHAPTER 6. THE RISK-TAKING BRAIN

The adolescent brain plays a significant role in reckless teen behaviors, and some mistakes (not all) teens make now can have lasting physiological effects.

### You've learned that . . .

- Teens are very susceptible to the dopamine rushes that come with taking risks
- Teens have trouble anticipating the consequences of their behavior because they rely more on the emotional amygdala than the rational frontal lobes
- Teens are extremely vulnerable to addiction and adolescent addictions are harder to break
- Technology can rewire the brain
- Cutting is a pleasurable, but unhealthy, habit
- Violence and aggression decrease with age

## CHAPTER 7. REACHING AND TEACHING TODAY'S ADOLESCENTS—TOMORROW!

Knowledge about the teenage brain and its unique characteristics should be reflected in how we run our schools and our classrooms. Middle schools and high schools need to reexamine how they are structured and how they can better help their adolescent population.

### Make school a place that . . .

- Eases the transition from child brain to adolescent brain and appeals to teenagers' innate interest in the world around them
- Feels more like a community than an institution and nurtures teens' burgeoning sense of empathy and compassion
- Allows teens to explore and develop a self-identity and to express themselves as individuals
- Provides the support and structure teens need to productively channel and invest their energy and enthusiasm

# Book Club
# Discussion Questions

**C**ongratulations on undertaking a book club study of *Secrets of the Teenage Brain.* Your desire to participate in a book club is a sure sign you are committed to the profession of teaching and have a desire to share information, common experiences, and strategies with your colleagues.

If your book club is just starting out, you may find the answers to the following questions helpful in ensuring that it runs smoothly:

1. Who will mediate? Will one person be designated the leader, or will you alternate the responsibility at each gathering?

2. Will you use a structured set of questions, semistructured (additional questions will be honored as they arise), or totally unstructured?

3. Will communication be casual, with people offering when they choose, or more formal, with each person responding in turn to the discussion question? (Some groups start with a general group discussion and then devote the last ten minutes to those who have not shared.)

4. Will you review the book in its entirety or divide it into one or two chapter segments? Whatever you choose, be sure to give enough time for everyone to complete the reading.

5. Do you plan to meet monthly, bimonthly, or once a semester? Do you want to have a set time each month, or will one person be in charge of arranging a convenient time to meet?

6. Consider online discussion groups if you can't find a group at your school.

7. Bring treats and have fun!

## CHAPTER 1. TEEN BRAIN: UNDER CONSTRUCTION

1.  What are some common, and not so common, adolescent behaviors you see in the classroom and outside the classroom?

2.  What surprised you most in this chapter?

3.  Choose the four most valuable points in this chapter. How will they impact you and your teaching?

4.  What have you learned or experienced in the last two months that grew dendrites in your brain?

5.  How are your students growing dendrites in and out of your classroom? Are they properly preparing their brain for the adult world?

6.  Do you think there is an appropriate balance between academics and other experiences and activities in your students' lives?

7.  What vicarious experiences increased your ability to be empathetic as a teacher?

8.  Are you a role model for your students: Do you demonstrate empathy and a desire to understand the intentions of others? If so, in what ways?

9.  What is one question you have after reading this chapter?

## CHAPTER 2. TEEN COGNITION AND LEARNING

1.  How do you gain students' attention in your class? What ways do you find most effective? What is one novel strategy you will try?

2.  Create a simile for the statement, "Teaching is like _____ because _____." (Group leaders may want to bring objects from their classroom or home to fill in the first blank. Pass out a flash drive, magic marker, puzzle piece, or clay so that each person has a different object.) For instance, Teaching is like *a puzzle piece* because _____, or Teaching is like *clay* because _____.

3.  What new instructional strategies from this chapter will you incorporate into your teaching? Will you make adaptations to the strategy?

4.  What is one new way you can include multiple intelligences in your classroom?

5. Refer to the heading "Making the World a Better Place." What examples of *pseudostupidity* and *teenage hypocrisy* have you seen in your classroom? How could you handle those situations in the future?

6. What is the status of physical education at your school? What changes if any, are needed?

7. How frequently do students actively participate in your class? What methods do you use to engage students in your classroom?

8. Share one fun or favorite mnemonic device.

9. How do you give feedback to your students' work, and how do they respond to your feedback?

10. What are some methods to assess your students that do not discourage them?

11. What role should schools play in teaching study and test strategies? What do you plan to do in your classroom?

12. What is something new you learned about students with ADHD?

13. What strategies have you found to be most effective when working with students with ADHD? Is there a new strategy you will try?

## CHAPTER 3. THE SOCIAL BRAIN

1. Telling stories is a favorite way to connect with students. What stories have you and your students shared, and what have been the effects?

2. Share a time you felt a natural dopamine rush.

3. How might you bring emotion into your classroom?

4. What are your views about expressing a sense of humor in the classroom?

5. Take the following identity inventory:

   a. My career is _____.

   b. My political stance is _____ (conservative, liberal, apathetic, moderate).

   c. My spirituality is _____ (Lutheran, Baptist, Muslim, Jew, agnostic, no formal religion).

   d. My personality is _____ (choose a few descriptors: fun, depressed, introverted, excited, bossy).

   e. My sexuality is _____ (heterosexual, homosexual, bisexual).

   f. My interests include _____ (choose a few: hobbies, sports, music).

   g. Intellectually I am _____ (academic, non-intellectual, middle of the road).

   h. My body image is _____ (I constantly criticize myself; I'm gorgeous; I may not be gorgeous, but I'm satisfied with myself).

   i. My ethnic or cultural affiliation is _____.

   j. I am (circle one) married, single, cohabitating.

In a nutshell these responses represent your identity. In what way (or ways) is your school or classroom supporting the identity formation of your students in each of these categories?

6. Discuss the cheating policy at your school or in your classroom. How does it fit with what we know about the brain and adolescent development?

7. Should moral behavior be taught in the school? If so, around what parameters?

8. Analyze the way gender is portrayed in televisions shows, movies, and magazines. Does your school add or detract from traditional gender role identification?

9. Discuss possible gender biases you have. Do you tend to prefer working with one gender over the other? If so, why?

10. Have you found strategies that meet the unique needs of girls? Of boys?

## CHAPTER 4. COMMUNICATION AND THE UNFINISHED BRAIN

1. What do you see as the central message of this chapter? How does it resonate with you and your students?

2. How do you incorporate writing and speaking skills into your classroom? What is the best thing about including them, and what is most frustrating?

3. Discuss teenager misunderstandings you have witnessed. How might you help to calm them down or reduce them in the future?

4. What stressors do you perceive your students have? Do they prevent them from moving ahead with their learning?

5. What can you do to help relieve your students' stress levels?

6. What stressors do you have that prevent you from taking risks in your life as a teacher?

7. From your experience, what words of wisdom would you like to share with someone entering—or in—the education profession?

## CHAPTER 5. SELF-CONCEPT UNDER ATTACK

1. In your opinion, what is the value of bringing information about puberty into your teaching? Is there content that you are uncomfortable incorporating into your subject area?

2. What ways have you found to value students' uniqueness?

3. How comfortable with your own body image are you? In what way does it impact your students?

4. How can you combat media messages about body image for girls? For boys?

5. Early bloomers and late bloomers: what are ways to help them feel more comfortable in their own bodies?

6. Share a story of a student who has faced an eating disorder. What role should the school play?

7. Discuss examples of students who have exhibited sleep deprivation. How did it impact their learning and their behavior? What can you do as a teacher to support good sleep habits?

## CHAPTER 6. THE RISK-TAKING BRAIN

1. In what ways do you facilitate positive risk taking with your students?

2. How do you define "difficult students" in your own teaching experiences?

3. How successful have you been in your efforts to deal with difficult students? What are some ideal ways to deal with them? What would you do differently?

4. List positive and negative contributions to education and life from technology. What are your views on how to control the negative impact?

5. How do you incorporate technology into your classroom? Do you believe it enriches or hinders learning?

6. Reread the passage on "Group Identity." Put the passage into your own words as it relates to your students.

7. Are schools and communities too strict with our teenagers? What role has the media played in sensationalizing teenage problems?

8. Compare and contrast veteran– and beginning–teachers' views on at-risk students. Are there differences? If so, speculate as to why.

## CHAPTER 7. REACHING AND TEACHING TODAY'S ADOLESCENTS—TOMORROW!

1. What are the most common academic interests of your students? How do you nourish their interests?

2. How do you encourage diverse students to work together?

3. What are your views about creating a sense of belonging in the classroom? What are the challenges? What are the workable strategies?

4. How do you ensure that students find your subject area meaningful?

5. In what ways do you and your colleagues support the transition between elementary school and middle school *or* middle school and high school? What is your opinion of current transition-support services? What changes would you recommend?

6. Who has been a mentor to you as a student or teacher? In what way has this person affected your views of yourself and your practices as a teacher?

7. What do you perceive to be the qualities of a good mentor?

8. What challenges do you face dealing with students' parents? How might relationships be strengthened?

9. List three strengths your school has in easing the evolution from child brain to adolescent brain and three areas where there is work to be done.

10. Will you change your teaching as a result of what you've read in this book? Why or why not?

# Glossary of Brain Terms

**amygdala.**   An almond-shaped area of the brain located deep in the temporal lobes that processes and remembers emotions; it is part of the limbic system.

**axon.**   A long extension coming from a neuron that sends information to other neurons.

**basal ganglia.**   A group of neural structures in the brain that controls voluntary movement (along with the cerebellum) and is involved with cognition and emotion.

**brain.**   Located in the skull, it is the main part of the central nervous system and contains gray and white matter. It controls mental processes and physical movements; it also manages emotions, consciousness, and memory.

**Broca's area.**   Associated with creating language, it is responsible for speech production and language processing. It is located in the left hemisphere of the frontal lobe and works in conjunction with Wernicke's area.

**cell body.**   It contains the neuron's nucleus.

**cerebellum.**   The part of the brain in control of voluntary motor movement (works in combination with the basal ganglia), balance, and muscle tone. Located at the lower back of the brain.

**cerebral hemispheres.**   The two symmetrical halves of the brain, referred to as the right hemisphere and the left hemisphere.

**cingulate system.**   Detects emotional meaning and allows a person to shift thoughts and ideas. It is part of the limbic system.

**cognition.**   Process of thinking.

**corpus callosum.** A network of neurons that connects the left and right hemispheres of the brain and allows communication between them.

**cortex (cerebral cortex).** Outer layer of gray matter that covers the cerebral hemispheres.

**cortisol.** The primary stress hormone. It is released with the "fight or flight" reaction.

**dendrite.** Branch that emerges from a neuron. Receives messages from other cell bodies; one neuron may possess thousands of dendrites.

**dopamine.** A neurotransmitter in the brain associated with pleasure, movement, and sexual desire.

**EEG (electroencephalography).** Technology that studies electrical currents in the brain.

**endorphins.** Opiate-like hormones that give a sense of well-being and euphoria and reduce pain.

**epinephrine.** A hormone released when individuals experience pain or fear. It stimulates the heart and opens up the lungs. It is also known as adrenaline and is initially released as part of the "fight or flight" response.

**estrogen.** A female hormone produced by the ovaries; involved with menstruation, breast development, and pregnancy.

**fMRI Scans (functional magnetic resonance imaging).** Technology that examines the functions of the brain.

**frontal lobes.** The executive function of the brain resides here. It is involved in decision making, language, problem solving, planning, and controlling sense of self. It is located in the front of each hemisphere of the brain, behind the forehead.

**glial cells.** Brain cells that digest dead neurons, create myelin, and provide nutritional support to neurons. They are not capable of transmitting nerve impulses. Glial cells make up ninety percent of the brain's cells.

**gray matter.** Refers to the nerve cell bodies and dendrites in the brain.

**hippocampus.** Plays a key role in memory processing and helps regulate emotion.

**hypothalamus.** Regulates the pituitary gland and is part of the brain in control of pain, pleasure, hunger, thirst, and sexual desire.

**leptin.**    A hormone that regulates metabolism, often associated with fat cells and appetite.

**limbic system.**    A group of interconnected structures in the brain involved in emotion, motivation, and the sense of smell. Structures involved include the amygdala, hypothalamus, and hippocampus.

**melatonin.**    A hormone released by the brain to cause and regulate the sleep-wake cycle.

**mirror neurons.**    A neuron that fires both when it does an act and when it observes the act being done by another.

**myelination.**    Fatty substance that insulates and protects neurons so they can communicate more efficiently.

**neuroscience.**    The study of the nervous system and the brain.

**neuron.**    A brain cell that sends and receives information to and from the brain and the *central nervous system.* It consists of dendrites, an axon, and a cell body. Neurons make up ten percent of the brain's cells.

**norepinephrine.**    A hormone and a neurotransmitter that increases heart rate and blood pressure, it releases energy.

**occipital lobe.**    In charge of visual processing in the brain. Located at the back of each cerebral hemisphere.

**oxytocin.**    A hormone that creates feelings of bonding and trust and is involved in reproduction.

**parietal lobes.**    A part of the brain associated with touch, temperature, and pain; located behind the frontal lobes at the top of the brain.

**PET scan (positron-emission tomography scan).**    A three-dimensional view of the brain that allows neuroscientists to observe the structure and functions in the brain.

**plasticity.**    The ability of the brain to reorganize itself as it gains information and has new experiences. It allows the brain to prune weak synapses and develop strong synapses.

**pruning.**    Elimination of weak and ineffective synaptic connections in the brain.

**serotonin.**    A neurotransmitter that regulates mood, it acts as a calming agent.

**synaptic connection.**    The space that connects one neuron to another.

**temporal lobes.**    A part of the brain involved with visual and verbal memory; located on each side of the brain, right above the ears.

**testosterone.**    A male sex hormone produced by the testes; it is the strongest of the male hormones and is required for sperm production and secondary sexual characteristics, such as facial hair and a deeper voice.

**Wernicke's area.**    Important in language development and works with Broca's area. Involved in recognizing and processing words that are spoken; located at the back of the temporal lobes on the left hemisphere.

**white matter.**    Myelinated neurons in the cortex.

# Bibliography

Adamson, L., Hartman, S. G., & Lyxell, B. (1999). Adolescent identity—a qualitative approach: Self-concept, existential questions and adult contacts. *Scandinavian Journal of Psychology, 40*(1), 21–31.

*Adolescent smoking statistics.* (2003). Retrieved from www.lungusa.org/site/c.dvLUK9O0E/b.39868/k.AFBF/Adolescent_Smoking_Statistics.htm

*After school for America's teens: A national survey of teen attitudes and behaviors in the hours after school* (An executive summary report by the YMCA of the USA). (2001). Retrieved March 26, 2004, fromwww.drugpolicy.org/library/bibliography/afterschool

Aguilera, A., Sanchez-Tomero J. A., & Selgas, R. (2007). Brain activation in uremic anorexia. *Journal of Renal Nutrition, 17*(1), 57–61. Retrieved from www.ncbi.nlm.nih.gov/pubmed/17198934

Aguilera, A., Selgas, R., Codoceo, R., & Bajo, A. (2000). Uremic anorexia: A consequence of persistently high brain serotonin levels? The tryptophan/serotonin disorder hypothesis. *Peritoneal Dialysis International, 20*(6), 810–816.

Alsaker, F. D. (1992). Pubertal timing, overweight, and psychological adjustment. *Journal of Early Adolescence, 12,* 396–419.

American Music Conference. (2007). *Music and the brain.* Available at www.amcmusic.com/musiceducation/social.htm Retrieved January 7, 2008.

Americans for the Arts. (2006). *Arts students outperform non-arts students on SAT: Average points better on SAT by arts students* [Data file]. Retrieved January 7, 2008, from www.artsusa.org/pdf/get_involved/advocacy/research/2007/SAT.pdf

Angelo, T., & Cross, K. P. (1998). *Classroom assessment techniques: A handbook for college teachers* (2nd ed.). San Francisco: Jossey-Bass.

Armstrong, T. (2000). *Multiple intelligences in the classroom* (2nd ed.). Alexandria, VA: Association for Supervision and Curriculum Development.

Arnett, J. J. (2001). *Adolescence and emerging adulthood: A cultural approach.* Upper Saddle River, NJ: Prentice Hall.

Aron, A., Fisher, H., Mashek, D. J., Strong, G., Li, H., & Brown, L. (2005). Reward, motivation, and emotion systems associated with early-stage intense romantic love. *Journal of Neurophysiology, 94*(1), 327–337.

Atallah, H. E., Frank, J. J., & O'Reilly, R. C. (2004). Hippocampus, cortex, and basal ganglia: Insights from computational models of complementary learning systems. *Neurobiology of Learning and Memory, 82*(3), 253–267.

Ausubel, D. P. (1968). *Educational psychology: A cognitive view.* New York: Holt, Rinehart & Winston.

Baird, A. A., Gruber, S. A., Fein, D. A., Maas, L. C., Steingard, R. J., Renshaw, P. F., et al. (1999). Functional magnetic resonance imaging of facial affect recognition in children and adolescents. *Journal of the American Academy of Child and Adolescent Psychiatry, 38*(2), 195–199.

Bangert-Drowns, R., Kulik, C. C., Kulik, J. A., & Morgan, M. (1991). The instructional effect of feedback in test-like events. *Review of Educational Research, 61*(2), 213–238.

Banks, W. A. (2003). Is obesity a disease of the blood-brain barrier? Physiological, pathological, and evolutionary considerations. *Current Pharmaceutical Design, 9*(10), 801–809.

Banks, W. A. (2008). The blood-brain barrier as a cause of obesity. *Current Pharmaceutical Design, 14*(16), 1606–1614.

Barbarich, N. (2002). Is there a common mechanism of serotonin dysregulation in anorexia nervosa and obsessive compulsive disorder? *Eating and Weight Disorders, 7*(3), 221–231.

Bartels, A., & Zeki, S. (2000). The neural basis of romantic love. *Neuroreport, 11*(17), 3829–3834.

Beckman, M. (2004, July 30). Neuroscience, crime, culpability, and the adolescent brain. *Science, 305*(5684), 595–599.

Benes, F., Turtle, M., Khan, Y., & Farol, P. (1994). Myelination of a key relay zone in the hippocampal formation occurs in the human brain during childhood, adolescence, and adulthood. *Archives of General Psychiatry, 51*(6), 477–484.

Blood, A. J., & Zatorre, R. J. (2001). Intensely pleasurable responses to music correlate with activity in brain regions implicated in reward and emotion. *Proceedings of the National Academy of Sciences, USA, 98*(20), 11818–11823.

Bloom, F. E., Beal, M. F., & Kupfer, D. J. (Eds.). (2006). *The Dana guide to brain health.* Available from www.dana.org

Bourgeois, J. P. (2001). Synaptogenesis in the neocortex of the newborn: The ultimate frontier of individuation? In C. A. Nelson & M. Luciana (Eds.), *Handbook of developmental cognitive neuroscience* (pp. 23–34). Cambridge: MIT Press.

Bourgeois, J. P. (2005). Brain synaptogenesis and epigenesist. *Medical Science (Paris), 21*(4), 428–433.

Brandt, R. (1999). Educators need to know about the human brain. *Phi Delta Kappan, 81*(3), 235–238.

Brandt, R. (2000). On teaching brains to think: A conversation with Robert Sylwester. *Educational Leadership, 57*(7), 72–75.

Bremner, J. D., Narayan, M., Anderson, E. R., Staib, L. H., Miller, H. L., & Charney, D. S. (2000). Hippocampal volume reduction in major depression. *American Journal of Psychiatry, 157*(1), 115–118.

Brendtro, L., Brokenleg, M., & Van Bockern, S. (2002). *Reclaiming youth at risk: Our hope for the future.* Bloomington, IN: National Education Service.

Breur, J. (1999). In search of . . . brain-based education. *Phi Delta Kappan, 80*(9), 648–657.

Brooks-Gunn, J., & Paikoff, R. (1997). Sexuality and developmental transitions during adolescence. In J. Schulenberg, J. L. Maggs, & K. Hurrelmann (Eds.), *Health risks and developmental transitions during adolescence* (pp. 190–219). New York: Cambridge University Press.

Brown, S. A., Tapert, S. F., Granholm, E., & Delis, D. C. (2000). Neurocognitive functioning of adolescents: Effects of protracted alcohol use. *Alcoholism, Clinical and Experimental Research, 24*(2), 164–171.

Brownell, S. (1999, August 9). Anorexia's roots in the brain. *U.S. News & World Report*, pp. 52–53.

Brownlee, S., Hotinski, R., Pailthorp, B., Ragan, E., & Wong, K. (1999, August 9). Inside the teen brain. *U.S. News & World Report*, pp. 44–54.

Buchel, C., Coull, J. T., & Friston, K. J. (1999, March 5). The predictive value of changes in effective connectivity for human learning. *Science, 283*(5407), 1538–1541.

Buis, J. N., & Thompson, D. N. (1989). Imaginary audience and personal fable: A brief review. *Adolescence, 24*(96), 773–781.

Caine, R. N., & Caine, G. (1990). Understanding a brain-based approach to learning and teaching. *Educational Leadership, 48*(2), 66–70.

Carney, R. N., & Levin, J. R. (2000). Mnemonic instruction, with a focus on transfer. *Journal of Educational Psychology, 92*(4), 783–790.

Carney, R. N., & Levin, J. R. (2008). Conquering mnemonophobia, with help from three practical measures of memory and application. *Teaching of Psychology, 35*(3), 176–183.

Carskadon, M. (Ed.). (2002). *Adolescent sleep patterns: Biological, social, and psychological influences.* New York: Cambridge University Press.

Center for Disease Control and Prevention. (2007). *Suicide trends among youths and young adults aged 10–24 years—United States, 1990–2004.* Retrieved September 3, 2008, from www.cdc.gov/mmwr/preview/mmwrhtml/mm5635a2.htm

Chambers, R. A., Taylor, J. R., & Potenza, M. N. (2003). Developmental neurocircuitry of motivation in adolescence: A critical period of addiction vulnerability. *American Journal of Psychiatry, 160*(6), 1041–1052.

Chugani, D. C., Muzik, O., Behen, M., Rothermel, R., Janisse, J. J., Lee, J., et al. (1999). Developmental changes in brain serotonin synthesis capacity in autistic and nonautistic children. *Annals of Neurology, 45*(3), 287–295.

Colapinto, J. (2000). *As nature made him: The boy who was raised as a girl.* New York: HarperCollins.

Coleman, O. D. (1996). An analysis of the perceptions of senior and junior students regarding the effectiveness of academic advisement in a teacher education program (Doctoral dissertation, Illinois State University, 1996). *Dissertation Abstracts International, 57*(06), 2441.

Compton, R. J. (2003). The interface between emotion and attention: A review of evidence from psychology and neuroscience. *Behavioral and Cognitive Neuroscience Reviews, 2*(2), 115–129.

Copley, J. (2008). *Psychology of heavy metal music: Effects on mood, aggression, suicide, drug use and intelligence.* Available from www.psychology.suite101.com/article.cfm/psychology_of_heavy_metal_music Retrieved January 4, 2009

Costa-Giomi, E. (1998, April). *The McGill Piano Project: Effects of three years of piano instruction on children's cognitive abilities, academic achievement, and self-esteem.* Paper presented at the meeting of the Music Educators National Conference, Phoenix, AZ.

Dagher, A., Bleicher, C., Aston, J. A., Gunn, R. N., Clarke, P. B., & Cumming, P. (2001). Reduced dopamine D1 receptor binding in the ventral striatum of cigarette smokers. *Synapse, 42*(1), 48–53.

Dahl, R. E. (2003). Beyond raging hormones: The tinderbox in the teenage brain. *Cerebrum: The Dana Forum on Brain Science, 5*(3), 7–22.

Dahl, R. E. (2008). Biological, developmental, and neurobehavioral factors relevant to adolescent driving risks. *American Journal of Preventive Medicine, 35* (3, Suppl. 1), S278–S284.

Damasio, A. (1994). *Descartes' error: Emotion, reason, and the human brain.* New York: Putnam.

D'Arcangelo, M. (2000). How does the brain develop? A conversation with Steven Petersen. *Educational Leadership, 58*(3), 68–71.

Davidson, R. J., Coe, C. C., Dolski, I., & Donzella, B. (1999). Individual differences in prefrontal activation asymmetry predict natural killer cell activity at rest and in response to challenge. *Brain Behavior and Immunity, 13*(2), 93–108.

Davidson, R. J., Putnam, K. M., & Larson, C. L. (2000, January 15). Dysfunction in the neural circuitry of emotion regulation: A possible prelude to violence. *Science, 289*(5479), 591–594.

Davies, P. L., & Rose, J. D. (1999). Assessment of cognitive development in adolescents by means of neuropsychological tasks. *Developmental Neuropsychology, 15*(2), 227–248.

De Bellis, M. D., Clark, D. B., Beers, S. R., Soloff, P. H., Boring, A. M., Hall, J., et al. (2000). Hippocampal volume in adolescent-onset alcohol use disorders. *American Journal of Psychiatry, 157*(5), 737–744.

De Bellis, M. D., Keshavan, M. S., Beers, S. R., Hall, J., Frustaci, K., Masalehdan, A., et al. (2001). Sex differences in brain maturation during childhood and adolescence. *Cerebral Cortex, 11*(6), 552–557.

Diamond, M. (1997). Sexual identity and sexual orientation in children with traumatized or ambiguous genitalia. *Journal of Sex Research, 34*(2), 199–211.

Diamond, M. C. (1988). *Enriching heredity: The impact of the environment on the anatomy of the brain.* New York: Free Press.

Diamond, M. C. (2000). *My search for love and wisdom in the brain.* Retrieved from www.newhorizons.org/neuro/diamond_wisdom.htm

Dietz, W. H. (2002). *CDC's role in combating the obesity epidemic before the Senate Committee on Health, Education, Labor and Pensions.* Retrieved from www.hhs.gov/asl/testify/t020521a.html

Doidges, N. (2007). *The brain that changes itself: Stories of personal triumph from the frontiers of brain science.* New York: Penguin.

Duke University Health System. (2008). *Monkey's thoughts make robot walk from across the globe.* Retrieved from www.dukehealth.org/HealthLibrary/News/10218

Dwek, L. B. (2002, July). Finding depression. *Psychology Today, 35*(4), 23.

Elkind, D. (1978). Understanding the young adolescent. *Adolescence, 13,* 127–134.

Epstein, H. T. (2001). An outline of the role of brain in human cognitive development. *Brain and Cognition, 45*(1), 44–51.

Fadiman, C. (n.d.). *Brainy Quote.* Retrieved April 20, 2009 from www.brainyquote.com/quotes/quotes/c/clifffadim165601.html

Fallon, D. (2002, March 19). *The amazing Miss A and why we should care about her.* Keynote speaker address at the Conversation between Foundation Officers and College and University Presidents, New York.

Feinstein, S. (2003). A case for middle school after-school programs in rural America. *Middle School Journal, 34*(3), 32–37.

Feinstein, S. (Ed.). (2006). *The Praeger handbook of learning and the brain.* Westport, CT: Praeger.

Feinstein, S. (2007). *Teaching the at-risk teenage brain.* Lanham, MD: Rowman & Littlefield.

Fernandez, A. (Interviewer), & Klingberg, T. (Interviewee). (2006). *Working memory training and RoboMemo: Interview with Dr. Torkel Klingberg.* Retrieved from www.sharpbrains.com/blog/2006/09/25/working-memory-training-and-robomemo-interview-with-dr-torkel-klingberg

Fishback, S. J. (1999). Learning and the brain. *Adult Learning, 10*(2), 18–22.

Fisher, H. E., Aron, A., Mashek, D., Li, H., & Brown, L. L. (2002). Defining the brain systems of lust, romantic attraction, and attachment. *Archives of Sexual Behavior, 31*(5), 413–419.

Flannery, D., Rowe, D., & Gulley, B. (1993). Impact of pubertal status, timing, and age on adolescent sexual experience and delinquency. *Journal of Adolescent Research, 8*(1), 21–40.

Friedman, I. A., & Mann, L. (1993). Coping patterns in adolescent decision making: An Israeli-Australian comparison. *Journal of Adolescence, 16*(2), 187–199.

Fuster, J. M. (2002). Frontal lobe and cognitive development. *Journal of Neurocytology, 31*(3–5), 373–385.

Gazzaniga, M. S., Bogen, J. E., & Sperry, R. W. (1962). Some functional effects of sectioning the cerebral commissures in man. *Proceedings of the National Academy of Sciences, USA, 48,* 1765–1769.

Giedd, J., Blumenthal, J., Jeffries, N. O., Castellanos, F., Liu, H., Zijdenbos, A., et al. (1999). Brain development during childhood and adolescence: A longitudinal MRI study. *Nature Neuroscience, 2*(10), 861–863.

Giedd, J., Blumenthal, J., Jeffries, N. O., Rajapakse, J., Vaituzis, A., Liu, H., et al. (1999). Development of the human corpus callosum during childhood and adolescence: A longitudinal MRI study. *Progress in Neuro-Psychopharmacology & Biological Psychiatry, 23*(4), 571–588.

Giedd, J. N., Castellanos, F. X., Rajapakse, J. C., Vaituzis, A. C., & Rapoport, J. L. (1997). Sexual dimorphism of the developing human brain. *Progress in Neuro-Psychopharmacology & Biological Psychiatry, 21*(8), 1185–1201.

Given, B. K. (2000). Theaters of the mind. *Educational Leadership, 58*(3), 72–75.

Goleman, D. (1995). *Emotional intelligence.* New York: Bantam Books.

Graber, J. A., Lewinsohn, P. M., Seeley, J. R., & Brooks-Gunn, J. (1997). Is psychopathology associated with the timing of pubertal development? *Journal of the American Academy of Child and Adolescent Psychiatry, 36*(12), 1768–1776.

Graham-Rowe, D. (2002, October 16). Teen angst rooted in busy brain. *New Scientist, 176*(2365), 16.

Greene, J. M., Ennett, S. T., & Ringwalt, C. L. (1999). Prevalence and correlates of survival sex among runaway and homeless youth. *American Journal of Public Health, 89*(9), 1406–1409.

Greenspan, S., & Benderly, B. L. (1997). *The growth of the mind and the endangered origins of intelligence.* Reading, MA: Perseus.

Gur, R. C., Alsop, D., Glahn, D., Petty, R., Swanson, C. L., Maldjian, J. A., et al. (2000). An fMRI study of sex differences in regional activation to a verbal and a spatial task. *Brain and Language, 74*(2), 157–170.

Gur, R. C., Gunning-Dixon, F., Bilker, W. B., & Gur, R. E. (2002). Sex differences in temporo-limbic and frontal brain volumes of healthy adults. *Cerebral Cortex, 12*(9), 998–1003.

Hardiman, M. (2001). Connecting brain research with dimensions of learning. *Educational Leadership, 59*(3), 52–55.

Healy, J. (1990). *Endangered minds: Why our children don't think.* New York: Simon & Schuster.

Heller, T. (2003). *Eating disorders: A handbook for teens, families, and teachers.* Jefferson, NC: McFarland.

Hennessy, J. W., King, M. G., McClure, T. A., & Levine, S. (1977). Uncertainty, as defined by the contingency between environmental events, and the adrenocortical response of the rat to electric shock. *Journal of Comparative and Physiological Psychology, 91*(6), 1447–1460.

Henningsen, M. (1996). *Attachment disorder: Theory, parenting, and therapy.* Retrieved from www.attachmentdisorder.net/Treatment_Links.htm

Hiort, O., & Holterhus, P. M. (2000). The molecular basis of male sexual differentiation. *European Journal of Endocrinology, 142*(2), 101–110.

Hotz, R. (1998, June 25). Rebels with a cause: Studies of adolescents' brains find possible physiological basis for turbulent teenage emotions. *Los Angeles Times,* p. B2.

Houdart, R. (1994). [Consciousness]. *Encephale, 20*(2), 159–168.

Howard, P. (1994). *The owner's manual for the brain: Everyday applications from mind-brain research.* Austin, TX: Leornian Press.

Hutchinson K. A. (1995). Androgens and sexuality. *American Journal of Medicine, 98*(1A), 111S–115S.

Huttenlocher, P. R., & Dabholkar, A. S. (1997). Regional differences in synaptogenesis in human cerebral cortex. *Journal of Comparative Neurology, 387*(2), 167–178.

Iacoboni, M. (2005). Understanding others: imitation, language, empathy. In S. Hurley & N. Chater (Eds.), *Perspectives on imitation: From cognitive neuroscience to social science* (pp. 11–55). Cambridge: MIT Press.

Iacoboni, M. (2008). *Mirroring people: The new science of how we connect with others.* New York: Farrar, Straus, & Giroux.

Ice, S. (2003). *Statistics.* Available from www.eatingdisorderscoalition.org

Jacobs, B., Schall, M., & Scheibel, A. B. (1993). A quantitative dendritic analysis of Wernicke's area in humans. II. Gender, hemispheric, and environmental factors. *Journal of Comparative Neurology, 327*(1), 97–111.

James, A. (2007). *Teaching the male brain: How boys think, feel, and learn in school.* Thousand Oaks, CA: Corwin.

Johnston, L. D., O'Malley, P. M., & Bachman, J. G. (2003). *Table 2: Trends in annual and 30-day prevalence of use of various drugs for eighth, tenth, and twelfth graders* [Data file]. Available from www.monitoringthefuture.org/data/03data .html# 2003data-drugs

Just, M. A., Kellera, T. A., & Cynkara, J. (2008). Listening to cell phones impairs driving, study. *Brain Research.* Retrieved January 4, 2009, from www .medicalnewstoday.com/articles/99696.php

Kagan, S. (1994). *Cooperative learning.* San Juan Capistrano, CA: Kagan Cooperative Learning.

Kalkowski, P. (1995). *School improvement research series: Peer and cross-age tutoring* (Close-up No. 18). Retrieved from www.nwrel.org/scpd/sirs/9/c018.html

Kaltiala-Heino, R., Marttunen, M., Rantanen, P., & Rimpela, M. (2003). Early puberty is associated with mental health problems in middle adolescence. *Social Science and Medicine, 57*(6), 1055–1064.

Keefe, D. L. (2002). Sex hormones and neural mechanisms. *Archives of Sexual Behavior, 31*(5), 401–403.

Kempermann, G., & Gage, F. H. (1999, May). New nerve cells for the adult brain. *Scientific American, 280*(5), 48–53.

Keshavan, M. S., Diwadkar, V. A., De Bellis, M., Dick, E., Kotwal, R., Rosenberg, D. R., et al. (2002). Development of the corpus callosum in childhood, adolescence and early adulthood. *Life Sciences, 70*(16), 1909–1922.

Kim, J. J., & Diamond, D. M. (2002). The stressed hippocampus, synaptic plasticity, and lost memories. *Nature Reviews: Neuroscience, 3*(6), 453–462.

Kimura, D. (1992, September). Sex differences in the brain. *Scientific American, 267*(3), 118–125.

Kimura, D. (1996). Sex, sexual orientation and sex hormones influence human cognitive function. *Current Opinion in Neurobiology, 6,* 259–263.

Kimura, D. (2002). Sex hormones influence human cognitive patterns. *Neuroendocrinology Letters, 23*(Suppl. 4), 67–77.

Kircher, T. T., Senior, C., Phillips, M. L., Rabe-Hesketh, S., Benson, P. J., Bullmore, E. T., et al. (2001). Recognizing one's own face. *Cognition, 78*(1), B1–B15.

Kirchner, M. B., & Gunther, N. (Producers). (2000). Alcohol, drugs and the brain [Radio series episode]. In *Gray Matters.* Joint production of Public Radio International and Dana Alliance for Brain Initiatives.

Kluball, J. L. (2000). The relationship of instrumental music instruction and academic achievement for the senior class of 2000 at Lee County High School (Doctoral dissertation, University of Sarasota, 2000). *Dissertation Abstracts International 61*(11), 4320A.

Koepp, M. J., Gunn, R. N., Lawrence, A. D., Cunningham, V. J., Dagher, A., Jones, T., et al. (1998, May 21). Evidence for striatal dopamine release during a video game. *Nature, 393*(6682), 266–268.

Koff, E., Rierdan, J., & Stubbs, M. L. (1990). Gender, body image, and self-concept in early adolescence. *Journal of Early Adolescence, 10,* 56–68.

Kohn, A. (1993). *Punished by rewards: The trouble with gold stars, incentive plans, A's, praise, and other bribes.* Boston: Houghton Mifflin.

Kreeger, K. (2002). Deciphering how the sexes think: It's not necessarily about who is better at what, but why the sexes process some stimuli in dissimilar ways. *The Scientist, 16*(2), 28–29.

Kulin, H. (1991). Puberty, endocrine changes. In R. M. Lerner, A. C. Petersen, & J. Brooks-Gunn (Eds.), *Encyclopedia of adolescence* (Vol. 2, pp. 897–899). New York: Garland.

Laitinen-Krispijn, S., Van der Ende, J., Hazebroek-Kampschreur, A. A., & Verhulst, F. C. (1999). Pubertal maturation and the development of behavioural and emotional problems in early adolescence. *Acta Psychiatrica Scandinavica, 99*(1), 16–25.

LeDoux, J. (1996). *The emotional brain: The mysterious underpinning of emotional life.* New York: Simon & Schuster.

LeDoux, J. (2003). The emotional brain, fear, and the amygdala. *Cellular and Molecular Neurobiology, 23*(4–5), 727–738.

LeDoux, J. (2007). The amygdala. *Current Biology, 17*(20), 868–874.

Leonard, J. (1999, May). The sorcerer's apprentice: Unlocking the secrets of the brain's basement. *Harvard Magazine, 101*(5), 56–62.

Lerner, R. M., Delaney, M., Hess, L. E., Jovanovic, J. D., & von Eye, A. (1990). Early adolescent physical attractiveness and academic competence. *Journal of Early Adolescence, 10,* 4–20.

Levy, J. (1983). Research synthesis on right and left hemispheres: We think with both sides of the brain. *Educational Leadership, 40*(4), 66–71.

Lurie, K. (2003, November 4). *Teen stress.* Retrieved from www.sciencentral.com/ articles/view.php3?language=english&type=&article_id=218392097

Lyvers, M. (2000). Cognition, emotion and the alcohol-aggression relationship: Comment on Giancola. *Experimental and Clinical Psychopharmacology, 8*(4), 607–608, 612–617.

Magnusson, D., Stattin, H., & Allen, V. (1986). Differential maturation among girls and its relation to social adjustment: A longitudinal perspective. In P. Baltes, D. Featherman, & R. Lerner (Eds.), *Life-span development and behavior* (Vol. 7, pp. 135–172). Hillsdale, NJ: Erlbaum.

Manisses Communications Group. (2003, May). What you should know about obesity in children and adolescents. *Brown University Child and Adolescent Behavior Letter, 19*(5), SI(2).

Marano, H. (2003, July). The new sex scorecard. *Psychology Today, 36*(4), 38–46.

Marzano, R., Pickering, D., & Pollock, J. (2001). *Classroom instruction that works: Research-based strategies for increasing student achievement.* Alexandria, VA: Association for Supervision and Curriculum Development.

Mason, M. (1998). *The van Hiele levels of geometric understanding.* Retrieved April 26, 2009, from www.coe.tamu.edu/~rcapraro/Graduate_Courses/EDCI%20624% 20625/EDCI%20624%20CD/literature/van%20Hiele%20Levels.pdf

McBride, D., Barrett, S. P., Kelly, J. T., Aw, A., & Dagher, A. (2006). Effects of expectancy and abstinence on the neural response to smoking cues in cigarette smokers: An fMRI study. *Neuropsychopharmacology, 31*(12), 2728–2738.

McClintock, M. K., & Herdt, G. (1996). Rethinking puberty: The development of sexual attraction. *Current Directions in Psychological Science, 5*(6), 178–183.

McCluckey, K., & Mays, A. (2003). *Mentoring for talent development.* Sioux Falls, SD: Reclaiming Youth International.

McEwen, B. (1999). Development of the cerebral cortex: XIII. Stress and brain development: II. *Journal of the American Academy of Child and Adolescent Psychiatry, 38*(1), 101–103.

McEwen, B. (2002). Estrogen actions throughout the brain. *Recent Progress in Hormone Research, 57*, 357–84.

McGivern, R. F., Andersen, J., Byrd, D., Mutter, K. L., & Reilly, J. (2002). Cognitive efficiency on a match to sample task decreases at the onset of puberty in children. *Brain and Cognition, 50*(1), 73–89.

*National Assessment of Educational Progress.* (2002). Retrieved from www.nces.ed.gov/naep3/

*National Longitudinal Study on Adolescent Health, 1994–2002.* (2008). Retrieved from http://dx.doi.org/10.3886/ICPSR21600

National Institute of Mental Health. (2000, September). *Depression in children and adolescents: A fact sheet for physicians.* Retrieved from www.nimh.nih.gov/ publicat/depchildresfact.cfm

National Runaway Switchboard. (2008). *National statistics.* Retrieved April 24, 2009, from www.1800runaway.org/news_events/call_stats.html

Neimark, E. D. (1975). Intellectual development during adolescence. In F. D. Horowitz (Ed.), *Review of child development research* (Vol. 4, pp. 541–594). Chicago: University of Chicago Press.

Nichols, M. (1996, January 22). Boys, girls and brainpower: The sexes differ in more than appearance. *Maclean's, 109*(4), 49.

O'Reilly, R. C., & Fran, M. J. (2006). Making working memory work: A computational model of learning in the prefrontal cortex and basal ganglia. *Neural Computation, 18*(2), 283–328.

O'Reilly, R. C., & Rudy, J. W. (2000). Computational principles of learning in the neocortex and hippocampus. *Hippocampus, 10*(4), 389–397.

Ormrod, J. E. (2000). *Educational psychology: Developing learners* (3rd ed.). Upper Saddle River, NJ: Merrill.

Ortiz, A. (2003). *Adolescent brain development and legal culpability.* Retrieved from www.abanet.org/crimjust/juvjus/resources.html#brain

Ostatnikova, D., Putz, Z., Celec, P., & Hodosy, J. (2002). May testosterone levels and their fluctuations influence cognitive performance in humans? *Scripta Medica (BRNO), 75*(5), 245–254.

Paus, T., Zijdenbos, A., Worsley, K., Collins, D. L., Blumenthal, J., Giedd, J. N., et al. (1999, March 19). Structural maturation of neural pathways in children and adolescents: In vivo study. *Science, 283*(5409), 1908–1911.

Paxton, S., Wertheim, E., Gibbons, K., Szmukler, G., Hillier, L., & Petrovoch, J. (1991). Body image satisfaction, dieting beliefs, and weight loss behaviors in adolescent girls and boys. *Journal of Youth and Adolescence, 20*(3), 361–379.

Pedersen, E., Faucher, T. A., & Eaton, W. W. (1978). A new perspective on the effects of first-grade teachers on children's subsequent adult status. *Harvard Educational Review, 48*(1), 1–31.

Perina, K. (2002, May). Mood swing: How feelings help and hurt. *Psychology Today, 35*(3), 17–18.

Piaget, J. (1970). *The science of education and the psychology of the child* (D. Coltman, Trans.). New York: Orion Press. (Original work published 1969)

Piphor, M. (1994). *Reviving Ophelia: Saving the selves of adolescent girls.* New York: Putnam.

Platek, S. M., Keenan, J. P., Gallup, G. G., Jr., & Mohammed, F. B. (2004). Where am I? The neurological correlates of self and other. *Brain Research: Cognitive Brain Research, 19*(2), 114–122.

Platek, S. M., Wathne, K., Tierney, N. G., & Thomson, J. W. (2008). Neural correlates of self-face recognition: An effect-location meta-analysis. *Brain Research, 1232,* 173–184.

Pollack, W. (1999). *Real boys: Rescuing our sons from the myths of boyhood.* New York: Henry Holt.

Puckett, M., Marshall, C., & Davis, R. (1999). Examining the emergence of brain development research: The promises and the perils. *Childhood Education, 76*(1), 8–12.

Putnam, J., Allshouse, J., & Kantor, L. S. (2002). U.S. per capita food supply trends: More calories, refined carbohydrates and fats. *FoodReview (A Publication of the Economic Research Service, USDA), 25*(3), 2–15.

Rapoport, J., Giedd, J., Blumenthal, J., Hamburger, S., Jeffries, N., Fernandez, T., et al. (1999). Progressive cortical change during adolescence in childhood onset schizophrenia. A longitudinal magnetic resonance imaging study. *Archives of General Psychiatry, 56*(7), 649–654.

Raz, N., Gunning-Dixon, F., Head, D., Williamson, A., & Acker, J. D. (2001). Age and sex differences in the cerebellum and ventral pons: A prospective MR study of healthy adults. *American Journal of Neuroradiology, 22*(6), 1161–1167.

Reiss, T. (1998). Wake-up call on kids' biological clocks. *NEA Today, 16*(6), 19–20.

Restak, R. (1994). *Receptors.* New York: Bantam Books.

Rice, P., & Dolgin, K. G. (2002). *Adolescent: Development, relationships, and culture* (10th ed.). Needham Heights, MA: Allyn & Bacon.

Saigh, P. A., Yaslik, A. E., Oberfield, R. A., Halamandaris, P. V., & Bremner, J. D. (2006). The intellectual performance of traumatized children and adolescents with or without posttraumatic stress disorder. *Journal of Abnormal Psychology, 115*(2), 332–340.

Sampaio, R. C., & Truwit, C. L. (2001). Myelination in the developing brain. In C. A. Nelson & M. Luciana (Eds.), *Handbook of developmental cognitive neuroscience* (pp. 35–44). Cambridge: MIT Press.

Santrock, J. W. (2003). *Adolescence* (9th ed.). Boston: McGraw-Hill.

Schacter, D. L. (1996). *Searching for memory: The brain, the mind, and the past.* New York: Basic Books.

Schiller, D., Ley, I., Niv, Y., LeDoux, J. E., & Phelps, E. A. (2008). From fear to safety and back: Reversal of fear in the human brain. *Journal of Neuroscience, 28*(45), 11517–11525.

Schneider, B. H., & Younger, A. J. (1996). Adolescent-parent attachment and adolescents' relations with their peers. *Youth and Society, 28*(1), 95–108.

Schwarz, J. (2006). *Researchers find physiological markers for cutting, other self-harming behaviors by teenage girls.* Retrieved from www.uwnews.org/article.asp?articleID=25024

Shaywitz, B. A., Shaywitz, S. E., Pugh, K. R., Constable, R. T., Skudlarski, P., Fulbright, R. K., et al. (1995, February 16). Sex differences in the functional organization of the brain for language. *Nature, 373*(6515), 607–609.

Siegel, D. J. (2001). Memory: An overview, with emphasis on developmental, interpersonal, and neurobiological aspects. *Journal of the American Academy of Child and Adolescent Psychiatry, 40*(9), 997–1011.

Siegel, D. J. (2006). An interpersonal neurobiology approach to psychotherapy: Awareness, mirror neurons, and neural plasticity in the development of well-being. *Psychiatric Annals, 36*(4), 248–256.

Smilkstein, R. (2003). *We're born to learn: Using the brain's natural learning process to create today's curriculum.* Thousand Oaks, CA: Corwin.

Smith, J. B., Lee, V. E., & Newmann, F. M. (2001). *Instruction and achievement in Chicago elementary schools.* Chicago: Consortium on Chicago School Research.

Sousa, D. (1998). Brain research can help principals reform secondary schools. *NASSP Bulletin, 82*(598), 21–28.

Sousa, D. (2001). *How the brain learns: A classroom teacher's guide* (2nd ed.). Thousand Oaks, CA: Corwin.

Sousa, D. A. (2003). *How the gifted brain learns.* Thousand Oaks, CA: Corwin.

Sowell, E. R., Thompson, P. M., Holmes, C. J., Jernigan, T. L., & Toga, A. W. (1999). In vivo evidence for post-adolescent brain maturation in frontal and striatal regions. *Nature Neuroscience, 2*(10), 859–861.

Spear, L. P. (2000). The adolescent brain and age-related behavioral manifestations. *Neuroscience and Biobehavioral Reviews, 24*(4), 417–463.

Spear, L. P. (2002, March). The adolescent brain and the college drinker: Biological basis of propensity to use and misuse alcohol. *Journal of Studies on Alcohol,* (Suppl. 14), 71–81.

Spearing, M. (2001). *Eating disorders: Facts about eating disorders and the search for solutions* (National Institute of Health Publication No. 01–4901). Retrieved from www.nimh.nih.gov/Publicat/eatingdisorders.cfm

Spice, B. (2008). *Carnegie Mellon study shows just listening to cell phones significantly impairs drivers.* Pittsburgh, PA: Carnegie Mellon.

Spinks, S. (Writer & Director). (2002, January 31). Inside the teenage brain (Program No. 2011). [Television broadcast]. In D. Fanning (Executive Producer), *Frontline.* Boston: WGBH.

Sprenger, M. (1999). *Learning and memory: The brain in action.* Alexandria, VA: Association for Supervision and Curriculum Development.

Squire, L. R., & Kandel, E. R. (2000). *Memory: From mind to molecules.* New York: Scientific American Library.

Stoleru, S., Gregoire, M. C., Gerard, D., Decety, J., Lafarge, E., Cinotti, L., et al. (1999). Neuroanatomical correlates of visually evoked sexual arousal in human males. *Archives of Sexual Behavior, 28*(1), 1–21.

Strauch, B. (2003). *The primal teen: What the new discoveries about the teenage brain tell us about our kids.* New York: Doubleday.

Sylwester, R. (2000). *A biological brain in a cultural classroom: Applying biological research to classroom management.* Thousand Oaks, CA: Corwin.

Sylwester, R. (2001). Unconscious emotions, conscious feelings, and curricular challenges. *New Horizons Online Journal, 6*(3). Available from www.newhorizons.org/journal/journa129.htm

Sylwester, R. (2007). *The adolescent brain: Reaching for autonomy.* Thousand Oaks, CA: Corwin.

Taylor, H., & Markow, D. (2003). Many high school students do not get enough sleep—and their performance suffers. *Harris Poll #24.* Retrieved from www.harrisinteractive.com/harris_poll/index.asp?PID=372

Taylor-Dunlop, K., & Norton, M. (1997). Out of the mouths of babes: Voices of at risk adolescents. *The Clearing House, 70*(5), 274–278.

*Teenage brain: A work in progress* (NIH Publication No. 01–4929). (2001). Retrieved from www.nimh.nih.gov/publicat/teenbrain.cfm

Thomas, R. (1993, February). *Cross-age and peer tutoring* (Report No. EDO-CS-93–01). Retrieved from www.indiana.edu/~reading/ieo/digests/d78.html

Thomas, R. M., & Peterson, D. A. (2003). A neurogenic theory of depression gains momentum. *Molecular Interventions, 3*(8), 441–444.

Thompson, P. M., Giedd, J. N., Woods, R. P., MacDonald, D., Evans, A. C., & Toga, A. W. (2000, March 9). Growth patterns in the developing brain detected by using continuum mechanical tensor maps. *Nature, 404*(6774), 190–193.

*Title IX at 30: Report card on gender equity* (2002, June). A report of the National Coalition for Women and Girls in Education. Retrieved from www.ncwge.org/pubs.htm

Udry, J. R. (1990). Hormonal and social determinants of adolescent sexual initiation. In J. Bancroft & J. M. Reinisch (Eds.), *Adolescence and Puberty* (pp. 70–87). New York: Oxford University Press.

Uekermann, J., Daum, I., Schlebusch, P., & Trenckmann, U. (2005). Processing of affective stimuli in alcoholism. *Cortex, 41*(2), 189–194.

Uekermann, J., Daum, I., Schlebusch, P., Wiebel, B., & Trenckmann, U. (2003). Depression and cognitive functioning in alcoholism. *Addiction, 98*(11), 1521–1529.

U.S. Department of Education. (2001). Societal support for learning: Parental involvement in schools (Indicator No. 54). In *The Condition of Education 2001* (Report No. NCES 2001–072, p. 93). Retrieved from http://nces.ed.gov/pubs2001/2001072.pdf

U.S. Department of Health and Human Services. (2002). *National Survey on Drug Use and Health.* Available from http://oas.samhsa.gov/nhsda/2k2nsduh/Overview/2k2Overview.htm#

Vedantam, S. (2001, June 3). Are teens just wired that way? Researchers theorize brain changes are linked to behavior. *Washington Post,* p. A1.

Volkow, N. D., Fowler, J. S., Wang, G. J., & Goldstein, R. Z. (2002). Role of dopamine, the frontal cortex and memory circuits in drug addiction: Insight from imaging studies. *Neurobiology of Learning and Memory, 78*(3), 610–624.

Volkow, N. D., Fowler, J. S., Wang, G. J., Swanson, J. M., & Telang, F. (2007). Dopamine in drug abuse and addiction: Results of imaging studies and treatment implications. *Archives of Nuerology. 64*(11), 1575–1579.

Wade, T. J., Cairney, J., & Pevalin, D. J. (2002). Emergence of gender differences in depression during adolescence: National panel results from three countries. *Journal of the American Academy of Child and Adolescent Psychiatry, 41*(2), 190–198.

Walkup, J. T., Labellarte, M. J., Riddle, M. A., Pine, D. S., Greenhill, L., Klein, R., et al. (2001). Fluvoxamine for the treatment of anxiety disorders in children and adolescents. *New England Journal of Medicine, 344,* 1279–1285.

Wang, A., & Thomas, M. (1995). Effects of keywords on long-term retention: Help or hindrance? *Journal of Educational Psychology, 87,* 468–475.

Wang, G. J., Volkow, N. D., & Fowler, J. S. (2002). The role of dopamine in motivation for food in humans: Implications for obesity. *Expert Opinion on Therapeutic Targets, 6*(5), 601–609.

Weissman, D. H., & Banich, M. T. (2000). The cerebral hemispheres cooperate to perform complex but not simple tasks. *Neuropsychology, 14*(1), 41–59.

White, A. M. (2003). Substance use and adolescent brain development: An overview of recent findings with a focus on alcohol. *Youth Studies Australia, 22,* 39–45.

White, A. M., & Swartzwelder, H. S. (2005). Age-related effects of alcohol on memory and memory-related brain function in adolescents and adults. *Recent Developments in Alcohol, 17,* 161–176.

Windle, M., Spear, L. P., Fuligni, A. J., Angold, A., Brown, J. D., Pine, D., et al. (2008). Transitions into underage and problem drinking: Developmental processes and mechanisms between 10 and 15 years of age. *Pediatrics* (Suppl. 4), 274–289.

Wingert, P., & Kantrowitz, B. (2002, October 7). Young and depressed. *Newsweek,* pp. 53–61.

Witmer, J. T., & Anderson, C. S. (1994). *How to establish a high school service learning program.* Alexandria, VA: Association for Supervision and Curriculum Development.

Wolfe, P. (2001). *Brain matters: Translating research into classroom practice.* Alexandria, VA: Association for Supervision and Curriculum Development.

Woolfolk, A. (2006). *Educational Psychology* (10th ed.). Needham Heights, MA: Allyn & Bacon.

Yoder, C. Y., Weitzen, S., Pickle, L. W., Grant, B., Herrmann, D., & Schnitzer, S. B. (2001). Cognitive functioning in the last year of life as a function of age, gender, and race. *Experimental Aging Research, 27*(3), 241–256.

Yurgelun-Todd, D. A., Killgore, W. D., & Young, A. D. (2002). Sex differences in cerebral tissue volume and cognitive performance during adolescence. *Psychological Reports, 91*(3, Pt. 1), 743–757.

Zeng, L., Leplow, B., Holl, D., & Mehdorn, M. (2003). Quantification of human spatial behavior in an open field-locomotor maze. *Perceptual and Motor Skills, 3*(Pt. 1), 917–935.

Zhou, J. N., Hofman, M. A., Gooren, L. J., & Swaab, D. F. (1995, November). A sex difference in the human brain and its relation to transsexuality. *Nature, 378,* 68–70.

Zhu, W., Volkow, N. D., Ma, Y., Fowler, J. S., & Wang, G. J. (2004). Relationship between ethanol-induced changes in brain regional metabolism and its motor, behavioural and cognitive effects. *Alcohol and Alcoholism, 39*(1), 53–58.

# Index